JUMP!

Tara

Keep exploring yourself.

Happy reading!

Much love.

Leonard

Visit Lenerd at lenerdlouw.com

First published by MFBooks Joburg, an imprint of Jacana Media (Pty) Ltd, in 2019

10 Orange Street
Sunnyside
Auckland Park 2092
South Africa
+2711 628 3200
www.jacana.co.za

ISBN 978-1-928420-48-4

Cover design by Anastasya Eliseeva
Editing by Sean Fraser
Proofreading by Linda Da Nova
Set in Sabon 11/15pt
Printed by ABC Press, Cape Town
Job no. 003522

See a complete list of MFBooks Joburg titles at www.jacana.co.za

JUMP!

An epic travel and soul adventure

Lenerd Louw

Contents

CHAPTER 1

Sex, drugs and Jacuzzis

There are three naked women dancing on my coffee table.

I'm on my back a few metres away, naked on a white feather duvet at the fireplace, cigarette in one hand and a glass of vodka and ice in the other. Their sexy bodies move to the rhythm of the music. Reflections of flames from the fire flicker over their smooth, tanned skin. The sliding doors leading to the deck and Jacuzzi are wide open. The music blares full blast, drowning out the crash of the waves on the rocks below.

I don't have to worry about complaints from the neighbours. Most of the multimillion-rand Clifton homes around mine stand empty out of season.

Here in my beach house I am king of my hood. I've lost track of time, but I know it must be late. The party started just before sunset when Sandy, a girl I've been recently hanging out with, arrives with a friend who has pretty eyes and long brown hair. Sandy knows how to keep my interest, bringing over new and beautiful women every weekend. Being with more than one woman at the same time does it for me.

Along with the champagne and sushi, as we lounge on the deck watching the sun set over the Atlantic there are lines of coke and MDMA capsules. I'm not a big fan of cocaine but the girls seem to like it. It keeps them awake, and there's more sex – which is an added bonus. I prefer MDMA, the main ingredient of Ecstasy. It's magical to have sex on. Even just a soft touch or stroke of your forearm feels euphoric, erotic. It's not long before all three of us are naked in the Jacuzzi on the open deck with its 360-degree views and the Atlantic Ocean stretching out like a jewel in front of us. The women are a perfect mixture of beauty and intelligence. Sandy has set fragrant white candles on the edge of the Jacuzzi. With the sound of waves crashing from the beach below, the setting is magical.

Later we find ourselves back inside, sprawled out on cushions near the fireplace. Pretty Eyes is on her back while Sandy, on all fours, has her head buried between her friend's outstretched legs, with me penetrating her from behind. I'm so involved I hardly notice when Sandy looks up and casually says, "Oh, look, there's a fire outside."

I glance to the left and find that the Jacuzzi's on fire, metre-high flames dancing skyward. For a while, I just stare. It looks surreal. Then it flashes through my mind that the Jacuzzi's on a wooden deck, that I live in a timber house and that all the houses around me are built from wood. The entire neighbourhood is about to burn down and I'm going to be the one who started it. Next thing the three of us are leaping around naked with cooking pots full of water, dashing between the kitchen sink and the Jacuzzi trying to douse the flames. It takes me a good 10 minutes to remember that I have a garden hose.

The weird thing is that as soon as I think we've put out the fire, it lights up again. I eventually look under the Jacuzzi to discover that there's a fire raging inside its walls, around the pump and motors. Maybe candles on the fibreglass edge were not such a good idea after all. I wonder how long it's been alight. We've been getting it on inside for at least two or three hours.

I've always found it fascinating how time seems to dissolve when you're having sex, especially when large quantities of alcohol and drugs are added to the equation. I finally manage to extinguish the fire, but the two girls have long since lost interest and are now back inside downing shots of tequila.

Not too long after, beautiful Mandy arrives to join the party. Shots of tequila, another gram of cocaine and a few more MDMA capsules later, Sandy and Mandy are dancing naked on the coffee table while Pretty Eyes is between my legs, performing incredible acrobatics with her mouth and tongue.

It is a night filled with flames. Unaware of how close we are to the fireplace, the next thing her hair catches alight. She's been so busy devouring me she doesn't realise it. For a split second I contemplate stopping her, tell her her hair's on fire, but I decide against it – I don't want the sensations pulsing through my body to stop. Instead I use the duvet to quash the flames. She reads it as a sign of my pleasure and moves her mouth up a gear. I will tell her about her singed hair later, but right now I'm back in my world of Pretty Eyes and her tongue.

After a while, she joins the other two naked nymphs dancing on the coffee table. Then, in my sexually charged MDMA-and-vodka haze, I slowly become aware of feathers floating around the dancing bodies. They are everywhere, drifting all over the open-plan living place, floating down the stairs that lead to the bedrooms below. They dance through the wide-open doors out to the deck, into the black night sky.

I suddenly get it. The feathers are from the duvet I used to extinguish the fire on Pretty Eyes's head. My gaze returns to the three women dancing on the table. The night is still young. The whole weekend lies ahead. I swallow some more MDMA and, greeted by loud cheers, I join the girls on the table.

Two years earlier, in May, the autumn of 2009, the month of my 45th birthday, I had moved from Johannesburg to Cape Town. It was not an easy move. I was heartbroken. I had just split up with the love of my life, Linda.

We had met a few years after my divorce and were good friends before we started going out. The relationship lasted almost four years. Although she was 16 years younger than me, she was mature beyond her years. With dark exotic looks, she was one of the most beautiful women I had ever met. She was highly intelligent, with a quick temper that was easily ignited but would just as readily subside. She was also a formidable businesswoman who started her own advertising agency at the age of 24, specialising in the internet arena. She would sell the business for very good money a few years later.

We lived together from the moment we started going out. We were inseparable. She took up golf so we could go on golfing holidays together. She became a mother to my young kids, who would spend every second weekend and school holidays with me.

But after a while, things changed. A few years into our relationship she decided that she wanted us to have children of our own, despite knowing I'd had a vasectomy a few years before meeting her. Unfortunately, she also knew that I had sperm stored at a laboratory. I had shared that with her when we were still friends, prior to us getting together. I had stored the sperm because I was only 39 when I had had the snip, as a backup if anything were ever to happen to my kids.

I made it clear at the start of the relationship that I didn't want any more kids. She'd agreed. So when she started trying to convince me otherwise, a big part of me was pissed off that she wanted to renege on the deal. Another part of me, though, felt deep compassion, as well as a strong dose of guilt. She was such a perfect mom to my own kids, how could I not give her one or two of her own?

The last few months of the relationship were a total mess as we drifted further and further apart. Anger, silences, constant arguing. It was clear that there was no solution. I knew she would grow to resent me if I made her give up her dream, and I would resent her if I was forced to father more kids. My children were already nine and 11 years old; there was no way I wanted to start another family. We both knew we had reached a stalemate. It broke her and it broke me too.

We were still living together in Johannesburg, but Linda would often go down to Cape Town on business during the week, but soon she began to stay weekends too. It felt like she was emotionally distancing herself from me. This made me feel very insecure. I was worried about how we were ever going to break up if we were both still deeply in love. Not for the first time in my life, I decided to override my heart and break it off once and for all. One sure way was to sleep with another woman, a one-night stand. I think, subconsciously, I left the telltale signs for her to see. It was the only time in our relationship that I had been unfaithful.

It did the job. But it broke her heart. As it did mine.

But it did much more than break my heart. It sent me into a spiral of self-loathing, guilt, shame and fear. Fear of being hurt again. I decided that, going forward, I would keep it superficial with any future women, no deep connections, just fun, fun, fun. And with that decision I shut off my feelings and moved even further away from my heart. Into a world of sex, drugs and Jacuzzis.

On the career front I was flying. The year before the breakup I was headhunted to start a direct insurance business for one of the big local financial services companies. The plan was that Linda and I would both move to Cape Town once the business was up and running. We decided to rent a house on Clifton beach, but after the breakup Linda moved down on her own and into the house that we were looking at. When I moved down a few months later, I could not bear living in the same area, so I rented a three-bedroom penthouse apartment in Mouille Point, a few kilometres away. Perched on the eighth floor, with a breathtaking view over the Atlantic, it was within walking distance of the new stadium they were putting the final touches to for the 2010 Soccer World Cup South Africa was hosting the following year.

I was very unsettled. But it wasn't just the breakup, the new job and the new city. There was something else. Something inside me had shifted. I could not put my finger on it, but it was very real and very confusing. I had an inner voice clearly telling me I should no longer be doing what I was doing. It made no sense –

this was everything I had worked and studied for. I had spent years at university obtaining three degrees: a bachelor's in commerce and law, an LLB and a master's in business administration.

What added to the confusion was that up until now I had really enjoyed what I was doing. I had a blast starting up, building and running businesses and being innovative in the market. I had successfully gone against the belief that it was impossible to sell life insurance directly to people, that you needed a broker. That didn't ring true to me so, after some thorough research, I backed my intuition and persuaded the private shareholders of the non-listed group I was working for to go with my idea to launch a direct life insurance company with an aggressive advertising and PR campaign. As the CEO and spokesperson, I took brokers and traditional insurers head on, often involving them in fiery debates on radio or TV. The business was a huge success. Success in business had come naturally to me. A few years earlier, in my mid-30s, I had been the director responsible for the advertising and marketing of the same big direct insurance group and brought a number of new brands to the market. During that time I launched the first car insurance brand for women only, and coined the phrase, "Save up to 40 per cent because women are better drivers" as the main message in a massive advertising campaign. The phones rang off the hook and the business was a huge success. Prior to that I'd worked in financial services in the UK for five years. For over two decades I'd been in love with what I was doing.

So what had changed?

I had no idea, but with each day, this voice of dissension grew louder and louder.

I was also finding it hard to fit in in Cape Town.

I had heard that it was one of the clique-iest places in the world, but that never bothered me – I had always fitted in very quickly in new places. Now, though, I felt lonely a lot of the time. It obviously had to do with having recently come out of the safety and comfort of a close personal relationship, but it was also more than that. I found it especially hard to form new male bonds in Cape Town because the guys were really quite different to the straightforward guys of Johannesburg.

Luckily, I had one good mate in Cape Town. Brother Lee and I had met 10 years previously in the advertising world and quickly became as close as brothers. We had so much in common. He was a good-looking guy, charming and with the gift of the gab, a great salesman and very good at what he was doing work wise. He also loved women and was as naughty as I was, maybe even more so. We often swapped war stories, thinking we were very cool.

As it turned out, Brother Lee had broken up with his short-term girlfriend just as I arrived in the Fair Cape. Three months was his average for a relationship. I think Brother Lee was as disconnected from his emotions and his heart as I had become. We were thus a perfect match. We both had no desire to take a girl to dinner and then have to deal with her expectations of a relationship. Besides, I was still heartbroken and deeply in love with Linda, who was living just a few kilometres down the road.

But while I didn't want to get involved with anyone else, I had a strong desire for intimacy, female company and conversation. So it was that Brother Lee and I came up with what we thought was a brilliant idea: to spend Friday nights – and sometimes even Saturday nights too – at a very upmarket gentleman's club in town. A strip club. We spent a ton of money there. On one extravagant night we wasted R23 000 between us on lap dances and booze... We soon became regulars and the girls flocked to us with our bulging wallets and clear appreciation of the female form. Plus, we were fun and treated them with respect. I had learnt respect from a young age, when my father told me to "look after the women" – meaning my mother and two younger sisters – while he was away overseas. I, at the ridiculously young age of six, deeply believed that I would fuck up anyone who tried to harm them. I didn't just love women, I really liked them on a very deep and respectful level. I quickly discovered that not all men do.

I liked hanging out at the strip club. These women were much more honest than some of those hanging out on the Atlantic

Seaboard or any of the other wealthier areas of Cape Town looking to catch a rich husband. There were some really fun, cool women working there, a lot of them from Central and Eastern Europe. Most were gorgeous. They were bright, interesting and great listeners.

In a way, lonely as I was, the club saved my life. It was a "safe" place for me to go. I could hang out with some really beautiful women without any pressure. I made some friends. But a deep conflict raged within me. On the one hand, I had made the deliberate decision that my mind would override my heart and I would not get into another relationship, while on the other hand I had a deep desire to connect at a soul level. It felt like I was being ripped apart at my core, and I had no idea how to solve that. Some of the women at the club must have sensed the genuineness in me and I think a lot of them had the same desire to deeply connect with another soul. My visits soon became less about the money and more about the need to just connect.

One of the girls who often sat with us was the Crazy Italian, a mad, hot girl with a heart of gold. One night, after multiple tequilas, she asked me to come home with her. She was gorgeous; it was an easy decision. When the club closed at 4 am, we left in her Audi TT convertible, roof down, speeding 200 kilometres per hour down the highway to her place in the northern suburbs. I remember looking at the speedometer, thinking, "I'm gonna die tonight." I thought momentarily to ask her to slow down, but I knew there was a very good chance that we'd have sex that night, so I decided not to risk it by not being the cool guy. And so I decided to face death instead. Seemed a fair trade-off. We arrived alive and we did have sex that night.

So it was that I woke the next morning in a strange suburban home with a massive Pyrenean mountain dog licking my face. There were cats everywhere and a colourful parrot prattling on incessantly in the kitchen. It was pretty surreal. After the Crazy Italian had made us breakfast, I took a taxi home, thinking that my world had gone pretty mad. But at least for a while I had stopped thinking of Linda.

CHAPTER 2

More madness

It was 2010 and South Africa was hosting the Soccer World Cup. The nation was aflutter with flags and anticipation. Nelson Mandela had played a vital part in securing it for the country a few years earlier in a well-contested bid. It was a big deal, leading to significant infrastructural improvements in the country. Prior to the World Cup our city airports had become tired and outdated. This investment meant that they were given a facelift, with new-look airport facilities in Johannesburg, Cape Town and Durban. Huge world-class stadiums were erected, roads were upgraded and the Gautrain, a state-of-the-art public transport system, was put in place in Gauteng.

The country was gripped with soccer fever. So was I. There was a cool restaurant and lounge bar on the ground floor of my building, facing the ocean. The games that I didn't watch at the new stadium down the road, I watched from there, flying high. Even today when I hear the anthem of that World Cup, performed by Shakira, I go into altered states of consciousness.

By now I had stopped going to our favourite strip club because I had met other gorgeous party girls in Cape Town. The good thing was that they too were not interested in any relationships or commitments; the bad news was that they were partying hard.

It wasn't just alcohol; suddenly there was a load of recreational drugs in the mix. I joined in. We would go out dancing and would often end up at my penthouse in Mouille Point late at night where the party would go on until sunrise. The hedonist in me knew no bounds. One night, we decided to play a game where I had four women naked on all fours on my triple extra-length king-sized bed, in a line facing the same way, while I moved from one to the other, fucking them from behind, one by one.

On the outside, I was living the life, but the voice in my alone time got louder.

The amount of drugs, mainly cocaine and MDMA, we took during that time was staggering. Almost everyone I knew did it. It was a pretty insane time. The whole country, especially Cape Town, went World Cup mad. But after the soccer-crazy foreigners left and the fever subsided, Cape Town came down from the high. I did not. I refused to, and I found plenty of fun women to join me in my crazy lifestyle. One of the women I was hanging out with was a Brazilian woman by the name of Ebony. She had been born in Mozambique but grew up in Brazil. I met her on a night out after watching a World Cup game. One of the first things I told her was that I was a black man in white skin. She thought that was hilarious but it grabbed her attention. Of course, it was a great pick-up line, but I was only partly joking. I had always felt that I was partly black and always had a natural, easy affinity with black people, especially black women. Ebony became a trusted friend; I looked out for her when we were out and she looked out for me when the party ended up at my place.

During the World Cup I had not seen much of Brother Lee, but one day he called to say it was time for us to hang out again and meet some new women. At the time, Ebony had a friend visiting from Brazil and wanted to introduce me to her. Like the good, sharing brother I was, I invited Brother Lee to join us. But when he and I walked into the cocktail bar in town to meet up with the two girls, we both gasped. They were standing at the bar counter, one very black, one lily white, both Brazilian, both breathtakingly beautiful, with bodies from a Victoria's Secret catalogue.

I was impressed with Ebony's taste in friends, but Brother Lee was even more so. Naturally, we all ended up at my apartment and while Ebony and I started making out in my room, Ivory and Brother Lee headed off to the guest bedroom. Brother Lee did not take any recreational drugs and was not aware that I was now heavily into them, so I was always sure to be very discreet. Ebony and I only started that part of the party once we were alone in my room. When Brother Lee woke the next morning and walked past the partly open door of my bedroom on his way out, Ebony and I were still high and wide awake. At that moment I was fucking her hard from behind. As he passed, we made eye contact.

When we chatted a few days later, he sounded concerned. "Bru," he said, "you looked like a demon fucking that girl. You had this crazed, wicked, wild look in your eyes."

I just laughed.

"I can't believe you were still awake," he continued. "You're a fucking crazy machine, brother!"

I took it as a compliment.

The following evening, rather than leaving Ivory alone in the room next door, Ebony and I invited her into the bed with us. My bed was certainly big enough; it was a massive designer piece, a third of the height of a normal bed, floating in a cream leather encasement with a large square cream leather headboard. Of course, I ended up making love to both women – Ivory had the most beautiful breasts – and fell asleep in between these two hot women, Ebony to my left, Ivory to my right.

In early 2011, I moved to one of the wooden houses on Clifton beach, often referred to as the Clifton Bungalows. Bungalow is a deceptive term, though, because these places are worth millions due to their prime positions in the most expensive neighbourhood on Cape Town's Atlantic Seaboard.

By now the voice in my head had become increasingly louder, constantly insisting that I should not be doing what I was doing in my life. This doubt in my head made no sense because I was making a lot of money, which in many people's books is everything. So I tried to drown the voice out. During the week that wasn't too hard to do because I was working pretty hard, often leaving work after 9 pm. However, over quiet weekends, it grew unbearable. So I decided not to be on my own. Ever. Copious amounts of alcohol, lots of sex and drugs did the job. For a while.

It was easy to be temporarily soothed by the scenery. Clifton is a magical place. Apart from the contrasting setting of the turquoise sea, white sandy beaches and towering mountains, it is also one of the few places in Cape Town where the wind seldom blows in summer – and that in a city where the South-Easter – the Cape Doctor – can blow you off your feet.

I felt like a king in my Clifton palace overlooking the beach and the entire bay beyond. And of course the Jacuzzi on the huge deck, adjacent to the swimming pool, was the centrepiece. In Mouille Point I had had a Jacuzzi installed on the patio and when I moved, it moved with me. It took the movers a few hours to get it from the road high above, down the steep steps to the Clifton place. It, however, was a non-negotiable. I had had a long history and love affair with Jacuzzis. Even in my single days in Johannesburg, between my divorce and meeting Linda, I always had a Jacuzzi at home. My Jacuzzi and I were inseparable.

The Jacuzzi was not only a great women magnet, but also a non-threatening way to get them naked. By now I wasn't interested in hanging around in restaurants, bars or clubs anymore. I had been to enough dark and dingy places to see the shadowy underbelly of Cape Town. So I would often recommend that we have the next drink in the Jacuzzi at my place or women would just come straight to my house for sundowners because the view from the deck of the sun setting over the Atlantic was otherworldly, lighting the sky and clouds up with magical hues of red. When it got to the point of getting into the Jacuzzi, I would just casually strip off my clothes, get in naked, turn away, to give them some space and look out over the sea. Most of the time they would just follow suit, not wanting to appear prudish.

Sitting in the Jacuzzi with a glass of champagne, overlooking the ocean, is an experience in itself... Sex or no sex, it always delivered. Perhaps that was the key – I was not too attached to whether the experience ended in sex. There was never any pressure on anyone; it just flowed. But, more often than not, sex was inevitable. There regularly would be me and two or three women Friday to Sunday – or early hours of Monday morning – having almost non-stop sex without any sleep. Part of that was about me living out a schoolboy fantasy of being with more than one woman at the same time; another part was that I had always had a very high sex drive but now, with the help of coke and MDMA, it had moved up a few gears and often one woman would not have enough energy to keep up with me.

And yet, despite round-the-clock parties and parades of women, deep down I felt really isolated and lonely. Apart from Brother Lee, I had almost no other male friends in Cape Town. I wasn't seeing him that often either because he was very occupied with his business and since he never used drugs, many of the parties weren't appropriate for him. A part of me was ashamed that he would find out I was using as much as I was, while another part felt responsible for protecting him from this lifestyle.

My isolation was intensified when I met a bunch of guys through a mutual acquaintance from Johannes-burg. They were a group of good-looking men, often with beautiful women on their arms. I really did not have that much in common with them but needed new connections and found myself hanging out with them in order to meet more women. My motives weren't that pure so I suppose I brought what happened on myself. At parties I began to notice that things were not what they seemed to be. I often got a feeling of being unsafe and became aware of whispered conversations happening behind my back. It soon became clear to me that a number of these guys were bisexual and that I was the topic of some of their secret conversations. I have never judged or held any prejudice towards bisexual or gay people. I grew up in a very liberal, open-minded home where my mother – involved in the television and movie industry – often had gay friends and colleagues over. Even though I grew up during apartheid South Africa of the '70s and the '80s, when racist and homophobic laws governed society, our home was a haven for free thought. In my early years my father was Director of Gymnastics at the South African Sport Foundation, a privately sponsored non-governmental body, and often had international gymnastic teams of different races touring the country. I remember him having to obtain permission from the Department of Home Affairs if he wanted to take his guests out to a restaurant. Prior arrangements would have to be made with an establishment not generally open to "non-white people", showing formal permission from Home Affairs, and still the guests would be seated in a different room or tucked away in a corner of the restaurant. Even if he had the visiting team over for a braai (barbeque) at our house on a Sunday, he would have to get permission from Home Affairs first. When I was a teenager at a conservative boarding school in Pretoria, I was sometimes called names for advocating "one person one vote" and refusing to judge gay people. In those days, in my beloved country one could easily be labelled a communist, or *kaffirboetie*, for views like these.

So I had no problem with these guys being bisexual; it was just that I felt like I was being secretively preyed upon, especially at parties when I was high on drugs, and thus vulnerable. The whole covert scene freaked the hell out of me, so I decided to give it all a miss.

I became less trusting, less open when it came to making new male friends. Cape Town was known for its gay community, but it was fascinating to notice how many bisexual men there were too – and how many were keeping it a secret from the women they were dating or married to.

On the work front, things were equally bizarre. I often found myself separated from within, looking at myself from the outside. I felt as if I were watching myself through a camera lens high up in the corner of the office while I played out the movie of my life as though I were in a TV reality show. It was like I wasn't living in my own skin, disconnected from myself. Ever since school and university days, and even more so when I started working, I was used to being seen as different. Even my good friends thought I was peculiar, but I had always felt like me, confident in my own skin. But now I felt like a great internal shift had taken place while I was sleeping. And, over time, the feeling grew stronger. And the louder the voice grew, the harder I partied. I had to try to drown it out.

Then I was introduced to Cat, otherwise known as Methcathinone. Cat was first synthesised in Germany in 1928 and was used medically in the Soviet Union as an antidepressant during the 1930s and 1940s. It went on to be used recreationally, especially in the '70s and '80s, and appeared to be a great alternative to cocaine. Coke really did not work for me. While it made every one else very confident and talkative, it made me insecure, paranoid and downright awkward. I seldom used it and when I did, it was often a bit of a social nightmare. Before Ms Cat came around, MDMA was my preferred drug. Cat is taken in the same way as cocaine, where you cut the lines with a bank card and then snort up a line with a rolled-up bank note. It gave me a lot of energy, made me feel like I was part of the social ritual, which was half the fun. MDMA is taken orally so does not involve the elaborate process of cutting, snorting lines and sharing rolled bank notes.

Ms Cat, however, made me pretty crazy. Some of my friends started calling me The Mask, as in the Jim Carrey movie. It wasn't an exaggeration. When high on Cat, I was off the wall and apparently very entertaining, sometimes crazily over the top and hyperactive. Another name for Cat is speed, which – considering the effect it had on me – made sense. I began to go on regular binges over weekends, when I wouldn't sleep for two days, speeding off my head.

CHAPTER 3

Snap!

And then I broke my cock.

I could hear and feel the tear when it snapped. She was squatting on top of me, moving rapidly up and down, fucking me madly. It was late Sunday night and while this was going down, I couldn't stop thinking, I should be sleeping, work tomorrow. But she was having such a good time, I thought I may as well go on a little longer. That's when I slipped out of her and when she came banging back I missed my mark and did not slip back inside her. Instead my hard cock collided full force with her coccyx. She came down on it full speed and with her whole weight. There was nothing for it but to snap. I immediately lost my erection. Seconds later, I was blue and swollen. We decided to call it a night and went to sleep.

The next morning when I woke, I was horrified to discover I was even more swollen, my cock now purple-blue. On my way to work I called my brother-in-law, a doctor in the town of George, to get advice. I was laughing when I explained what happened, still thinking it couldn't be too serious. His reaction put an end to my attempts at light-heartedness. "Lenerd," he said, "get to a doctor immediately – it's very serious. If you aren't treated immediately, there can be permanent damage."

I immediately called the urologist he recommended, one of the best in South Africa.

The very next morning I was being operated on. I had what is known as a penile fracture, a tear in the tunica albuginea. This is the rubbery sheet of tissue below the skin that allows the penis to increase in width and length to produce an erection when blood is pumped into it. It was a horrific operation. They made a circular cut all around the tip of my penis, sliced the skin in half, pulled the bottom piece all the way down to the base and then repaired the tear by stitching it together internally. My tear was close to the base so they had to pull the skin all the way down. It's even more complicated if you are not circumcised. The urologist had asked me whether he could do the operation in such a way that afterwards I'd be circumcised, because that would make it less complicated. I told him no way, I didn't want to lose any skin. I had always been grateful that my parents had never put me through the horrific experience of circumcision at a few days old. I also enjoyed the heightened sensitivity around the tip of my penis. If you're circumcised you can become desensitised with it constantly rubbing against clothing.

I was discharged from the hospital the next day with a row of stitches all around the tip of my penis where the skin had been stitched together again. It looked horrific. I winced every time I looked at it. I had been under anaesthetic for quite a few hours, so I did not feel great physically either. Before the operation I had the courage to ask the urologist what "permanent damage" meant. He explained that there was no guarantee and that in some cases the operation could be unsuccessful and you would never have an erection again. I was shocked, but immediately put it out of my mind – a life without sex was not even an option.

The urologist warned that, to allow for a full recovery, I could not have intercourse for a whole month. I didn't wait that long. Two weeks later I was fucking again. When women asked about the scar when it was still visible, I jokingly told them that I had a penis reduction, which was the reason I no longer had a nine-inch cock – they had simply taken off all of an inch. I did not tell anyone else about the operation, not even Brother Lee.

Of course, in retrospect, this was a clear lesson and a powerful message. But back then I did not get any of it. It all went straight over my head.

In May that year my advertising agency gave me a copy of Jordan Belfort's *The Wolf of Wall Street* for my birthday. The book covered his crazy party life in New York, and the inscription in the front read, "Happy birthday, Len, the Wolf of Adderley Street." I laughed when I read the book because, as far as the party side was concerned, the comparison wasn't far off. I, however, missed all the subtleties, rather thinking how cool and glamorous I was, just like the Wolf. Ironically, when I read about the insane things he got up to, the book made me feel more normal. I would later learn from the agency's creative head, who became a good friend, that he had given me the book to warn me how living that life could end up. Jordan Belfort ended up in jail for two years.

During these crazy years I had two strict rules. One, I always, without exception, used condoms and, two, I never allowed anyone to take photos. And I think that what kept me alive and operating during this time was that even though I partied really hard with almost no sleep over the weekends, I would not party at all during the week. I would not even have a beer, a glass of wine, or a cigarette.

I was also exercising a lot. I did martial arts and my third dan black belt Taekwando instructor would come to my house before work at 7 am during the week and train me hard on my deck or on the beach. I would start on Tuesday mornings because the hangover was far too bad on Mondays. Actually, it was worse on Tuesdays, but by then I had at least caught up on some sleep. We used to call it Steak-Knife Tuesday, because the come-down and the hangover was so bad that you felt like taking a steak knife and slitting your wrists. The training, however, helped a lot. It almost killed me and it was really tough, but I think it played a big part in cleaning my system out.

At one point I pulled a calf muscle when I leapt off a table at a weekend party and, because of all the kicking involved in martial arts, I gave it a break for a while and took up boxing training, which was the hardest workout I'd ever done in my life. Often, I would also swim a kilometre at the gym pool or do a workout there. And then over the weekends I would have hours and hours of sex with little or no sleep. My other weekend exercise was running up the steep Clifton steps to meet drug dealers at the top, on the road, because I never allowed anyone to come to my house. Despite all the partying, physically I was in the best shape of my life. I was fit, lean, strong and had a hard, ribbed six pack.

But beneath the toned muscles, I was in a terrible state. A total mess. I remember sitting on my own on my deck one day, thinking, what was the use of it all? I didn't get as far as actually considering suicide, but I wasn't far off. I would have been quite happy if my life was to end at that moment. I simply couldn't see the meaning. The best I could come up with was to maybe sell one of my four luxury apartments in the Victoria & Alfred Waterfront Marina Residential and, with a portion of the proceeds, buy an Aston Martin sports car. Maybe that would help. I already had a BMW convertible, but after seeing James Bond driving one in a movie, I always loved the Aston Martin. Maybe becoming a little more like James Bond would make me feel better. I seriously considered this for a few weeks, but then I realised that neither the Aston Martin nor James Bond would solve the problem and give meaning to my life. It was a close call though.

So I decided to see a psychiatrist. The voice inside was pretty loud by now, the out-of-body feeling intense, and I was seriously wondering whether I had gone mad. The therapist turned out to be a complete waste of time. After two sessions, she confirmed that I wasn't crazy – well, not clinically at least. And she had no further advice, apart from warning me to lay off the drugs. She had no compassion, no recommendations about any kind of inner journey or talking to someone else. Nothing. She had nothing. At least she didn't prescribe antidepressants, though. Not that I would have taken them. I was very clear in my head even before going there that I was not going to take medication. I had seen what it had done to friends and family, how it had blunted them to life. I was very aware of the irony in feeling so strongly about not taking any legal drugs, but having no hesitation in taking copious amounts of illegal ones. I left the psychiatrist even more distraught and in an even bigger mess.

Very soon after that, however, I decided to part ways with Ms Cat. I was starting to get really paranoid and neurotic, and one night I had this vision of standing on the edge and a clear realisation that I could go two ways, either stand back or go over. I instinctively knew that I wasn't far from stepping over the edge with Cat, so I decided to leave her there and then, and to never touch her again.

By this point, I had started to feel less and less authentic. As a business leader, everyone looked to me for motivation and inspiration. I would get up on the sales floor at prize-givings, which the whole company always attended, mic in hand and deliver a motivating speech that would get everyone worked up, while at the same time feeling like a Hollywood actor delivering the performance of his life in some off-the-wall movie. For some strange reason, Leonardo DiCaprio – of *The Wolf of Wall Street* fame – sprang to mind. I would give it my best shot, knowing throughout that I was not speaking from the heart and therefore not being authentic to myself and anyone else. I felt like such a fraud, which tore me apart. I felt as though my intestines were being shredded in a blender, terrified that everyone would see right through me and tell me to stop acting and sit down. In reality, everyone would be shouting, highly motivated and inspired. This made it even worse. I wasn't being authentic about where my heart was and people didn't see that.

In the spring of 2012, in the month of September, I met Jade. She was pretty, had long dark hair, a body to die for – thin, lean, athletic and very sexy. I had never seen a flat stomach and six pack like that on a woman before. She was very tall, almost as tall as my six-foot height. She had a big personality and an even bigger sex drive, as big as mine, maybe even bigger.

It was good timing, too, because I had become jaded, tired of all the partying and all the people wandering around my house. I was ready for a relationship with one person, to take it a little easier. But, although we soon found ourselves in a relationship, we didn't take it any easier. Jade was a party animal. The intensity of the weekends remained much the same, except now it was with just one woman. I didn't need more though – I had met my match.

Our lovemaking was intense and varied. We would ravish each other for hours on end. We spent hours in role-play. She loved to dress up in sexy costumes and we would laugh our heads off afterwards at some of the stuff we came up with. We became very good friends too. She had warned me at the start of the relationship that she was a bad girlfriend and that I should not lose my heart to her. I never understood why she had said that, but it made me decide once again to keep some protective layer around my heart. What she did not bargain for was falling in love with me though, which she did. Totally. The way we made love made falling in love even easier: she had deep, intense orgasms, which I later would learn were cervical orgasms. And the way that I made love, which was all consuming, and she had not come across that before, intensified as she became physically addicted to me. I wasn't aware that I was doing anything differently because I thought all men made love like that. Although I loved her, I kept a back door open with that layer of armour firmly in place.

Although we partied hard, Jade brought a little stability to my life, but nothing else changed. The voice continued, getting louder and louder, the deep pit of loneliness growing ever bigger. It actually felt as though my life had gotten even worse. One day I was walking on Clifton beach, looking at the world around me. After just five minutes, I was bored out of my mind. I realised that what I was seeing must be beautiful: white powdery sand, crystal-clear turquoise waters, blue skies with flecks of cloud and Table Mountain towering high above. But I could not see the beauty in it. It did not move me at all. I felt a huge heavy emptiness within. At the pit of my stomach there was this dead weight and in my chest a tight contraction.

I had hit rock bottom. I was a mess and I knew I was in big trouble.

CHAPTER 4

The first surrender

And so I surrendered.

I realised I wasn't going to beat the Voice, so I stopped trying. I had been running from it for so long. I had no problem fighting the good fight, but there was no sense in fighting a fight you cannot win. So I gave up. I surrendered to the Voice that was telling me to stop everything I was doing. Telling me that this life, this job, this career was no longer for me.

I stopped partying too. There was no need for that anymore. Why put a lot of stuff into your system and suffer horrible hangovers and depressing comedowns if it can't drown out the Voice?

So it was that I just woke up one morning in late December 2012 and stopped taking all the drugs and, apart from the occasional beer, stopped drinking too. Jade was shocked. I told her that I needed to be sober and clear-headed to listen and understand the Voice.

In a way, it was a miracle that I was able to stop immediately like that. That I never developed a dependency, a substance addiction. But it was never just about the sex, or the drugs and alcohol; it was all a way for me to distract myself from the Voice. Alcohol was never a real problem anyway; I was drinking relatively little when partying, more sipping a drink or having a beer when thirsty. Drugs could have been a problem, but in a way sex saved me there.

If you take too many drugs, you lose your erection, so I almost always controlled my intake – not because I was responsible but because I didn't want to lose my hard-on. I took drugs mainly to give me energy and to keep me awake to have a lot of sex. It was fucked up, yes, but the sex was a saving grace. I wasn't 20 years old any more, and I just got tired. Alcohol made me even more tired. Drugs solved the problem for a while, and they definitely gave me the energy to operate. Like a good friend of mine used to say, "It's not pussy, it's chasing pussy that kills you."

Jade and I still had a lot of fun, but the dynamic was now different. At 2 am or so, on weekends, I would want to sleep because I was tired and there were no foreign substances to keep me awake.

Jade was really funny when she said, "My whole life I went out with only good boys. I kind of walked all over them. Now that I eventually found myself a bad boy, he turns good on me. What the fuck!"

I just laughed and shrugged my shoulders.

Eventually, after a few weeks of sobriety, I was finally ready to listen. I summoned up all my courage and asked the Voice, "So what should I be doing then?"

Silence.

That was a little disappointing. I expected more than that.

I repeated the question, "You said I shouldn't be doing what I am doing. So … what should I be doing?"

Again, silence.

For the next few weeks I walked around thinking about this. I was clearly very bored with what I was doing at work. I started thinking about alternatives. What other job should I be doing? What other business, or what about an entirely different career? I asked the Voice, only to be met with an empty silence.

Eventually I decided to take a different angle and asked, "How can I find out what I should be doing?"

This time there was an immediate answer: "Clear out all of the old to create space for the new."

"What the fuck does that mean?" I asked.

Again, silence.

I got the message though. I instinctively knew that this was the right thing to do. My life was so cluttered, I was in such a rut, in such a comfort zone, that there was probably no way I was going to figure it out in the state I was currently in.

I knew, too, that the first step in the process of clearing out the old was leaving my job. Making that decision was surprisingly easy. It took me no more than three seconds to get there. It was kind of logical. What wasn't that easy was actually doing it. That took another six months, the reason being the responsibility I felt toward the senior team I had brought on and to all the staff. The business started with just me, but by this stage we were over 400. My personality and informal, friendly entrepreneurial style of management were also closely woven into the culture of the business. This weighed heavily on me.

In the months between reaching my decision and final departure, I started reading some spiritual books, one of which was *The Monk Who Sold His Ferrari* by Robin Sharma. I never had the Ferrari to sell – although I did almost have that Aston – but the part where he had a heart attack in the courtroom in New York grabbed my attention. Also, the part where, prior to his heart attack, he would tell himself that he needed at least $300 million in the bank in order to retire. I decided to get out before the heart attack and realised the absurdity of putting a figure up there to slog towards rather than authentically living one's life. I, of course, had my own ridiculous figure up there. I was surprised how easy it was to drop all of that. I agreed on an exit from the business and by the end of July 2013 I was out of there.

By now I had kind of stopped asking the Voice specific questions, but continued to listen – and the messages came floating in. The Voice and a deep inner knowing became one. The Voice told me everything I already knew.

I knew leaving the job was only the start. I knew that without a shadow of a doubt.

I knew I had to clear out *all* of the old.

I knew that it would not help sitting in Cape Town, waiting for the new to come in. I had to get out of my comfort zone, out of the known, out of the old. That meant leaving the country for a while. Somehow I knew that that was a critical, important move to make. The only thing that could potentially stop me was my children. I thought long and hard about that.

When they were younger and we all lived in Johannesburg, I would have them every second weekend and for a part of their school holidays. When we got divorced, my son was four years old and my daughter two. I was the single dad with the nappy bag and the small, hyperactive kids running around all over the show when we went out. My daughter was still in nappies when we separated, but I was used to changing them – I was also a very active dad, getting up at night, bottle feeding them and changing nappies. When they were 10 and eight years old, my ex-wife revealed that she and her new husband wanted to move to Ballito, a small town just north of Durban, in order to enjoy a better quality of life. I did not like the idea because it meant I would see less of the children, but promised I'd think about it. After a few days, I relented and gave them my blessing. I knew intuitively that it would be a better quality of life for the children. Durban was only an hour's flight away from Johannesburg, so I flew there every third weekend and still had them for their school holidays. That's how it ended up that I set the company up in Cape Town. If the kids were still living in Johannesburg I would have set it up in Johannesburg, never in Cape Town. The fact that they were already in a different town opened up other options.

From a business perspective, there were very attractive reasons to be in Cape Town instead, so I went with that. The arrangement of flying up to them for weekends and getting them down to me for school holidays remained in place. In fact, those were the only sane times in an otherwise mad time for me. When I had the children for those two weeks or so, I never had people over, never held parties at home and never introduced them to any of the women I was hanging out with. We had great times on Clifton beach, swimming in the sea and in my pool and having braais on the deck.

Over the last few years in Cape Town the frequency of me flying up for weekends to Durban to see them had slipped. They were in a top private school in Ballito and the pressure on them to perform increased as they got older and advanced into the senior years. My son, especially, was very competitive and one of the top students at school and would just say to me that there was not much sense in me coming up because he would have to study the whole weekend, work on projects or have school stuff to attend to. The pressure on the kids was crazy. In the last year, when they were 16 and 14, I was seeing them mainly for the school holidays. So I decided that it wouldn't make much difference if I went overseas and just flew them out to me to wherever I was in the world, just as I would get them out to me in Cape Town. By now they were frequent and confident flyers and used to flying on their own.

My children had their summer school holidays in December and I wanted to spend that time with them travelling up the Cape coast, so I decided to stay in South Africa for the last few months of the year and to leave only in January.

Initially I thought to go to New York and live there a few months, check out new businesses and innovations and maybe study. It was a very confusing time; I was bored with the type of business I was in, so I thought I had to find new and innovative ideas. But when I looked at the temperature charts for New York, January temperatures were sub-zero. Growing up in Africa meant a strong aversion to the cold, so the Big Apple wasn't going to work for me. I noticed, though, that the weather improved later in the year and was acceptable around May. So I decided to stay in the southern hemisphere for a few months – maybe South America or South East Asia – where it was still summer, and then maybe make my way up to New York in about May.

What I also knew was that I had to do this journey on my own. As tough as it was going to be, I had to do it solo. And I needed to keep it open ended. There would be no plan, no return date, no commitments, no preconceived ideas, just totally open for whatever needed to come in. That meant I had to break up with Jade. Travelling with a partner would not allow me to dig as deep as I needed to. And I knew I'd have to dig deep, very deep. I would miss her terribly and would have to resist the temptation to call her to join me when it got lonely, but this was something I needed to do.

Jade was amazingly supportive and, even though it broke her heart, she understood that I could only do this journey on my own.

I also knew I had to declutter my life, so apart from a few investment properties, I sold or gave away all my possessions. At one point, I had owned seven Blue Chip investment properties. I sold most of them – right at the bottom cycle of the market. Financially, it wasn't a great decision because the value would increase over the next few years, but I didn't want to sit with all that money so I kind of gave it back to the Universe. All of a sudden, money wasn't that important any more. And, on some deep level, I felt it was probably a good idea to still have a certain amount of pressure on me to have to earn and learn in the future. I knew there would be temptations to return to the life I knew and I had visions of myself touring on my own yacht with lots of beautiful party women and a few bags of recreational drugs, with some old buddies joining us occasionally. I knew that that wasn't what I wanted and that I'd probably not have survived for much longer living like that, but I knew too that the pull was still strong and that the temptations would be there. I had always had a good relationship with money and was sure I'd be able to make more if I needed to.

I also sold my Jacuzzi. More like gave it away to my Jacuzzi guy for all the service he had given me over the years and for all the hard times I had given him. I had often called him or messaged him at 4 am on a weekend morning when there was a problem and would insist that he come over immediately or as soon as he woke up.

As far as the decision between South America and South East Asia, in the end I just flipped a mental coin. I had always been fascinated by Inca history and thought it would be cool to see the lost city of Machu Picchu, so South America won the toss. I checked on the map where Machu Picchu was and went, "Aah, it's in Peru... That's where I'll go then."

I had absolutely no idea what I was going to do with the rest of my life, but at least I knew what my first destination was. I hesitated for a second before I hit the pay button on the screen of my iPad: a one-way ticket to Lima, Peru.

Jade helped me with the final arrangements, like buying a giant blue-grey backpack. I bought the biggest one I could find and in it packed the remainder of my worldly possessions. Jade and I knew it was the end of our relationship. It was very emotional for both of us; we were together until the very last day. She sat with me at the airport before I flew out. As I settled into my seat on the plane before take-off, I was struck by the insanity of it all. Then I felt a surge of immense gratitude for having the financial means to be able to go on an adventure that would – hopefully – give me a new lease on life.

CHAPTER 5

A leap of faith

I landed at Jorge Chávez, Lima's international airport, at 2 am on 22 January 2014. Walking out of the arrival lounge with my bare-necessity backpack, I waved down the first taxi I saw and asked him to take me to a hotel close to the Spanish school in the Miraflores neighbourhood of Lima. Apart from my air ticket, I hadn't pre-booked anything at all, not even a hotel for my first night.

One thing I had decided was to do this journey in the flow and take it day by day. I no longer had a house in South Africa to return to, and the stuff that I hadn't sold or given away I had put in storage but felt no attachment to it. So, in a way, my only possessions were those on my back.

I was on a continent where I could not speak a word of the native language, with absolutely no idea why I was really there and no plan for what I was going to do there. Without knowing why, I intuitively knew that giving up control was going to be a big part of my journey.

I came across the term "surrendering to life" in most of the spiritual books I started reading a year before, but had no clear idea what that really meant. But what I did get was the notion of giving up control and that no planning could play a role in getting to that point. I had no idea to what extent I would get to understand that over the years to come.

Waking up in Lima the next morning and then walking the streets was pretty surreal. On my second day I enrolled at the Spanish school but walked out of the group class after just 20 minutes. It was terrible. They followed this old, inflexible method by writing all the verb forms out on the board. I did two years of Latin during my law studies at university – not that I could remember much from those days – and this reminded me of that formal way of learning. I then tried some individual classes for a few days, but found those too tough.

After a week in Lima, I decided to get going to Machu Picchu and took a flight to Cusco, high up in the Andes. Cusco was the capital of the Inca Empire from the 13th to the 16th century, and I was very excited to see it. I had been warned about altitude sickness – Cusco is 3 400 metres above sea level – but thought it was probably psychological, all in the mind. I was in for a surprise.

I was advised that the best way to prevent altitude sickness, or at least minimise the effect, was to do minimal physical activity and to avoid alcohol for the first day or two. I did neither. I took a taxi from the airport into town and by the time I found a hotel it was already after midnight, but there was absolutely no way that I could have gone to sleep anyway. The place was simply breathtaking. It was like arriving in an ancient Inca city lost in time, the only difference being that this one was occupied by people of the 21st century. The city was magical, lit up like a fairy tale, spotlights unveiling ancient buildings revealing massive blocks of stone that make up the walls, giving them a soft golden hue. Some of the stone blocks were taller than me, and not just square but a variety of shapes. The fascinating thing was that they fitted perfectly together without even the slightest gap. I had read that no mortar was used in the construction of these buildings and you can't even insert a note or credit card anywhere between the stones – that's how perfectly they fitted. Naturally, I took my debit card and tried for myself... It was all true.

By this time, the restaurants and bars were closed, so I could explore this magical place entirely on my own. I walked the steep roads and alleyways until the early hours of the morning. My heart was racing in total wonder. I felt like a boy again, on an exploration mission and had stumbled upon a magical lost city in the middle of the jungle. By the time I got back to my hotel it was almost sunrise. I was exhausted and crashed into bed.

I only woke up in the late morning and immediately set out for brunch. After, I ventured out again to explore further and, later in the day, came across a little bar with live music and decided to chill there for a while. I was offered the traditional drink for that part of Peru, and when in Rome... The drink, Pisco sour, is made with Pisco, the Peruvian clear brandy, lime juice, a little syrup and a tablespoon of egg white mixed together in a blender. It was an interesting taste to say the least, but not too bad. I had a few of those – the live music was good – but it must have been a pretty strong drink because I felt its effects on my walk back home and had to focus to keep in a straight line.

Unsurprisingly, then, I woke the next morning with what I thought was a terrible hangover. And it partly was, but I soon discovered that it was mostly due to altitude sickness. I experienced a panicky feeling, like I couldn't draw enough oxygen into my lungs, so I was constantly having to take short breaths. I felt nauseous, had no energy and struggled to walk far without stopping to rest. The worst was still to come. I found out when I went to bed that it was impossible to sleep because my body kept thinking it was suffocating. I would manage to sleep for no more than a few seconds and would then startle awake to catch a deep breath. That went on the whole night.

The next day I googled it and spoke to a guy at my hotel who said that in severe cases it was necessary to go to the hospital to get an oxygen bottle to assist your breathing. He recommended drinking coca tea, a popular tea in Peru. It certainly helped, but I didn't know that it is also a stimulant that gives you a lot of energy and so makes sleeping difficult. The Incas are famous for having walked for days over mountains without eating, chewing leaves of the coca plant for energy. The coca is also the plant from which cocaine is made... Little wonder I slept even less that night.

I googled more the next day and found that another way to alleviate the sickness is to drop altitude by a few hundred metres. I checked and saw that the Sacred Valley, where Machu Picchu is situated, is a few hundred metres lower. The valley is long and narrow and starts at one end at the town of Písac on the west side, dropping down lower to end at the village of Aguas Calientes in the east, from where you could then make your way straight up the mountain to the city of Machu Picchu. Písac, at 3 000 metres, was only 400 metres lower than Cusco, but I thought I'd start there and if it still wasn't low enough I'd travel farther down the Sacred Valley until I began to feel better.

I decided to give it one more day, hoping my breathing would improve and allow me to see as much of Cusco as I could, taking into account how sick I felt. I even went for another Spanish lesson at the local language school, but that only added to my frustration. That night I had another night of disturbed sleep. By the next morning I decided to hit the road and organised a taxi to take me the 30 kilometres or so to Písac.

Dropping down into the valley was extraordinary. With every metre we dropped I started feeling better. I was amazed at how so little could make such a big difference. Halfway down, the nausea and anxiety began to subside. I began to breathe easier. The view was spectacular and the valley was completely different to how I'd imagined. It was narrow, probably only a kilometre wide, and stretching left and right as far as the eye could see. The mountains on either side were high but the valley floor was perfectly flat, as flat as a table top, and remarkably green.

I found a hotel on the outskirts of town and, after dropping off my rucksack, set out to explore. That night I slept like a baby.

The next morning at breakfast I could not help but think about my extremist nature and how much fun, enjoyment and pleasure it had brought me, but also how much pain and suffering too. If I had taken all the advice, I would probably not have encountered altitude sickness, but the strenuous exercise and abundance of alcohol, all within 24 hours of arriving at high altitude, really messed me up.

Moderation had never been my thing. For me it had always been about getting the most out of each moment, pushing the envelope and wrenching the last drop of juice out of everything. I think I was born that way. I, however, also had a strong influence in my life that helped enforce that – my father. When warned by my mother or others about the dangers of smoking 60 cigarettes a day and drinking red wine or brandy daily, he would say he would rather live for 50 years than die for 80. He had certainly put 80 years of living into the first 50 years of his life, and he was already 74 years old. I was probably doing much the same.

It turned out that Písac had its own set of ruins high above the town, built at roughly the same time as Machu Picchu. It was a relatively tough walk and arduous climb to reach them, but I was feeling good again and enjoyed the walk up. I was very fit and in top physical condition. Those six months between leaving the job and leaving South Africa I had been exercising extra hard. Because it was not an easy walk, there were no crowds and no gates to pass through. I had the entire ruin almost to myself. The view of the Andes mountain ranges and the Sacred Valley below were astonishing. The ruins themselves were ancient and spectacular and even though the place had been abandoned hundreds of years ago, water still ran there in some of the waterways and canals. I was in awe; it felt like I had travelled back in time, like I was a citizen of this ancient city. Engrossed, I spent the whole day up there. I just made it off the mountain and back to town before dark.

After a few days in Písac, I started down the Sacred Valley toward Machu Picchu. I travelled from village to village, staying in hostels or local homestays by night, exploring the mountains and ruins by day. The length of the Sacred Valley was just 100 kilometres, but it took me a month to complete the trip.

It was a very strange time. On the one hand, my life was filled with adventure. I was exploring a strange, distant land, travelling back in time, witnessing unsolved mysteries in breathtaking nature. I was immersed in an adventure. On the other hand, I was very aware that I was experiencing all of this on my own. I often wished that there was someone next to me, someone I could experience the beauty with. Someone who could witness it along with me and with whom I could share my thoughts and impressions. I started to feel achingly alone. I was not used to being on my own, definitely not for such a long period. My demons came to the fore. My mind became really busy; I began to feel a deep paranoia. I started to wonder whether it was the long-term effects of all the partying, all the Cat I'd taken, the substances I'd imbibed. Also, the local people were not that friendly, especially if you were not buying from them. I internalised that too. Deep down I knew that it was a resentment they held toward all Westerners, since the days the Spaniards had invaded their lands, slaughtered their people and destroyed their scared buildings and temples. But I took the antagonism and hatred I saw in their eyes personally.

In the Sacred Valley, four weeks after leaving South Africa, I hit rock bottom. I was sitting high on the rooftop of a small local restaurant eating something basic, when this overwhelming feeling descended over me. This was too much for me to do. It was too much for me to do on my own. I was sad, depressed and alone. I had been thinking about Jade a lot over the preceding weeks, especially when I saw or experienced something special. It would have been so good to turn to her, to laugh about it, talk about it. I often thought about calling or messaging her to join me. I knew that if I asked, she would have been on the next plane.

I reached for my phone to start typing her a message. I sat with it in my hand for a few seconds, thinking of how to word the message. And then I looked up. It took my breath away. In front of me, spanning the entire sky, was the most beautiful rainbow I had ever seen. What made it even more magical was that it had the Andes as a backdrop and was straddling the Sacred Valley. All choked up, I dropped my phone in my lap. Then I noticed something else. On roof of the building in front of me there was a cross. The cross was right in the centre of the rainbow, stretching across it.

I could not move. I just stared at that picture: the rainbow, the cross, the mountains and the valley in front of me. It was spellbinding. And then my mood lifted, my heart filled with joy. I felt an immense gratitude for being on this journey. I smiled, then started laughing. I knew that something significant had just happened. That it was a sign. I didn't understand it, but I knew that I had got some help at a critical point when I had almost abandoned my journey. I knew that getting Jade to join me meant that I would be abandoning myself, in the same way as getting on a plane back to South Africa would have been. I could only do this on my own. I could only go deep inside, on my own. I knew that without any doubt. The Voice told me so. My heart told me so.

I continued down to the bottom of the Sacred Valley, arriving at Machu Picchu a week later. Standing on top of the world, in this ancient lost city high up in the Andes, was surreal. Built atop a mountain peak and surrounded by a number of other peaks in close proximity, it is covered with dense, dark, green jungle. It's a whole different world, magical and mysterious. I wandered the ruins of the city for hours, mesmerised, as if in a trance, imagining life as a citizen here all those years ago.

A week later, having returned from Machu Picchu, with a stayover at the floating islands of Lake Titicaca, I found myself in the surfing village of Máncora on the north coast of Peru, a few kilometres from the Ecuadorian border. I found a basic little hotel right on the beach, very rustic but in an amazing location. My room overlooked the ocean; after taking two steps from my door I was on the sand.

One night I was sitting on the balcony of my hotel, sipping white wine and reading a book, *Finding Your Destiny*, when I heard laughter on the steps, a conversation in Spanish. A guy and three women. They stopped when they saw me sitting in the middle of one of the two big couches, taking up most of the space there, and then turned to find some other place to sit. But there were only a few other uncomfortable chairs on the balcony, so I moved to the side of the couch and waved them over. I immediately carried on reading. As they sat down the guy asked whether I cared to join them for a drink. I was really enjoying my own company but before I could even open my mouth to decline, he'd already poured me a drink. It was a stiff one and he proudly showed me the label of the bottle; his favourite whiskey, he said, and asked whether I'd had it before. The label read Grand Old Parr, which I had never heard of, but they were friendly and clearly a few drinks strong already so I relented. They were Peruvian but, fortunately, their English was good, because my Spanish was nonexistent. One of the women was the manager of the hotel, one the surfing instructor and the third a guest, as was the guy. They asked what I was reading and what I was doing in Máncora and Peru. I showed them the book and told them a bit of my story. They found it very funny, convinced that from the picture on the book it was clear that my destiny was to stay in Máncora, get a boat and become a fisherman. I ended up sharing quite a few Grand Old Parrs with them and by the end of the evening I had been offered the job as the new barman. The previous guy had left earlier in the day and Paloma, the hotel manager, insisted that it was my destiny to be the barman at her hotel. In that moment, it sounded like a good idea, so I accepted.

The next morning Paloma moved me to a room with an even better view and alongside that of the guy from the night before. He was from Lima but clearly a regular here, and he and I would become good friends; he became Amigo Jorge – both the *j* and the *g* pronounced as a guttural *g*.

In the sober light of day, though, I confessed to Paloma that I was probably not a good choice as a barman – I wanted to read a lot of books. She just laughed and agreed to find someone else. As it turns out, though, the Peruvian guy she hired was a disaster. When he opened the beach bar at 10 am, he'd immediately start playing hectic rap, the lyrics consisting mostly of "fuck", "fucking" and "nigger" and combinations thereof. Amigo Jorge and I explained nicely that that music was too distracting when having your breakfast on the deck on the beach and asked whether he could wait and rather reserve his music for the late afternoon. He agreed, and would do that for a day or so, but then quickly revert to his old ways. Amigo Jorge and I told Paloma that we needed to find her a new barman, that we'd recruit from the supply of gorgeous young European tourists staying in or travelling through the village. That's how Crazy Dutchie became the new bar lady. Everyone was happy. She was gorgeous and didn't play rap music over breakfast. She and I became good friends and hung out a lot.

It was at this point that I started noticing that there was something strange happening to me. Crazy Dutchie was clearly into me but I just could not bring myself to get physical with her. I was definitely attracted to her – she was beautiful and sexy – but something was holding me back. And it wasn't just her ... I noticed the same thing when it came to all the other women in the village. And I came across quite a few because Amigo Jorge turned out be a good wingman. He was roughly my age, half Spanish Peruvian and half Croatian and very good looking; the blonde Europeans especially liked his dark Spanish looks. He and I would often go out for dinner in the village or for drinks at the hostel across the road, and we met a lot of women that way. It was a surfing and party village, which meant that there were a lot of beautiful girls passing through or even staying long term. After being on the road for such a long time, mostly on my own, the female company was great. Naturally, I'd be physically attracted – my body would respond with an erection – but the moment I realised it was heading towards sex, I would withdraw, both emotionally and physically. I would even do idiotic things like – perhaps subconsciously – spill drinks in a woman's lap – clearly a stern internal voice warning me against sex with them. It was all seriously confusing; this had never happened to me before. It was really frustrating, too, because I missed making love. It was also really confusing for the women, of course, because one moment I seemed to be into them and the next not. It looked as if I was playing games, but I really wasn't.

And so my period of celibacy started. It was never something I had consciously decided on, rather something that happened by listening to the Voice. It didn't make any sense to me at all, but by now I had got used to listening to the Voice so, as difficult as it was, I went with it.

After three weeks in the place, it was really difficult to leave Máncora. I felt a strong pull to stay in the village forever and could understand how many visitors who arrived there on holiday ended up staying a lifetime. I knew, however, that I had to keep moving, that there was a lot of learning ahead of me. Although the temptation was great, I realised that staying in Máncora would be another way of abandoning the journey. I knew it. The Voice said so. My heart agreed.

So late one afternoon, on the spur of the moment, I bought a bus ticket for the same day, and a few hours later I was on a bus heading for the Ecuadorian border. Paloma, Amigo Jorge and Crazy Dutchie thought I was crazy to be leaving so abruptly, but I knew I had to … I was getting too comfortable. Otherwise, I would still be there.

CHAPTER 6

Next stop, Ecuador and Colombia

I spent a month in Ecuador, the first week up in the high mountains around the town of Baños and the last part in the surfing village of Montañita, travelling north from there up the coast towards Colombia.

It was in Ecuador that I came across an online Spanish course designed by an Australian guy living in Mexico. It spoke to me, simply because it was a more modern, more intuitive way of learning a language. I was also moving around quite a bit and found that stepping into a different language school in every new town was really difficult because there was no continuity. So I bought the programme and spent time almost every day learning a little more. I was shocked at how difficult I was finding learning a new language. For some reason, I had thought learning Spanish would be a breeze. I was, after all, already fully bilingual. Although my mother tongue is Afrikaans, I was fluent in English and I thought adding a third language would be a cinch. It was not, and my self-confidence took a serious knock. I was starting to wonder what had happened to my brain over those last few years in Cape Town. Maybe all the drugs had altered the chemistry in my brain; maybe being so bored with my job meant that my brain had become lazy. So, internally, I was going through a few challenges. Externally, though, the adventure continued, which did help calm the whirlwind in my mind. This was truly a gorgeous country: spectacular vistas, towering mountains and vast white beaches. I was connecting more and more with nature and slowly that connection grew and I was able to see and appreciate the beauty in everything around me. It was difficult not to.

By now I was known as Leonardo or Leo because the pronunciation of Lenerd seemed just too difficult, too soft for Spanish speakers. Within a month or so of my travels around South America I was already introducing myself as Leonardo – it was so much easier and saved a lot of time. Lenerd would almost always be followed by the same sequence of questions and answers, and I'd end up repeating my name a few times without success: "Lenerd … like Leonardo, but without the *o* at the end."

Then there would be the inevitable, "Aah, Leonardo!"

I would go, "Si!"

They would go, "DiCaprio?"

I would go either, "Si!" or, "I wish!"

Then everyone would crack up laughing, including me, and from then on I'd be known as Leonardo. It was a great icebreaker, but the whole process took a long time, so I eventually just defaulted to Leonardo, got used to it and actually started liking the name. I was really enjoying the wonderful sense of humour of South Americans. There was almost a childlike innocence in a lot of the people I encountered.

So Leonardo arrived in the village of Montañita after walking the high mountains of the interior for a week. It turned out that Crazy Dutchie had also made her way to Ecuador, further south down the coast, but was planning to travel up to Montañita when she heard I was in town. That made me really happy because I'd been missing the friends I had made in Máncora and was looking forward to seeing her.

I was in the village for only a few days, however, before I was man down for almost a week, an extreme case of diarrhoea and vomiting. I had definitely picked up something, probably from a fruit smoothie bought on the side of the road. The water system in Ecuador, especially down at the coast, was a bit of a mess and the sewerage system and water system often got mixed. Vendors are supposed to use bottled water for the smoothies, but of course there was never any guarantee. Within a few days I had been sapped of all my energy. There was no doctor in the village and with the language problem it would, in any event, have been difficult to have had a meaningful discussion. So I just went to the local pharmacy and got some stuff to make me feel slightly better.

A few days later Crazy Dutchie arrived with two friends in tow, another Dutch girl and an Australian. They were in their 20s and having a blast touring South America. I had a big room with a few beds, so they all crashed with me. By now I was no longer staying in expensive hotels, but in hostels or budget hotels because they were much more social; here you came into contact with the people of the country as well as other travellers. I, however, was way beyond staying in dormitories and always got my own room. There were often single private rooms available and, if not, I'd just book a double or triple room for myself.

I had fun hanging out with the girls, but once again it was never more than just friendship – a strange experience because previously this would have been sexual nirvana for me. After a few days, Crazy Dutchie and I decided to travel further up the coast, making our way from village to village. It was great the first few days, but then I think she started taking it personally that I wasn't having sex with her. I had told her about my escapades in Cape Town, so she knew that I loved women. I'd also explained that I was taking a much-needed break from sex, that this strange internal voice was insisting I not engage sexually with anyone. I don't think that made any sense to her though. She was like 26 and I didn't blame her – at that age, it would not have made any sense to me either. And, truth be told, it actually didn't make much sense to me, but I wasn't following logic, I was just following the Voice.

Crazy and volatile as she was, this made her even crazier. She would challenge me at every turn, argue about everything. Eventually, we decided to remain friends but rather part ways, so she moved on further north while I stayed in the village of Mompiche. It was wonderful to have peace and quiet again and I spent my time walking on the beach, swimming lengths in the sea and reading my books.

Something wasn't right though. My health wasn't great and I started to suspect that I had picked up a parasite – or amoeba, as they're called in South America. I was often out of energy and was losing weight. There were never any doctors in the tiny isolated villages along the coast so I decided I would see a doctor once I was in Colombia, the next country on my itinerary. I had heard amazing things about the place from the other travellers who were making their way south and had just come from there.

So I agreed with Amigo Jorge, who was in Lima at that stage, to meet in Cartagena on the north coast of Colombia and for us to travel together for a few weeks. He had never been to Colombia and because he owned a few investment properties that he rented out, he was flexible and could work from his laptop anywhere. I then made my way from the coast to the capital, Quito, spent a few days there, and then caught a plane to Cartagena.

When I walked into the foyer of the hostel in Cartagena, he was already there. He jumped up when he saw me and shouted in his thick Spanish accent, "Leonardo, what the fuck you doing?"

I laughed – I had no idea what he meant.

He just pointed at all I was carrying and asked, "What you doing with all this shit?"

I immediately clicked. I carried my large, overfull backpack on my back, another small one with my books and iPad in my left hand, and in my right a large black dustbin bag filled to the brim. I could barely walk under the weight of it all and had basically stumbled into the hostel foyer. I laughed and explained to him that I had bought some new stuff to wear but still had the old worn stuff in the bag.

The next day we went through my bag and almost halved everything I was carrying. In my bag I even had an expensive sports jacket that I planned to wear in New York. We weighed it and that jacket was almost a kilogram on its own. It was already May, the month I was supposed to have touched down in New York. In fact, I was starting to suspect that I was never going to see New York, at least not in the foreseeable future. I just didn't feel like going there.

I instructed Jorge to put on the jacket. "That looks great on you, amigo," I told him. "I think you're going to get lucky in that – you can have it." The rest of the stuff I gave to the hostel's barman. When we left the next morning, I walked out with a much lighter load, both my hands empty. I felt amazing, light and free. It was as if I had just started another adventure all over again. It felt as I had just offloaded a few houses, cars, boats – the obligations that were weighing me down. It was a beautiful message of learning. My struggling down the road with all of that weight on my back was a metaphor, a vivid picture, a reminder of what all the stuff we own does to us on a daily basis.

Amigo Jorge and I toured the coast for a few weeks and then boarded a flight to the city of Medellin, in the heart of Colombia, which was once the murder capital of the world and the home of Pablo Escobar. An infamous place.

We did our research though. I had spoken to a number of travellers who had come down from Colombia and had visited Medellin, and I was enthralled by their tales of an enchanted, friendly, modern, sophisticated city. No longer dangerous and very welcoming to travellers simply because, following all the bad press over the years, they were still not getting many tourists. And, coming from South Africa, I knew what bad press could do to tourism. I also knew that there often is a lag, where the situation in a country has improved but people still remember the reports from a few years ago, which puts them off visiting. Travellers from the USA and Europe were especially scared of places they perceived as dangerous. People from South Africa much less so – probably because we live in a pretty dangerous place ourselves. So, for me, being in Colombia and on my way to visit what was previously the murder capital of the world wasn't that big a deal.

Medellin was even better than the stories I'd been told. Amigo Jorge only stayed a week before going back to Lima, but in that week we saw a lot. Evergreen and nestled in a long valley with high mountains on either side, it's known as the City of Eternal Spring because the weather is great virtually throughout the year. Never too hot or too cold, temperatures always in the low to mid-20s. There are small rivers and streams running throughout the place, with lots of lush vegetation everywhere. It was so unlike the other South American cities I had seen up to then. Lima and Quito each had over 10 million people, while Medellin had just 1.6 million inhabitants. Being much smaller made it much more personal.

After Amigo Jorge left, I decided that I was going to stay in the city for a while to experience more of the place, soak up more of the atmosphere. I also heard this was a good place to study Spanish. The way the Colombians speak the language is certainly much easier to understand than the Spanish I had come across in Peru and Ecuador. They spoke slower and much clearer, and for the first time I could have at least some sort of conversation with taxi drivers and other locals. It was still extremely basic and limited, but I saw a tiny light at the end of the language tunnel.

I researched study options and opted for Universidad Pontificia Bolivariana, also known as UPB, a beautiful university located in the suburb of Laureles, an area of the city where there were almost no tourists or foreigners. Up until then I had been staying at a hotel in the Poblado neighbourhood in the touristy part of the city. I decided to move to be close to the university and found myself an apartment not far from it. It was clear from the start that this was going to be a fascinating experience. I would walk down the street and people would stare at me. They were not used to seeing foreigners. I started dressing the same as the Colombians and even cut my hair in the same short style that was popular and fashionable there. Medellin is a sophisticated and fashionable city, the people always very well dressed. No shorts or slops. Always long pants with shoes. I still stood out though. At first I couldn't fathom it but eventually realised that my complexion gave me away. I wasn't that fair, but still much more so than their swarthy looks.

My apartment was only a few blocks from the rooftop where Pablo Escobar was shot 20 years prior. This city must have been a crazily dangerous place at one time; I was told that there was a law that a motorbike, irrespective of the size, was not allowed to carry a passenger. Reason being, the passenger was presumed to be an assassin. I never felt unsafe though. I suppose growing up in Johannesburg helped. From an early age, you would always be very aware walking down the street, conscious of what was going on around you, especially behind you. You'd observe without giving it away, without coming across as nervous. On the contrary, you would try to come across as assertive, fearless, aggressive almost. A clear sign that you were not an easy target. That would quickly become second nature, without much thinking. I think because I walked with that same energy in the cities of South America I never had any trouble. The closest I came to any real risk was one night in quite a dangerous part of Lima and I at some point sensed danger; I crossed the street and carried on walking on the opposite pavement. Out of the corner of my eye I could see a few guys behind me also crossing over. Then I knew for certain. It was already after midnight and my intuition told me not to take a chance. I immediately jumped into the first available taxi and got him to drop me off a few blocks away.

I would cycle to university every day, lock my bicycle in the bicycle shed, go to class, eat in the cafeteria with the other students, swim some lengths in the university pool and cycle back at the end of the day. It was surreal. I felt as if I was 19 again.

The Spanish classes were hilarious. You could do individual or group classes, and I enrolled for the group ones. The classes were limited to 10 students, but for some reason there were only two in my class: me and this guy from Trinidad. He was of Indian heritage but had this strong Caribbean accent, which was very funny to me because I was used to Indians speaking with an Indian accent. What made it funnier was that I had a strong South African accent and our Spanish teacher could not speak a word of English. Essentially, class was a comedy of errors. We were not very advanced, so half the time we wouldn't understand what the teacher was saying and when it was impossible for us to get clarity from him, we would just start talking and guessing between ourselves in our respective Caribbean and South African accents. Every now and then I would crack up laughing at the absurdity of the situation. That we learnt anything in these classes was a miracle. Amigo Brian, as I started calling him, and I became good buddies and would practise our broken Spanish in the cafeteria with some pretty women students – and there were many. They were happy to speak to us; we stood out and they found us strangely fascinating.

I also decided to take salsa dancing classes. In my six months in South America, it had become very clear to me that if you can't dance, you have a problem. Dancing is big. Everyone dances. Everywhere. In South Africa, as in most English-speaking countries, you can get away with leaning against the bar counter with a beer in hand, looking all cool, macho or tough, whilst others are dancing. In South America, if you do that, you just look stupid – the only one standing at the bar, looking silly, sad, insecure.

What made it more difficult for me was that I was never much of a dancer. At university we would sometimes arrive late in the evening, a few drinks strong at the organised dances on campus. These were called *sokkies*, and would entail dancing with a partner, doing waltzes, two-steps and so on. Traditional Afrikaners were all very good at this, a little like the Spanish-speaking people, spinning, twirling and moving together with their partners all over the show. My mates and I, however, thought we were too cool for this, so we never really learnt.

My salsa teacher was a colourful, energetic, passionate Latin woman with bright red hair. She spoke not a word of English and my Spanish was very limited, but that did not stop her; she spoke rapidly in long sentences, explaining and showing the dances, loudly counting the steps from one to eight in Spanish. I understood very little of what she was saying and told her so, but she just continued unperturbed. She decided that I should not only learn salsa, but bachata and merengue also. I enjoyed bachata the most and, to my own surprise, ended up having a lot of fun, dancing for the sake of dancing. I never became very good at it, but at least I have the confidence to step out on the dance floor.

I had never been in a city with so many beautiful women as in Medellin, a melting pot of different genes. At one point there was an influx of Italians, which together with the Spanish was a deadly combination. There was also a theory that Pablo Escobar apparently "imported" beautiful women from all over the country when he was living in Medellin. They stayed and their genes spread too. I, though, didn't sample any of the women. I had now been celibate for half a year. I still had no idea why; I was just following the Voice. Even though I wanted to – there were times when I was really horny – I just couldn't bring myself to do it.

My first two months in Medellin were quiet. Very quiet. I focused on my Spanish studies, salsa classes and the spiritual books I was reading. It was here that I fell in love with Paulo Coelho and read every book of his that I could find. I read the *Warrior of the Light* probably 10 times. But I was also still sick and losing a lot of weight. When I initially arrived in town, I confirmed my suspicions when I tested positive for parasites in my system. I was prescribed antibiotics, but the condition did not go away. I would end up having four courses of antibiotics, to no avail.

I could feel my strength, my weight and health deteriorating. I had to be very careful about what I ate and could not touch alcohol, sugar or any rich or spicy food. All I could really eat were grilled chicken breasts and dry rice. Anything else and I would stink up the place. I could only drink water because fruit juice, cold drinks and alcohol all contained sugar, and parasites love sugar. I didn't see the humour in that at the time. Even when eating basic foodstuff I could still sense the parasites converging on the food as it hit my stomach. It was a terrible feeling to know that my body and even, to some extent, my consciousness were being taken over by foreign bodies. I googled parasites and amoebas and watched videos. It was very disconcerting. I felt terrible.

Added to that struggle was that I realised I wasn't going to see my children for their July school holidays. I had planned to fly them out, but it turned out that getting them to South America wasn't that easy. There was no direct flight to Medellin and I wasn't comfortable with them catching connecting flights in South America. The only other option was to fly them to São Paulo in Brazil and meet them there, but with the upcoming Soccer World Cup taking place in Brazil, flight options were limited and there were also a few security scares around the World Cup. My ex-wife was understandably very sceptical about them flying alone to São Paulo during this time. The only other option was for me to fly to Durban and see them there. I, however, had a deep knowing that this would bring an abrupt end to my travels. Being back in South Africa at this critical point in my journey would not have worked. I didn't think I would have had the courage to leave again. To remain on this journey, I had to pay another price. This time that price was not seeing my kids. I also knew that I would not see them for their October school holidays either because those were too short, only one week, and that they wanted to use some of that time to study. The next available opportunity would thus be the December holidays. That would mean that I would not see them for almost a year. I was heartbroken and torn in two. Whatever I decided would have a serious downside. I mulled it over for a few weeks, trying hard to find alternative options, but to no avail. Eventually, I turned to the Voice. The Voice was clear, "Stay on your journey."

It was one of the hardest things I have had to do. I knew that I would be missing out on a critical time in their young lives. I also knew that they were taking strain not seeing me, especially my daughter. I called her to discuss the issue with her. "Daddy," she said, "it's important that you do what is right for you. You must look after yourself. If this is important for you, then you must follow that. I understand."

I put the phone down, all choked up. She was only 14 years old, yet she sounded so mature, so wise, so selfless. I felt so much love for her, so much connectedness. I missed them both terribly. I knew, too, that as difficult as it was, I had to stay on the journey, not just for me, but for them. The Voice told me that I was not doing this just for me. I did not understand that entirely, but I clearly felt the truth of it.

So I stayed on the journey.

And then the 2014 Soccer World Cup kicked off in neighbouring Brazil. And with that the austerity of my current existence was all but abandoned. Fuck this, I thought. I'm not getting better by trying to be good … I might as well just join the party.

And what a party it was.

The whole of Colombia went mad. Their team did very well and the intensity increased with every game they won. I very soon realised that this was "mad" on an entirely different level. During the first few games in the capital, Bogotá, so many people died in the celebrations, caught in the line of stray bullets fired in celebration, that they enacted a "dry law". On the day of a game, no alcohol could be sold or served right throughout the city. That law was not enforced in Medellin, the city having escaped the fatalities of the capital.

So Colombia's team became my team. South Africa was not playing in the World Cup. We didn't even get close to qualifying for it. I also soon realised that studying Spanish and wholeheartedly supporting your team in the World Cup didn't go together. The courses were running monthly, so after the soccer started, I didn't renew for another month. I explained to Amigo Brian that he was on his own with our teacher and that I was dedicating my efforts to becoming a full-time supporter.

By the second game I had bought myself a yellow Colombian soccer shirt and was going crazy with my fellow countrymen. I became Colombian. After each game, after each goal we scored, I danced in the streets with them. Naturally, I made a lot of

Colombian friends. The people, especially in Medellin, are sociable and friendly. When walking in the street or a park in the evenings and over weekends, you would often be stopped and offered a shooter of aguardiente, the local drink. It's a white rum made from sugar cane and has an anise flavour. It reminded me of Sambuca, which we drank often in university days. With the World Cup now in full swing, being offered aguardiente happened regularly. I don't think it was very good for my condition, but by now I was trying not to think about that too much and was enjoying the party.

My team did really well – until we were "cheated out of it" in the quarterfinal against Brazil. With the rest of the country, I went into mourning, and then rejoiced a week later when justice was served and Germany fucked Brazil up properly in the semifinals with a 7–1 win.

During this time, in full party mode, I made some good friends, brothers.

Brother California was as big as a mountain, six foot four with biceps almost as thick as my thighs. He was born in South Africa, but his parents had left when he was two years old to move to Los Angeles. A bald but good-looking guy with a well-trained gym body, he looked a lot like the The Rock, the movie star Dwayne Johnson. He had a soft heart and a small dog he was crazy about.

Then there was Brother Italy, a stylish Italian who spoke fluent Spanish but never touched a drop of alcohol. He loved women though – he was in Medellin mainly for the women. He was employed by a university in Miami, but worked online from Medellin.

Brother Germany was a very lean, six-foot-five German in his late 20s and an excellent sportsman, having come fifth in the international Ironman competition. We often swam lengths in the large pool at the sports complex close to the university. He thought my form was terrible. I agreed. He was in Medellin to give English classes and to study Spanish. He had a tiny Colombian girlfriend half his height, who he was very serious about.

Brother America was a smooth, good-looking American – a

direct marketing specialist working online from Medellin, and also there mainly for the women.

I was now living at the edge of the Poblado neighbourhood, in a tenth-floor one-bedroom apart-ment, which had a magnificent view of the whole of the city and mountains beyond. I moved there because I no longer needed to be close to the university and because, with a lot of cool bars in the area, it was a good place to watch the soccer.

My international brothers introduced me to a side of Medellin I hadn't seen before, having been a good, studious boy who didn't go out much. It turned out that a lot of guys come to Medellin for the beautiful women. Some looking for love and a wife, some just to play around. Especially the Americans, it seemed. I had many Americans tell me how women in their country had become so masculine and full of shit that they preferred the more feminine, more passionate Colombian women. I, however, found out very quickly that when meeting women it was a big advantage if you were not American – the gringos did not have a good reputation in town. Being from Europe or elsewhere was much more interesting and exotic. Being from Africa was extra exotic. Being white *and* from Africa was extremely exotic and a mind fuck for most. I had many a discussion where they could not understand and refused to believe that I was from Africa. The number of times I heard, "Pero, no eres negro!" ("But you are not black!") was like Groundhog Day.

If you were a foreigner, there was an assumption that you were a gringo, so one of the first things I did when I met women was to point out that I was not from the USA. That always sparked the interest. I was enthralled by the women of Medellin, but I was also still celibate. That did not stop me looking at them, though, speaking to them and wanting to meet more of them. I was really torn. I was longing for some connection. Some intimacy. Some feminine company.

So I ended up going on a dating site, aptly named Colombia Cupid. I met only one woman in person. She was the dream: a famous DJ in Colombia, in her mid-20s, and sexy. She was glamorous too, performing on stage in revealing outfits that showed her beautiful breasts. Unlike most of the women on the website, she was making her own living and doing that really well. She was often flown to Panama to play in clubs there. We ended up kissing, but before taking it any further she wanted to know whether I was going to be in Medellin long term or not.

I was torn in two. I could see myself with this woman. She was beautiful and bright, and we had a great connection. I could see myself hanging with her, accompanying her to Panama for gigs and having a blast with her in Medellin. I also knew that that would mean abandoning the journey. I would probably never leave Medellin. And I knew there was more learning on the journey ahead. The temptation was huge. A part of me wanted to say, "Fuck it!" and stay put, take the pressure off, be with the girl, fuck the journey. It took me a few days to decide, but eventually I told her I would probably continue my journey in a few months. My international brothers thought I was fucking insane. Firstly, they could not believe I'd managed to get her interested in me. Secondly, they could not believe that I didn't just tell her I'd be there long term, get to fuck her and then see where it went.

A part of me thought the same, but another part really just wanted to be authentic, to treat her right and not create more karma for myself.

When the World Cup came to an end, I considered my options and was finally swayed to stay on in the City of Eternal Spring for a number of reasons. Firstly, over the following few weeks there were some cool events happening. Colombiamoda is a glamorous Fashion Week that takes place every year, attended by models from all over South America. It turns out Medellin is the fashion capital of South America. Feria de las Flores is the annual flower festival with parades and festivities. I decided I could not leave just before these two popular events.

Secondly, Brother Italy – the non-drinking Italian – introduced me to the strip clubs of Medellin. We did the range, from the upmarket to the decidedly rough. It was an eye opener. It was also my introduction to the white gold of Colombia, and came with the territory I was now hanging out in. The famous white powder of Colombia. This was the real stuff. Not the cut-down stuff they sell in South Africa or Europe. It was crazy strong, very pure. One line could fuck you up. Properly fuck you up. It did. I also got fucked properly. Literally. It seemed Colombian cocaine can bring a cessation to mysterious celibacies. It can drown out the Voice, override internal guidance systems. Very soon I was back in my Cape Town pattern and often landed up at the end of the night with two girls at my place, doing long lines of cocaine on each other's bodies, fucking our brains out.

Brother America turned out to be an excellent wingman. He and I would go out on the town, have drinks, meet women, dance with them, drink with them. Yes, I was also drinking now. My condition was still not better, the parasites still lurking. Maybe I could drown the motherfuckers...

Brother America's Spanish was much better than mine, although he spoke it with a heavy American accent, which was quite funny. Half the time he sounded as though he was speaking American English rather than Spanish. My accent was much better, but my Spanish was very limited. We got by though; most of our conversations were far from intellectual. Basic Spanish did the job.

The dating scene worked differently to what I was used to. Women seldom paid for anything on a date or night out. Even when a group of friends went out, the women would pay nothing at the end of the night. It's custom for Colombian men to foot the bill, whether it's a date or just a group of friends having dinner. On a date, the guy would often be expected to pay for the woman's taxi ride there and back. I found it very peculiar. But this was Colombia. Things worked differently here.

There was never a shortage of women ready to party, which meant that we were out most nights. It was as if my life in Cape Town was replaying itself. Walking away from a possible long-term relationship with a cool girl, only to find myself in casual encounters with party girls, fucking and getting fucked.

Colombiamoda was a lot of fun. The international brothers and I – excluding Brother Germany, because he had a girlfriend – went almost every day, attended the evening functions and practised our Spanish on the models there. We were like four boys in a candy store. Much the same was true of the colourful Feria de las Flores, and Brother California and I hung out there regularly. His Spanish was quite good and we made a few good Colombian friends.

At the time, Brother America was living in a high-rise building with a great view over the city, so we partied there a lot and got to know quite a few women who enjoyed hanging out with us. I met some really great women with whom I connected – and not just on a physical level. A few became good friends.

Once again, none of my international brothers partook of the white powder, just me and my female friends. The brothers were living long term in Medellin and using it was frowned upon by the upmarket community there. It was seen as a low-class drug – quite the opposite to Cape Town, London, etcetera, where it's very much considered a high-society habit. It was crazy cheap also. I commented to one of the girls how cheap it was at just $10 or sometimes $5 per gram, compared to Cape Town at around $50 per gram. She said I was crazy to pay so much; she could get it for us at $2 a gram, which she did and it was even better quality.

When Feria de las Flores ended, I knew it was time for me to move on. I had been living in Medellin for three months and had had an amazingly varied experience there. I knew, too, that there was a purpose to even the last few weeks of going off the rails. It had been a touch of the old life. The old life I didn't want anymore. I wrote it off to research. I suppose I had to double check.

CHAPTER 7

Paying the price

I went to detox in the coffee region.

After Medellin, I travelled south and stayed on a coffee farm for three weeks. The amoebas were eating me up. Handfuls of antibiotics had failed to kill off the parasites and my partying had made it much worse. They really loved the sugar in the alcohol!

Now that the parasites seemed to have multiplied, I started to look for alternative solutions. I had come across ayahuasca earlier in my journey in Peru, as a lot of travellers I met on the road had come specifically to do day-long ayahuasca plant journeys. I hadn't understood what that was all about and wasn't especially interested in the plant then, but now heard that it was good for cleansing your system, flushing it out and ridding you of parasites. That got my attention. I was pretty fed up with the way my condition had been deteriorating.

I ended up doing ayahuasca with some locals on two consecutive Saturdays at a venue not far from the farm where I was staying. Before the ceremony I did proper research. Ayahuasca is a brew made from a vine found in the Amazonian jungle of South America. Medicine people have been using it for thousands of years as a spiritual healer and as a shamanic means of communication. It is meant to summon the unconscious and bring otherworldly processes to the surface. You have to follow a strict diet the week before the ceremony and are not allowed to have any meat, salty or spicy food, alcohol or marijuana and little to no food on the day of the ceremony. After drinking it, there is usually a purge – heavy vomiting often accompanied by diarrhoea – before the journey starts.

None of this sounded like fun to me, but I badly wanted to get rid of my uninvited companions of the last six months. And, of course, the purging sounded logical – a good way to get rid of them – so I decided to give it a try.

It was terrible. Terrible. A few minutes after drinking the vile mixture from a ceremonial cup, I started feeling nauseous. Fifteen minutes later, I found myself hanging over the wall of the open-air boma where we were holding the ceremony, throwing up heavily. Not long after, I had to dash to the toilets with severe diarrhoea. There were only two toilets for 30 people. Luckily, most of the group were Colombians who had been performing the ritual regularly, so they mostly vomited and skipped the diarrhoea. We were only three foreigners in the group. We did both. Extensively. Especially me, probably because of my parasites. I often did both at the same time. I would get up from the toilet, turn around, throw up in the bowl and then sit down again, my bowels emptying. I would make my way back to the boma and collapse on the little bed I had made up with blankets on the concrete floor between the others. Finding your own spot was not easy because it was dark. But as soon as I lay down, I'd be up and running, sprinting off to the toilet again. This went on right throughout the night. I had no idea where all the fluids were coming from. They just ran out of my body. I wasn't drinking much water because I was just too nauseous, but still the fluids continued streaming out of me. At one point the liquid was clear. I had clear water running out of my body. I was fascinated by that. Where did all this clear fluid come from? Then I remembered that I had read that our bodies consist mostly of water, like 70 per cent or something. I wondered how much of me was going to be left over after all of this.

In the middle of the night we were offered another ceremonial drinking. Whoever felt up to it could have another cup of the vile-tasting mixture. I didn't feel up to it at all, but went along anyway. With my alpha male personality, I wasn't going to sit back. Also, I thought, let's really fuck these parasites up now! I may die in the process, but at least they would be dead too.

Because of the parasites in my system, I was mainly purging and not journeying much. However, at some point in the early hours of the morning, I was able to lie down for a while without having to leap up and sprint to throw up and take yet another shit. That's when I had something of a journey. In my vision, I was standing close to the edge of a very high cliff and the message I received there was that the use of cocaine determines how close one gets to the edge. So I'd imagine myself refusing the drug and would find myself moving away from the edge, then I'd imagine myself taking it and would shift closer to the precipice. I spent quite a lot of time moving back and forth until I decided to see how close I could get without falling. I imagined using more and more and the next moment I was teetering, leaning over the abyss, losing my balance and struggling to reclaim it. The experience shook me to the core. It was so real, the images so vivid. I managed to regain my balance and immediately dropped the association with the drug and I was swiftly shifted far back from the edge. It was a clear warning.

The following Saturday evening I had an even worse purging experience because I had faltered on my diet. That morning I ate a small amount of a bean dish, which was allowed as long as it was at least six hours before the ceremony. What I did not realise was that there were bits of bacon and fat in the dish. I thought I was having a perfectly healthy vegetarian meal, only to find out later that I had eaten meat and fat. That meant a severe reaction to the plant medicine. I was purging right throughout the night. It was brutal. I never ate pork again after that night.

After some time on the coffee farm, I made my way further south to the city of Cali where I stayed for a month with a Colombian family, renting a room in their house. On the ground floor was a guy who treated me with magnets to get rid of the parasites. The ayahuasca experience had improved the parasite condition, but only temporarily. They were still there. I could feel it. I was now desperate and looking at all other alternative methods. I had found this guy on the internet when I googled natural cures for parasites. It turned out that the magnets didn't offer a cure either, although they improved my condition for a while.

It was an interesting time with the Colombian family; no one spoke a word of English, but the stay definitely improved my Spanish. I was also studying my internet Spanish course daily, so that helped too. Included in the rent were three meals a day, which I ate with the family. To assist with the fight against the parasites, they served very basic food. I also was drinking no alcohol again, for the same reason.

The wife was very outgoing and friendly, and wanted to introduce me to her friends, but I was back on my celibacy path. They had two sons, aged nine and 13; I taught them a little English and they practised on me. We all grew very close and I would go with them on family outings on Sundays, sitting in the front of the big 4x4 with the husband, while the wife and the kids sat in the back. They all loved talking to me and would shout loudly "Leo! Leo!", competing with each other for my attention. They were colourful characters, and my time with them was pretty chaotic in that Latino kind of way. I loved it, though. It was a special time.

Both boys gave me a present when I left. The 13-year-old gave me a Colombian armband and the nine-year-old three of his gold medals, which he had won in table tennis tournaments. I was deeply touched. I gave each of them an English edition of Paulo Coelho books that I had in my bag. Finally, when it was time to leave and the wife and the younger of the boys dropped me at the airport, they cried. It was very emotional saying goodbye to them.

Because I had been in the country for almost six months and you are only allowed six months in a single calendar year, I had to get out of Colombia. The question was, where would I go? For some reason, I felt that it had to be north. Maybe because that was the original idea, to travel north to New York. I, however, had no desire to make my way to the Big Apple – I just didn't feel it. But still the "going north" thing stuck.

Then I remembered what Brother Germany had told me about the magical lake in Guatemala, where he had stayed and studied Spanish for a few months. When he originally told me the story, I felt something stir in me. I could feel it in my future. It was a strange feeling, out of the blue. A call of sorts. And, with that, I booked a ticket – with a week stayover in Panama City to – Guatemala City.

The week in Panama was a total mess.

I went off the rails again.

It started when I met some Colombian girls. And the party was on.

Then I ran into Crazy Dutchie. She'd seen on Facebook that I was in town and invited me to visit her and a group of friends at the hostel where they were staying in the old town. Facebook is a great connector when travelling. I arrived at the hostel and walked straight into a raucous party. Everyone was drinking and already a few lines strong. After a couple of drinks, Crazy Dutchie, a Swedish girlfriend and I decided to go out, but we hadn't got far down the road when Crazy Dutchie mumbled something, turned angrily and sped back to the hostel – upset, I think, that I was paying too much attention to her friend. Frankly, I did not have the energy to try to figure it out.

The Swede was pretty, with a really sunny, easy disposition, and we ended up chatting to a group of Panamanians who invited us to join them at a cool club.

A tall young guy, asked, "You want some party stuff?"

"Sure." I said. "Why not?"

Tall Young Guy handed me a small, rolled-up parcel of cocaine. We were having a blast, partying and dancing, but I was getting a little tired and thought the cocaine would give me energy – which it did, as it always does. I kept the parcel in the pocket of my jeans and bought a round of drinks to return the favour.

Next thing two police officers walked in. They were dressed

in military uniform, handguns strapped to their waists. My heart almost leapt out of my throat. They immediately instructed Tall Young Guy, who was closest to the door, to empty his pockets and began searching him. I managed to casually reach into my pocket, retrieve the rolled-up paper and slip it under the cushion I was sitting on. And so I just sat there, as if there was nothing wrong, chatting nonchalantly to the Swede. In truth, however, my heart was racing. The next moment, Tall Young Guy was handcuffed and marched out of the room. Minutes later I audaciously retrieved the parcel from under the cushion and we continued partying up a storm until the early hours. The vision I had had during the ayahuasca ceremony was far from my mind.

However, when I woke the next morning, I knew that I was fucking with my life now. Seriously. In a jail cell in Central America was not the way I intended to end this journey, and by the way my life was going, that was now a distinct possibility. Apart from a ruined business and social reputation, what hit me hardest was how this would affect my kids, even more so than my parents, who would have been destroyed. I would have failed my kids, irredeemably. I felt it in the pit of my stomach, an intense shame at the core of my being. It was a terrible feeling. I knew I had to do some serious rethinking on where I was heading.

CHAPTER 8

When the student is ready...

"Look at the energy leaking out! No wonder you have parasites…" he said, pointing at my stomach and lower back.

Okay, I thought. I've been told that Dr Bill's a bit crazy, but this is just damn weird.

When I had asked at the hostel in Guatemala for anyone who could help with the healing of parasites, the owner had recommended Dr Bill. That's how I found myself in a room in a house above a store in a tiny Mayan village by the name of San Marcos in Guatemala, on the shores of beautiful Lago Atitlán. Lago is the Spanish word for lake. The lake is surrounded by volcanoes, one of them still active.

I looked down at my stomach and then tried twisting around to see my lower back. "I don't see anything," I said.

"No, there! Look there. You losing energy out of that area, man!" Dr Bill replied.

He then turned his head towards the door and called, "Ben, come and look here!"

With that, a scrawny 20-something kid peered around the corner.

"You see that, Ben?" Dr Bill asked.

"Yes, he is losing energy there," the scrawny kid said, pointing.

My instinct was to get the hell out of there fast, but something made me stay. The Voice was back. I was desperate. I was sick. I was disillusioned. I was totally fucked and broken. I had hit rock bottom.

It had been nine months since I'd left South Africa. For the last seven, parasites had been my constant companion, eating me alive. When I started out, I was a lean and fit 82 kilograms, the perfect weight for my height of six feet, but by the time I arrived in Guatemala my weight had dropped to 72 kilograms. I had lost 10 kays of pure muscle in seven months.

I had been through four courses of antibiotics, with absolutely no result other than the dramatic side effects. The antibiotics were going to kill me long before they'd kill the parasites.

Dr Bill was my last hope. He continued to point at my "energy leak".

"You must release your emotions. Not be so hard on yourself," he said.

That took me by surprise. I had always thought of myself as a happy-go-lucky kinda guy.

"Yes!" he continued. "You must emotional release and have a good cry! When last did you cry?"

I started mumbling something about primary school, but he jerked upright and raised his voice, his finger wagging in my face. "And you must get laid!"

Whoa! How could he have known about my weird celibacy? How every time it got close to sex I'd hear a stern voice inside me saying, "No, not now, take a break!" Yes, it had been confusing, but it felt right, so I had listened. And now there was this strange guy picking up on all of it.

Dr Bill poured something he called colloidal silver water and insisted I drink. At this stage, I was prepared to do anything.

Before I left, he told me he would introduce me to an Englishwoman who lived up the hill and that she would be able to help me further. And then, a few days later, Dr Bill walked me up the hill to introduce me to Grace, who I dubbed the English Girl of The Lake. There was a brief introduction about her being part of some international group doing great work and then he left. Next thing I'm telling her my life story, and she's taking notes. I couldn't help but wonder how this was going to help rid me of my parasites, but decided to go with the flow.

An hour later Grace asked me whether I had heard about emotional release tools. No, I told her. She gave a long explanation about how critical it is to release our emotions and how as kids we are taught not to express our emotions but rather to suppress them, which causes them to settle in the cells of our bodies, creating tension and energy leakage and making us sick.

She then told me she'd illustrate the tools to me. I was sceptical about all of this, but had already paid for the session – plus, desperation is a great motivator. And so, over the next hour, I found myself screaming into cushions, punching cushions, fucking cushions, power stomping around the room, wailing at the top of my voice, "Why, God? Why me?", my hands stretched out above me, doing hand screams – screaming into the palm of your hand to muffle the sound – and finally on my back on the bed, throwing a tantrum like a two-year-old, kicking and hitting the bed while shouting, "I want an ice cream! And I want it fucking *now*!"

In the beginning, I could not help scanning the room for hidden cameras – I was convinced I'd probably feature on some reality TV show. But after a while, I decided to let it rip and gave it my best.

When I woke the next morning, everything was different; for the first time in seven months, it felt like the parasites had left me. It was astonishing, an amazing sensation. Like something deep down had shifted, like my life would never be the same again. The Universe, God, Divine Consciousness – whatever you want to call it – got my attention. For me to move from the left brain, the physical form, the material and controlling world, I needed shock treatment and my getting sick was that for me. I suddenly realised that the parasites had simply been a reflection of what was going on inside me. A catalyst. Within just a few hours I had emerged into the real world, the world of energy. It felt like I had been reborn, like my eyes had been opened. But now the real hard work would begin, where I could start to really look at myself and question everything I believed in.

Dr Bill and I became good friends and regularly went for walks through the village, stopping to talk to people on the way. I learnt that he was a qualified medical doctor with a master's degree in psychology. There were many stories about him in the village; one was that when the president of Guatemala was seriously ill, he'd send his chopper out to fetch Dr Bill.

Dr Bill (everyone called him that) was from Canada and even though he was Caucasian in appearance – bright blue eyes – his grandfather was a Native American. He told me that, as part of a traditional ceremony at the age of eight, he was buried alive and when his grandfather took him out of the ground, he was able to recount everything that had gone on in the ceremony. That was confirmation enough for them that he was a See-er – one who sees – and from then on he was known as Blue-Eyed See-er of the North. Dr Bill was certainly not your normal, run-of-the-mill physician. He would hold talks most mornings at 11 am on his patio in front of his house, and they'd be well attended by travellers passing through the village because San Marcos was well known as a spiritual community. His reputation preceded him.

At one of his talks, Dr Bill colourfully demonstrated how he once pulled an alien – or some kind of entity – out of someone's ass by placing his foot on the person's bum and then yanking it out by force. He had then told the person, wagging his finger at him, that the entity had warned that if he took ayahuasca outside a ceremonial setting again, he would return to kick his ass!

Dr Bill was an extremely colourful character and a lot of fun to hang out with. But he also had amazing gifts of insight and his direct, no-nonsense but charismatic style suited me perfectly. As the saying goes, "When the student is ready, the teacher appears."

I spent some time looking through his books. One engrossing

one made the point that all – like 100 per cent – diseases and sicknesses are related to emotions or rather blocked emotions and that they correlated with the part of the body affected by a specific emotion. Once again, without having any previous experience in this area, I instinctively knew this to be true.

On one of our walks, he asked, "What's your DOC?"

I was confused.

"Your drug of choice," he explained.

I laughed. It was funny. It was the first time that I had heard that.

And so I told him about my party days in Cape Town when my DOC had been MDMA. I also said that that was now behind me and that I would never take drugs again.

He turned and looked straight at me. "That means you should go right now and take a lot of drugs! Because saying *never* – and in the way you said it – means there is still a charge in your body. Only when there is no charge in your body and you feel neutral about it, will it work."

"Okay..." I said. I had to think about that.

"And you do know that a DOC does not have to be a substance? It can be a sport, work, sex, yoga, anything really."

At that moment I wasn't sure what he meant, but he had planted a seed deep within me and in time all would become clearer.

I stayed a month in San Marcos, renting a room in a grand wooden house right at the water's edge. I had the whole house to myself. Apart from hanging out with Dr Bill and occasionally with Ben, the scrawny kid with astonishing telepathic gifts, I pretty much isolated myself, reading and experimenting with different morning meditations.

It was a magical setting. The water was less than 10 metres from the raised wooden veranda and across the vast lake towered the massive volcanoes on the other side. Often, Mayan fishermen would fish right in front of the house, their canoes dug out of tree trunks, exactly as they had for thousands of years.

There are theories that The Lake – as I came to call it – was in fact an imploded volcano and that there was an ancient city at the bottom of it. I definitely felt the power of the energy that emanated from the place. It was tangible. I knew, too, that The Lake would play an important role in my life in times to come. At the time, I didn't understand why I felt the way I did; it was just a deep knowing.

Naturally, I wanted to stay longer but had agreed with an old friend prior to leaving South Africa that I would meet him in October in Las Vegas, where he was attending a conference. I had no desire whatsoever to leave the tranquillity of San Marcos and considered calling him, offering to pay for his ticket to Guatemala to join me there. But I knew he would probably refuse, so I decided to honour the commitment and booked a flight to Vegas.

CHAPTER 9

The seat of the soul – America and back

I touched down in Las Vegas at 11 pm on a Friday night. Good God! From the tranquillity and isolation of a month at The Lake to arriving in Las Vegas! In the cab from the airport I was met with surreal images of strangers running around in Dracula costumes. It was Halloween.

Vegas was interesting. Of course, it was great catching up with my old friend, Philip, but whereas I would usually have gone crazy, having a debauched time in the gambling capital of the world, I was kind of bored. I wasn't into gambling and after months of not touching a drop of alcohol, I had lost the taste for the stuff and struggled to drink more than one or two beers. I also had no desire to go to a strip club – an aversion that was completely new for me. We did end up going to one and I was intrigued by how uncomfortable I felt and how strange I experienced the energy there. We didn't stay long.

What I did enjoy was hanging out with Philip. We had been friends since varsity days, golf partners, and had a deep connection. After almost a year among strangers in South America, it was great to see someone from the homeland. But after Philip left, I was at a loss for where to go to. I wanted to go back to The Lake, but I was so close to California that it made sense for me to check it out first before returning to Guatemala. It took me two weeks to make up my mind. I was staying at the Riviera Hotel, which had been a grand old hotel in its day, but was a little dated now, although it was in a great location, right on the main strip. The daily rate was crazy cheap, like $19 per day. I think it was slightly out of season and most of the hotels offer good rates because they bargain on making it up with the gambling and drinking. I wasn't doing either so I don't think I was their ideal guest.

I spent much of my time at the Riviera reading and found myself fascinated by information on Tantra, one of the things Dr Bill had recommended I look into. So I ended up googling Tantra yoga and found myself in a class on the other side of town. I cracked up laughing when I imagined that I must be the only guy who goes to Vegas to do yoga.

I also booked a Tantric massage for the first time in my life. It was a remarkable experience. My masseuse gave me a book, *Tantra Spirituality & Sex* by Osho, an author I hadn't even heard of. That gift was the catalyst for what would turn out to be a life-long love affair with Osho.

Eventually I decided it was time to head off to California. I rented a convertible Mustang and drove through Death Valley in Nevada to Los Angeles in California and then up north on Highway One to San Francisco.

All the time in the States I had this feeling deep inside that I didn't want to be there, that I wanted to be back at The Lake. I knew that I would go back to The Lake at some point, but something told me to stay in the States just a little longer and, for some reason, make my way up to San Francisco. In San Francisco I visited friends I made in Mompiche in Ecuador and ended up at a dinner party.

At some point during the course of the evening I walked over to the bookshelf in the lounge area and, without hesitation and without looking at any titles, reached out at a book, opened it and started reading *The Seat of the Soul* by Gary Zukav. I was immediately entranced and only stopped about 15 minutes later when I realised that I was being rude reading at a dinner party held in my honour. So I put the book down and rejoined the rest of the guests.

A few hours later, when we were saying our goodbyes, the hostess, Pamela, said, "Here … take your book with you."

"Oh," I replied, "I couldn't just take your book."

"No," she said to me in a strange, authoritative kind of way, "it's *your* book. Take it. Pass it on when you're done with it."

I left with the book in my hand and a clear realisation in my head that this book was the sole reason I had come all the way up to San Francisco – and to the USA, for that matter. It was to come and get this book. That experience in front of the bookshelf had been surreal. I knew that I hadn't chosen it, the book had chosen me. I didn't even fully know what that meant then, but I knew that it was true and that I would understand in time to come.

Later that same evening I booked a ticket back to Guatemala and two days later I was sitting on the veranda of the grand wooden house overlooking the calm waters of The Lake, *The Seat of the Soul* open on my lap.

I had often found that reading a book is an interesting intellectual exercise where you can evaluate and consider the concepts and views it reveals.

Reading *The Seat of the Soul* was none of that. The best phrase I can come up with to describe the experience is, "I remembered." It was like that for me, a homecoming. Some ancient memory, a connection to how it is.

I was fascinated to discover that the book had been written way back in 1989. I started googling and, to my astonishment, found that the 25-year anniversary second edition had just been published that same year, 2014. The second edition was word for word the same book, the only difference being a new foreword by Oprah Winfrey.

This book was transformational for me ... I immediately started questioning all my belief systems and set out on a process of throwing off layers up on layers of conditioning.

I began to understand the difference between external power and internal authentic power and realised that, although I had a lot of external power in the world, I did not have much internal power.

Zukav explains that the pursuit of external power has always been part of the evolutionary process of humankind, but that we are now going through a transitional time and that the next stage in our evolution is the pursuit of authentic power. According to Zukav, external power is the manipulation and control of people and things. That can be done with reverence for life or without it. Doing it with reverence has served us well because it has meant advancement, safety and comfort. Doing it without reverence has brought immense pain, suffering and damage.

In the book, he says that the time for both has now passed and that the pursuit of authentic power, the alignment of the personality with the soul, is the next step in our evolution. He explains that we are evolving from five-sensory humans to multisensory humans. Our five senses, together, form a single sensory system designed to perceive physical reality. The perceptions of a multisensory human extends beyond physical reality to the larger dynamical systems of which our physical reality is only a part. From the perception of the five-sensory human, we are alone in a Universe that is physical. From the perception of the multisensory human, we are never alone and the Universe is alive, conscious, intelligent and compassionate. From the perception of the five-sensory human, the physical world is an unaccountable given in which we find ourselves, and we strive to dominate it so that we can survive. From the perception of the multisensory human, the physical world is a learning environment created jointly by the souls who share it, and everything that occurs in it serves their learning.

For me, this book laid the foundation for deep work to follow and started to help clear up some of the confusion I felt when the shift happened in me in Cape Town. I had already – albeit nervously – stepped over the threshold, but reading Zukav's book catapulted me head first into this new world. Gary Zukav would become an important guide and ally on my journey.

CHAPTER 10

Tikal

Having settled into a life at The Lake that saw me absorbing all I could from Gary Zukav, I decided to leave The Lake for a few days to travel north to Tikal, to the ancient Mayan city and its temples. What prompted me was a formal reading I had had with Dr Bill that lasted more than two hours in which he said some of my guides were popping into the room and that he was channelling messages for me.

He told me that in previous lives I had been involved in the construction of a few of the Mayan cities in northern Guatemala and southern Mexico and advised me to go up to Tikal to check them out. I was fascinated when he revealed that my Mayan star sign was the Jaguar. The jaguar is a predator cat found in the jungles of South America. In primary school, I had for some reason been enthralled with South America and jaguars, and for three years running did my orals in both the English and Afrikaans classes about jaguars. I researched everything about them and loved talking about them. I was 12 years old.

According to Dr Bill, a guide by the name of Sarah also appeared. She was very fond of me, she said, and that she'd once worked with me at a big research station in the Belt of Orion where I was responsible for some part of it and that we got into trouble because I blew up part of the place when researching laser technology. Dr Bill told many such stories and I just laughed; it sounded like something I could have done, but I didn't take it too seriously.

Another interesting revelation by Dr Bill was that I would meet and work with a number of women practising and teaching conscious sexuality and that, in time, I would help a lot of my friends and business associates in the consciousness space.

So, having made my decision to venture out again, I flew up to the north, stopped over in the beautiful island city of Flores and, at 3 am the following morning, left for Tikal.

It was with a sense of mystery that a small group of us walked in pitch dark – we had to get special permission to enter before sunrise – and sat below the Temple of the Jaguar before making our way to one of the other pyramids and climbing to the top. There we sat in dead silence, high above the treetops of the jungle, waiting for sunrise.

What followed I shall never forget for as long as I live. It was still pitch dark when the jungle slowly started to come to life. The sounds of birds and monkeys slowly began to filter in and became progressively louder as the sky turned from black to golden. Emerging from the pitch dark and dead silence to the light of sunrise and the sounds of the jungle slowly creeping out of that darkness, breaking that silence, was an experience that touched and stirred my soul.

As it became lighter I could see far away over the treetops and started to make out the tops of two pyramids in the distance. And then, when the sun appeared, it edged out from behind and slightly to the left of the pyramid on the right. Suddenly, I realised that the placement of the two pyramids in relation to the one I was sitting on was to pinpoint the position of the rising sun on the summer and winter solstice. I was blown away and remained on the pyramid after everyone had left, in awe and wonder.

Later in the day, wandering among the temples and pyramids, I remembered that when my journey started in January of that year I had wanted to be in New York a few months later, in May. I could not help smiling. It was November; almost a year had passed and New York and business – despite being a huge passion in my old life – were the furthest from my mind. It all made a lot more sense now. I understood that I had not been going crazy when I heard the Voice; I understood that this was always supposed to happen.

Dr Bill had also suggested I read up on the Mayans. I had known about the ancient Mayan calendar that only ran up to 21 December 2012, but now I realised the significance of that on a personal level. The shift that started to occur in me a few years prior to 2012 had reached a peak around that date in December 2012 when I made the decision that I was going to leave. It was simply impossible for me to keep on doing what I had been doing, and by July 2013 I had resigned. I was often told that it was so brave of me to do what I had done, making those massive changes. In reality, I didn't think it was brave; I simply had no choice in the matter – it was impossible not to make those changes. I knew deep, deep down that I simply had to.

I realised, too, that what was happening to me on an inner, personal level was also happening on an outer level in the world. This was the end of one cycle and the start of a new one, where in our evolutionary process we got to leap into higher consciousness, from five-sensory humans to multisensory humans.

The out-of-body feeling I had also made much more sense to me now. There had been a significant shift in my soul path, yet my body and personality continued much as they had before, so there had been a massive disconnection – an out-of-body experience, as though watching myself in a movie.

And when I read up about crystal and indigo children – another of Dr Bill's homework assignments – everything became even clearer. Firstly, I sensed that my kids – and most, if not all kids born today – are crystal children born into a higher consciousness. It was very clear to me when I spoke to my children. I was often blown away by the wisdom and connectedness of my teenage daughter to nature, to animals, to the invisible world. My teenage son was less vocal about it, but as connected.

I also clearly recognised myself as one of the indigo kids born in the '60s. Yes, the previous century. That seemed such a long time ago, and yet I still felt like a teenager most of the time. The role of the indigo kids was to pave the way for the crystal kids, with their warrior energy, to make changes in the world and lay the foundation for a new and higher consciousness. Some of the indigo kids would only awaken to this role later in life, but the skills they acquired in the first part of their life would be vital for that role later. Once again, I could relate.

On my return from Tikal, I spent another three weeks at The Lake, mainly reading and catching up with Dr Bill every now and then.

During one such interaction, he taught me the Emotional Freedom Technique, which involved tracing the meridian points on your body using the fingertips of your left hand to tap along the edge of your right hand, for example, while repeating something like, "Even though I did XYZ, I completely accept, love and forgive myself." You would insert something you did or something that happened to which you had a related emotion, such as guilt or shame. The first few times I felt a bit daft, but after a while, I got the hang of it and found it extremely effective in shifting some of the issues that were bugging me.

Then I became one of the founding members of the San Marcos Men's Sacred Circle, an initiative started by two guys in the village who I'd connected with. I went to the first meeting to support the guys and to find out what it was all about. It was really cool; we sat around making music and would take turns sharing our vulnerabilities. It was the first men's group I had ever gone to, but it immediately resonated. We met on Monday evenings and I went to all of them while I was at The Lake.

I met Keith, the Chocolate Shaman, when I went to one of his Sunday cacao meditations. This was my first experience with cacao and it would start a life-long involvement with this remarkable plant. Keith was quite famous in conscious circles around the world for the cacao beans, which he sourced from the best organic farms across South America, and would then process and package it in blocks and ship it across the globe for people to use in meditations and dances. He gave us a little background, explaining the power of the plant and how it helps you connect with your pure heart energy. Then we were each given a glass of warm cacao with a pinch of chilli, which helped with the slightly bitter taste of the raw cacao. Even though chocolate is made from the same plant, raw cacao isn't sweet so it doesn't taste at all like chocolate. We each had to express our intentions for the ceremony and then drink it with awareness before going on a guided mediation. It was an extraordinary introduction to cacao and, later on my journey, I would often attend cacao dance events and found that they gave me a natural high and connected me to my heart. And so hot chocolate would become my new DOC.

I again met with Grace, the English Girl of The Lake, who had previously showed me the emotional expression and release tools, and we had a fascinating chat about the group of people she was working with. She explained that their mission was to help others lift the shame, fear and guilt around sexuality and assist them to live authentic lives and in full presence. That caught my attention. I asked her to expand further. She told me that they would have their next training in Hawaii in January of the following year and proposed that I join them. The training was a seven-day Level 1 residential course on spiritual sexual shamanism hosted by her organisation – let's call them the Transformational School (TS). She suggested I check out the website and videos on YouTube.

This all sounded pretty crazy and out of this world, but by now I had come to expect nothing less on this journey of mine.

I shared with Grace the strange bout of celibacy I was experiencing. She said that it was vital that, even if I was not having sex, I masturbate regularly – or self-pleasure, as she called it – or one could easily be disconnected from one's own sexual energy. She explained that rather than using porn or even fantasising, it'd be better to simply celebrate, touch and love your own body when self-pleasuring. I could not help wondering how interesting it was that my search for a cure to my parasites had lead to a frank and open discussion about how to self-pleasure. Naturally, I checked out the website and videos and found myself strangely drawn to the idea. Deep down, I sensed I would end up in Hawaii in two months, but first I was travelling to Europe to meet up with my kids.

"So, Daddy, when d'you think is a good age to have sex for the first time?" – my 15-year-old daughter.

We were sitting high up in the mountains of Catalonia, at the thousand-year-old Santa Maria de Montserrat Abbey and Monastery, not far inland from Barcelona. I had left The Lake to meet my son and daughter in Europe where they were on vacation with my ex-wife and her husband. The five of us spent Christmas together in London and then I met the four of them a few days later again in Paris for New Year. The following day the kids and I toured down to Spain for another two-week holiday, just the three of us. I was ecstatic to see them. I had missed them terribly. It had never been the plan to not see them for 11 months. It was a heavy price to have paid for the continuation of my journey.

My 17-year-old son looked up from the book he was paging through. It was after dinner and he and I were having a beer, my daughter a hot chocolate.

I kept a straight face but internally I was jumping with joy, blown away that she was comfortable enough to ask me, especially in front of her elder brother. I noticed that he, too, seemed quite relaxed about the question.

"Well, my baby," I said, "I'm not sure that there *is* a right age or a specific age. You – and only you – will know when the time's right. You need to ask yourself. Ask your body, your heart, your mind, your spirit whether it's the right time. If it's not a unanimous yes on all levels, then it's not the time. What is important is not to listen to anyone telling you that the time is right. It's not their decision, it's yours. Don't get tricked into the peer-pressure thing. In fact, if anyone tries that, tell them to fuck off."

"You shouldn't swear so much, Dad," she said sternly.

"Sorry, my baby," I said. "Tell them to get lost then."

"Aah, much better…" She smiled at me.

"Shouldn't you be at least 17 or 18?" my son chirped.

I laughed loudly. "Agh, don't play the big brother now! There's no specific age, no right age, kiddo. And the same applies to you. It's your decision – don't let anyone tell you it's time."

"I wish someone will tell me that. But that's not happening," he snorted.

"I love you, my boy," I said, smiling at my tall, good-looking son. "It'll happen. I have seen how those beautiful Spanish girls stare at you."

What followed was an hour-long discussion on the subject. I knew that neither had had sex before, so it was perfect that they had initiated the discussion rather than me because it allowed me to make my point without the pressure of sounding like a father doling out instructions.

I had always had a good relationship with my kids, but I knew without a shadow of a doubt that my daughter would not have asked me that question a year previously. I realised then that the journey I was on was changing the energy of the relationship between us, allowing more to be shared. I felt so grateful and inspired and knew that this was only the beginning of many more open discussions and deep soul connections with them.

CHAPTER 11

The Big Island

I only bought the ticket to Hawaii two days before I said goodbye to my kids in Spain.

I had left my departure flight open because I had gotten into the habit of not planning too far ahead. That meant that I often ended up paying more for tickets, but I loved the freedom that that gave me. I was starting to embrace giving up control and going with the flow wherever the Universe was taking me.

I was also not 100 per cent certain I wanted to do the Hawaii TS Level 1 training suggested by Grace, the English Girl of The Lake, back in Guatemala; it sounded pretty intimidating, so I left it to the last moment. But, as the time drew nearer, the call was strong, so I did what I became accustomed to doing: I jumped.

I arrived on the Puna Coast of the Big Island, Hawaii, just in time for the Hawaii Tantra Festival taking place the week before training. Of all the islands in Hawaii, the Big Island – and it really is the biggest – was the least touristy. The Puna Coast was even more off the beaten track, close to an active volcano which experienced a series of minor eruptions in the weeks before I arrived. It was the home of a bunch of alternatives, hippies and, of course, local Hawaiians.

By the time I arrived, I still hadn't committed to the TS training and I had no idea what to expect from a Tantra festival either. In fact, I had only come across the word *tantra* for the first time two months prior and had very little understanding of what it meant. And yet here I was...

The only person I knew in Hawaii was Grace, and it was great seeing her again. She was extremely supportive and encouraging, and introduced me to a lot of people. She was such a wise woman and became a real soul sister.

I had a feeling that the Tantra thing and the Spiritual Sexual Shamanism training were going to be a further stretch out of my comfort zone. I had no idea how much.

I eased myself into the Tantra Festival and signed up for only a few workshops, spending most of my time hanging out on the volcanic black sand of "clothing-optional" Kehena Beach.

In the workshops there was a lot of eye gazing, sharing and hugging, but I had always been a very tactile person so that came easily to me. What leapt out at me, though, was the notice on the website, as well as on the event programme and at the dance venue: "Strictly no alcohol or drugs." That made sense to me when it came to the workshops and yoga, but I was trying to imagine how one could go dance in the evening without at least a drink or two. At the dance, I found I was really out of my comfort zone. Since university days, we would have a few drinks before or at the dance or club. And here I was dead-cold sober!

The other rule was, no talking on the dance floor. So when we got onto the floor and the music slowly started, we were invited to listen, to feel it, to allow our bodies to move the way they wanted without limitations. It seemed that everyone was doing their own thing, oblivious to the next person. That put me at ease and I decided to just let go, to enjoy myself, to allow the music to move me. I felt so empowered that I never actually needed that drink. It made me think about society's dependence on alcohol in order to relax, to be one's self.

But it wasn't just about dancing. I had some beautiful conversations. People who understood when I opened up about certain aspects of my sexuality. Ten years prior, I had stumbled upon orgasm without ejaculation. At the time, I was in a deep, loving four-year relationship with Linda. She had a high sex drive – to match mine – so we made love a lot and for long periods. On her 26th birthday, we set a target that, over the course of the weekend, she would have more orgasms than her age. And we did it; she had 27. I learnt to hold my ejaculation for long periods and my body eventually understood that ejaculation and orgasm were two entirely different experiences, that you can combine them, but that you can also split them. It was an amazing experience, but I didn't really understand what was happening and I had no one to talk to about it. In those days, certainly in my circle, guys didn't really discuss the details of their sexual experiences with each other, so I assumed that most guys made love like that.

During the party years in Cape Town, I experienced the same but took it to another level. I found that the recreational drugs I was using over the weekends made it easier to control and postpone ejaculation. It also heightened my senses and allowed me to feel the sensations in my body much more intensely. I would have loads of orgasms over the weekend but would only ejaculate late on Sunday night.

The difficulty, though, was that none of my friends could relate to making love for four hours non-stop and for a whole weekend without sleep. They must have thought I was either talking nonsense or just a little crazy, weird, a freak of nature.

But here, in Hawaii, were people who were doing the same sexually. It felt like I had come home. It was here that I really began to learn about Tantra and Taoism, ancient practices from thousands of years ago devised by the Tantrics in Ancient India and the Taoists in Ancient China.

What amazed me was that I had come across this quite naturally long before I had even heard about Tantra or the ancient practices. I had a deep sense, however, that my body, my DNA code, carried an ancient memory of it and how to do it. I could not help but think what a different world we would be living in if everyone engaged in sex this way; it leads to a much deeper loving connection with your partner and with yourself. I wondered how this could be brought to the lives of more people.

Even though I was from a world very different to that of most others at the festival, I felt at ease and was welcomed with open arms. It was during that week that I decided to do the TS Level 1 training that I had flown halfway around the world to "maybe" do.

At the opening circle of the TS training, we all shared our backgrounds and why we were there. In the group of 35, apart from one guy who was also a businessman, I was the only one who wasn't in the field of sexuality, bodywork, yoga, massage or a related area.

I was blown away by the training. I realised the extent to which we have all been conditioned when it comes to our sexuality and how that has disempowered us and made people so easy to control and manipulate. I started to understand the extent of the shame, fear and guilt around sexuality, the way people were being cut off from their authenticity and creative life force energy.

Growing up, I'd been exposed to damaging, regressive thinking around sex.

In 1980, I was 15 years old and at a prestigious all-boys school in Pretoria.

"If you have sex before marriage, you will burn in hell for all eternity. Having sex before you are married is a sin against God and you will be punished for that."

This was the constant refrain every Sunday morning and Tuesday evening, when we were marched off to hear the *dominee* preach fire and brimstone. The first time I heard that, it simply didn't ring true to me. Eventually, though, they got to me. I don't know whether it was the sheer repetition of the statement continuously over the three-year period that I was at boarding school there or whether it was the "burning in hell for all eternity" thing. I could maybe handle taking the punch for a limited time, burning for a while, but burning for eternity ... that was a bit rough. So, despite being fiercely independent, never scared to speak my truth, they still got to me. By the time I was in my final year of school, I had been brainwashed enough to decide that I was not going to have sex before marriage. The eternity thing was a powerful deterrent.

After school, I arrived at university in Johannesburg with the no-sex-before-marriage refrain firmly entrenched in me. University life was a blast. All of a sudden, I was free to do whatever I wanted, but still I minimised my contact with women – I didn't trust myself, not sure I'd be able to restrain myself. I was trying to avoid the burning for eternity. I was really horny, though, so I masturbated a lot.

Then, at the age of 21, in my third year at university, I cracked when she pushed her tongue in my ear. I was at my parents' place with a friend and two girls we had met the previous weekend at the infamous bar across the road from the university grounds and invited over that Friday evening. She was a year or two younger than me, but clearly much more experienced. The moment she shoved her tongue in my right ear, my mind went, "Fuck that! I'll burn in eternity if I have to, but I am going to have sex ... now!" It was like a switch. I made a conscious decision to accept the risk of burning for eternity if that was the price I was to pay. I immediately took her down to my cottage – I think I came before I was even fully inside her. We had sex many times that night. She was both fascinated and thrilled when I told her, after the first time, that I had been a virgin. For the rest of the night, she took it upon herself to educate me and I was a very willing student.

The next day there were two conflicting emotions. On the one hand, I felt it was all bullshit because surely something as beautiful and pleasurable as this could not be wrong. On the other hand, though, I was just waiting for the bolt of lightning to strike me down.

I learnt a lot in the following few weeks. I was, however, ridden with guilt and when I developed a slight rash on my upper thigh I was convinced that the punishment had started and broke it off with her. It was a terrible mixture of guilt, shame and fear. It would take me many years to throw the conditioning off and even when I thought I'd succeeded, I would uncover further layers.

Here in Hawaii I was able to face the deep layers of that fear-based conditioning. What I learnt was much broader than the mind could articulate. The training was much more experiential than theoretical, and included a lot of exercises, rituals and ceremonies. Because this was a residential training – everyone stays at the same venue for the full six days – it was fairly intense; apart from the busy programme, every day from 7 am to around 10 pm, we were also constantly in each other's space, with most trainees sharing rooms.

The first day was spent learning how to say no and how to set and communicate boundaries. This created a sense of comfort and safety because it made it clear that no one need do anything they didn't want to. It all sounded very obvious, but I realised that the reality was that most of us don't know how to say no or when we say no we feel compelled to make excuses for why. Also, most of us are terrible at setting and communicating boundaries and when we feel they have been infringed we so easily slip into victim mode, which has a detrimental effect on our internal authentic power.

On the morning of the second day we were shown the seven tools of emotional release that I learnt at my time at The Lake. Good God, the combined effect of 35 people together in one room at the same time punching and fucking cushions, doing hand screams, throwing tantrums, stomping around and wailing at the top of their voices was insanely intense.

Afterwards, we gathered in a circle again and there was opportunity for sharing. But then, while someone was sharing, I just burst into tears ... for no specific reason. I wasn't sad or angry. It was just a spontaneous explosion of emotions. I didn't hold back either; I just let it flow and it proved to be a wonderful release. I put my hand up to share and, in between sobs, told the circle that this was the first time I had cried since primary school.

As I talked I could feel my body vibrating to its core. It wasn't shaking, just a vibration from deep inside and I could feel the tangible energy between my hands. I could actually make a ball of it and play with it. I shared that too and could not help cracking a joke between the tears: "I thought you were all bullshitting when you said you could tangibly feel energy, but now I feel it and believe it."

Everyone laughed and the women on either side of me gave me a hug.

I was relieved I could cry. I had known for a while that it was important to be able to, but was convinced I was long past that, that I had blocked my emotions so much and for so long that there was no way back.

It was also important that I shared, because deep down I knew that revealing my vulnerability was an important step forward. I learnt, too, that by moving emotions you also activate the emotional body and that that creates the vibrations you feel in your physical body. As a male growing up in apartheid South Africa, we were taught to suppress our emotions. Boys were told it was not okay to cry; girls were taught to suppress anger. If a boy cried he was a baby or a sissy and was told to man up; if a girl showed anger she was a bitch. So, from childhood, we learn to suppress these emotions, but of course they don't just go away – they hide in the cells of our bodies, where they cause tension and disease.

One of the facilitators gave the example often seen in nature: after a deer escapes an attack from a predator, it shakes its body in order to release the stress. After that, it casually continues to graze as if nothing has happened. Because of societal conditioning, we humans have stopped doing that, with the result that the stress lingers in our bodies long afterwards. I wondered why these ideas were not being taught at school.

Later in the day we did dialoguing exercises where you kneel on a pillow with another pillow in front of you. You then place an imaginary someone or something on the pillow in front and start a communication process – anything you would like to resolve or understand better. You could just talk to the cushion or touch it or punch it or scream into it using the emotional release tools to make it more effective. After a while, you reverse the position and kneel on the cushion that was in front of you previously, facing the cushion you had been on. You then take on the identity of the person or thing you were talking to before and "answer" or communicate back at yourself using the same tools.

The important thing was not to delve deep into your mind but to allow things to come up spontaneously. You then continue to switch positions, back and forth, keeping the "conversation" going. I was blown away. I placed a few family members on the cushion and was astonished at the answers and insights. I know for sure I would not have had the same result by talking to them because this went right to the source of the information, bypassing ego and pride. Sometimes I started the process in anger but ended up feeling compassion, which made it so much easier to drop the version of the story I had carried around in my own mind for so long. I saw their insecurities, what they were suffering through.

I had absolutely no idea how all of this worked – all I knew was that it was working because I felt the truth in the communication. Sometimes you just know. I could feel it drop in from somewhere much higher, much deeper. Later in my journey I would grow to believe that you are actually tapping into the universal field of consciousness and thus straight into the consciousness of the person, because everything's connected. But back then, I didn't try to understand it, realising that whatever terminology we use to describe this is irrelevant – that was just the mind wanting to find a rational explanation, whereas any explanation of how it works is not really important.

One of the most significant realisations I came to over those six days was that we all have masculine and feminine energies, whether we are born in a male or female body, and that if we don't honour both and balance the two we'll never be integrated human beings. I realised, too, that I had been living predominantly with my masculine energy and had failed to honour my inner feminine energy, always looking for and interacting with the outer feminine. It suddenly dawned on me why I had been pulling away from sexual interaction with the outer feminine in the last year of my journey through South America. Was I – maybe even prior to this training – subconsciously laying the foundation for acknowledging my inner feminine?

I distinctly remember that on the first day of the training, when we were sitting in the opening circle getting to know each other, I had two movies playing simultaneously in my head. In one I could see myself sleeping with at least four of the girls during the training week and I already knew who they were going to be. I could pinpoint them just by looking around the circle. In the second movie I wasn't going to sleep with anyone. And what's more, I knew that it was all going to be determined by that first evening. I had met a beautiful woman at the Tantra Festival who was also doing the training course and there was an understanding that we'd get together that evening. I knew without any doubt that if we did connect sexually that night, my movie would be movie one; if we didn't, it would be movie two.

Naturally, I was tempted but understood too that it would be good to break the pattern, that maybe it would maximise my learning, so I went with movie two and withdrew both emotionally and energetically from her during the course of the evening and we did not connect that night. I did not sleep with anyone else either, even though the facilitators encouraged us to engage sexually with each other in order to put the learnings into practice. I wasn't even sure why I did it; I had simply been listening to some internal voice leading me. And, as we continued through the week, it became much clearer because I was dropping deeper into the learnings.

CHAPTER 12

Beyond the comfort zone

On the third last day of training I was chatting to Grace, the English Girl of The Lake, and thanked her for introducing me to the training, for encouraging me to give it a try. She smiled and said, "I hope you still feel the same after the last few days and don't want to kill me." I had no idea what she meant but suddenly I started feeling a little uncomfortable, nervous even.

After the opening circle the next morning, the facilitators began discussing the events of the day. There was a nervous energy in the air. I could see the concerned faces around the circle and realised that I probably looked much the same. As the discussion continued, the looks turned from concern to anxiety and even fear. We were told that the group was to split into two, one male and one female, and that the last two days were to be spent giving and receiving sacred spot massages.

I had absolutely no idea what a sacred spot massage was – it was the first time I had heard the term. All I knew was that it sounded foreign to me and felt very intimidating. I wanted to ask but decided to rather not.

It very quickly became clear, however. They explained that the women's sacred spot ceremony meant that the guys would prepare a temple environment for the women inside the meditation hall while the women waited outside. As the women came in they would each be paired up with a guy who would lead her to the space he had created for her with a mattress, sarongs, cushions and flowers. You would then sit with your partner, sharing your boundaries and intentions for the ritual. It was again made clear that no one was compelled to do anything that made them uncomfortable, but that this was an opportunity to use this powerful ritual for whatever you wanted. The man would then give the woman a full body massage to relax her and to shift her energy. In the boundary discussion, the woman would express whether she was comfortable being naked and what parts of her body the man could or could not touch. At a certain point, the massage would move to the groin area, then around the vagina – or yoni, as it's generally referred to in Tantra circles. After a while, the focus would move to the lips of the yoni, massaging them and tugging them softly. Only when the woman was completely relaxed and aroused would one start touching or putting the fingers lightly against the opening of the yoni.

We had a long discussion about this critical part of the exercise and it was emphasised that the man was not to enter the yoni with his finger until the woman was ready and told him so, either verbally or with her body. As the lead facilitator explained, you could just rest your finger at the opening and if she was ready, your finger would be sucked into her without you doing anything. He explained that so many women had been penetrated unconsciously or too early and that her experiencing penetration in this sacred way would be very healing for her. I immediately remembered reading that the number-one complaint for many women in the sexual space was being penetrated too early. Once inside the yoni, there was not much you had to do but locate the G-spot area, the slightly ridged area not far in, at the roof of the yoni, and hold the pressure there with your finger. You could check with your partner whether she wanted the pressure harder or softer.

We were told that the goal was not to give pleasure or to assist in orgasm but just to hold space for the woman to have the experience she wanted or needed at that time. We were assured that experiencing pleasure or an orgasm was also not a problem, and to simply allow whatever came up.

The facilitators explained that the yoni, and especially the G-spot area, holds so much tension as a result of trauma and past experiences in our lifetime or previous lifetimes – and even in the lives of our ancestors – that applying pressure in that area allows the tension to be released. For some women that area may be numb due to the tension being stored there and you may have to apply considerable pressure for her to feel it.

I could not help thinking every now and then during discussion how the pairing was going to work. Many thoughts were running through my mind: Will they pair us up? Do we have to ask a person? How do you choose? How do you ask? What if they say no? The pairing process alone was pretty intimidating. Eventually someone asked the question I'm sure we were all thinking about. The answer was, "Nature selection." Of course, that still meant nothing to me.

But when they explained it, I was fascinated. In essence, there would be two trays of items from nature – leaves, flowers, rocks or whatever. What was important was that the two trays would mirror each other; in other words, a similar flower, rock or leaf on the second tray, identical to that on the first. The women would choose from one tray and the men, in another room, from the other tray and that would determine the pairing. Rock with rock, flower with flower, leaf with leaf. I thought that was pretty crazy, but I was going to learn the magic of this method over time. We weren't given much time to prepare before the ceremony, which was probably a good thing because I was happy not to think about it too much; I'd much rather just get into it. I could not help thinking, though, that I was really managing to constantly push myself beyond my comfort zone. Crazily so!

After a short break, the women got together under a tree outside while the men met in the meditation room and started preparing their individual massage places for their prospective partners. I was in awe of the attention and detail and care the guys were putting into their spaces, draping flowers and branches around the space, placing colourful cushions and other items around it. But then I noticed I was doing the same. There was a sacred, very respectful atmosphere and energy in the room.

When we were finished, the women were called to enter the room one by one. We stood in a line inside and they had to make their way down the row of men with their nature item held in front of their chest until they found a man with the similar item and then stop in front of him. The man would then take their hand and lead them to the space that he had prepared.

When a woman in her late 40s stopped in front of me I could see that she was even more nervous than I was. I took her hand and led her to our space and invited her to sit. She gasped when she saw the space and immediately said, "Thank you, you have made it so beautiful." I could see her visibly relax. We sat down and shared our intentions and boundaries. I expressed to her that my intention was to be there for her and to hold space for her and to allow her to have whatever experience she wanted or needed.

I really took my time with massaging her whole body, allowing her to relax completely. When I finally rested my finger against the lips of her yoni, it wasn't long before my finger was sucked deep inside her.

I had experienced much the same with girlfriends and lovers before because I had vowed to rather penetrate a woman too late than too early. I had always been intuitively aware of the collective wounding of women around too early penetration. I found that if you took your time and waited for her, she'd eagerly draw you in when she was ready.

After entering her, I curled my finger upwards and immediately found the ridged area of the G-spot and then, slightly deeper, the softer spongy A-spot area. I moved my finger slightly back to the ridge and slowly started applying pressure, steadily increasing it.

My intuition told me to do it quite hard right from the start and to hold it like that for a while before asking her whether to go harder or softer. She asked that I go even harder, so I went as hard as I could – but she wanted it even harder. I illustrated to her, by pressing with my other hand on her upper arm, the level of pressure I was already applying. She gasped at the pain of that pressure on her arm and I could tell by her eyes that she realised how numb her G-spot area was.

Keeping the pressure constant for such a long time, my hand and arm were starting to ache, but I just dug deep. What happened over the next half-hour, hour, or more – I actually have no idea how long – was a deeply spiritual experience for me. I watched as she went through a range of emotions, from crying to laughing to screaming, and then all of it all over again. I witnessed her face change in front of my eyes; at one point she was a 16-year-old girl, at another time a 60-year-old woman.

Watching as all of this unfolded in front of me required me to stay fully present and, at one point when she was screaming like crazy, her body shaking, I had to call in my warrior masculine to stay with her, to calmly hold the space for her to release whatever she needed to. I never looked up from her, not once, but was at the same time very aware that the room, everything around me, had gone crazy. There was a lot of screaming, crying and even crazy laughter, loud music in the background, with one facilitator guiding the process over the microphone. The energy was alive, intense.

That went on for quite a while before the facilitator slowly brought the ceremony to a close. I covered my partner with a sarong and sat silently at her head as slow soft music played. I felt such compassion for her, such pride in myself for my part in this. I realised, too, how little I and most others really know about anything. I was also astonished at how unsexual the entire experience had been. There was some sexual energy, yes, but I was surprised to find that after penetration, while applying pressure on the G-spot, there was none, that it had changed into something else entirely. Something profound, something sacred, something significant.

I was also aware that if I ever told someone that I gave a woman a G-spot massage and that it was not at all sexual, it was going to be very challenging getting my point across. The fact is, though, that it wasn't.

I was exhausted and slept like a baby that night.

The following morning I woke up very aware that today was the day the men were to receive sacred spot massages. The day before, I had thought briefly about what that meant, but because of the intensity of the exercise and the need to be fully present and focused when giving, there had been no time to explore it much further. Now I was to be on the receiving end and had a bad feeling that I was about to be pushed even further beyond my comfort zone. I had no idea how much.

When the three facilitators started discussing the day's activities at the morning opening session, it was clear that it was going to follow the same ceremonial structure of the day before and that the same nature selection would apply to pairing people.

Eventually we got to the part on everyone's mind: "What does sacred spot mean for men?"

The short answer was that men's sacred spot massage entailed massaging their prostate. The facilitators explained that, similar to the G-spot in women, a lot of tension, trauma and blocked emotions are stored in the prostrate and that massaging it or putting pressure on it can release that blockage. Access to the prostate is via the anus – not always easy because a lot of men hold a lot of tension in that area. And, much like a woman's yoni, you can't just force your way in but have to slowly massage around it until it opens naturally. They explained about the outer and inner rings of the anus and how to slowly slip in and then locate the prostate. I looked around the room; the women, who were to give the massage, were as nervous as the men who were going to receive it.

Even with all the explanation, I could not imagine how having

94

someone put their finger up my ass was going to advance my spiritual path or be good for me in any way. There were, however, proven health benefits apparently; having this regularly helps prevent prostrate cancer, for one. This massage would also allow men to access their feminine energies and even unlock a personal power that may be locked there. This made even less sense to me, but I had committed to this training and I needed to keep an open mind. What the hell, I thought, I'm here now and already some way down this crazy path, so no sense stopping now.

This time I was on the receiving end, walking into the room with my nature object at my chest, looking for the partner who was going to put her finger up my bum. When I found her, I was kind of relieved. She was a tiny, pretty young woman from Europe with whom I'd had a few discussions earlier in the week; we'd made a good connection. I learnt so much from that massage.

After a long body massage, she asked whether I was ready and for permission to penetrate me with her finger. In that moment, I understood women's vulnerability as far as penetration was concerned. Lying there with my legs open and raised, I felt extremely vulnerable.

I was nervous and tight throughout the entire process, but managed to relax enough for her to at least enter me. Apart from the occasional visit to the doctor for a prostrate check – which was quick and unpleasant – I had no reference point of how it would feel if my anus was entered and my prostrate touched. So I don't know to what extent my partner actually touched or massaged my prostrate, but to be honest I was happy when it was over. The funny thing, however, was that when she covered me with a sarong afterwards, I was quite emotional, overcome with compassion for women for all the wrongs committed against them for thousands of years. This was not something from the mind; it came from a very deep place within me and I felt it intensely, personally connected to it. It started bubbling up more and more until I could no longer hold back the tears. I had never experienced anything like it before. I was tapping into a deep level of the feminine, as if

I was part of the female, as if deep inside I could connect with the collective consciousness of womanhood, with the woman in me.

The week-long training had been powerful and groundbreaking, but I was left with a nagging thought about why all of this wasn't being brought into the mainstream. That's where it was so needed. It's all good and well helping and training people already in the space, but what about the rest of society? I kind of knew the answer. The mainstream market was not going to google "spiritual sexual shamanism". No way! Even I, who had always considered myself an out-of-the-box thinker, wouldn't have. But now I began to think about how this beautiful message could be spread wider.

With the course over, I stayed for another three weeks on the Big Island, hitchhiking up and down the coast. Luckily, the locals believe that Pele, the goddess of the volcano, also hitchhiked and if you don't pick her up you're in for some big trouble. So lifts were easy.

I often went to Uncle Robert's, an open-air food and music market a few kilometres down the coast from where I was staying. It's a magical place. Prior to the volcanic eruptions of 1991, which extended the land about 800 metres into the sea, Uncle Robert's was basically on the beach, but now you had to cross black volcanic rock to get to the "new" beach. It's a surreal landscape, with bright green ferns starting to grow out of cracks in the black rock. I was fascinated by the fact that I was walking on earth that was much younger than I was. Locals tell of how, during the eruption, the flowing lava diverted when it reached the house of Hawaii's royal family, wound its way around it and then backtracked towards the beach and retreated into the sea. This wasn't strange for Hawaiians because they believe lava has a consciousness of its own. I was starting to feel much the same.

In that period after the training, I tried to practise what I had learnt on the course, specifically the principle of masculine-feminine energies. By this time, I had come to know a few of the islanders and hung out with them on Kehena Beach, at Uncle Robert's and at some of the Ecstatic Dance evenings. Most of the time, however, I kept to myself and went for long walks on the beach at sunset. I would joke with myself that I was taking my inner chick out on a romantic date. After one such date, I wrote a piece in my journal. It was almost a love letter to myself.

I had an awesome date last night.

I went for a walk across the black lava fields to the beach and then along the beach. I sat on the black sand and black volcanic rocks with the waves crashing underneath and listened to the swirling sound of water on pebbles as waves retracted back to the ocean. I watched the sun set whilst smelling the ocean, feeling the breeze on my skin and tasting the salt on my lips.

What an awesome date. With myself. With the beautiful girl in me that I never knew about. I'm integrating the masculine and feminine inside me. What a journey. As a friend mentioned last night, the longest 18-inch journey you'll ever take is the journey from the mind to the heart.

I have been blessed with having had amazing, wonderful, beautiful women in my life and I know I will have that again, but for now I am in love with myself, making love to myself, to the universe. It is beautiful.

I would crack up laughing at the craziness of it all, but deep down I knew it wasn't that crazy, that I had touched on a deep essence within myself. I still had a lot of work to do in integrating my energies, but there was a sense of excitement for the journey ahead. I began to realise how the masculine energies were a lot about the mind, about control, directing, holding space for others, driving projects, getting things done, penetrating to the core of a problem. Well, I was pretty good at all of that. My whole life had been about achievement and control. The feminine energies, on the other hand, were about the heart, emotions, surrender, the nurturing of others and yourself, relaxing and listening to your body. Well, I was pretty bad at all of that.

The best way to learn, I thought, was to throw myself into

those feminine energies. I knew that this needed inner work, a journey that I could do only on my own. So I continued to stay away from the outer feminine – in other words, all the gorgeous young women running around on Hawaii's Big Island.

CHAPTER 13

The Pacific – embody the learnings

In my last days on the Big Island I was faced with a difficult choice. I felt a strong call to return to South Africa. I'd been away for more than a year, and now my dad was ill. I was worried about losing him. Physically, my mom was fine, but taking strain, and I worried I may lose her too. I was even more afraid, though, that I would arrive back in South Africa and be sucked back into my old life.

I knew intuitively that I needed to deepen and solidify my learnings and new habits before returning home. That's when I spotted on the TS website that there was another intensive Level 1 course at the end of February 2015, just a few weeks away, in Byron Bay, Australia, and then a Level 2 initiation the following month in New Zealand. I decided to sign up; that meant that I could then go back to South Africa in April, visit my parents and spend time with my kids over their school holidays.

One of the best ways to fly to Brisbane, the closest airport to Byron Bay, is apparently via Fiji. And because I had a few weeks open before the training, I decided to stop over there rather than simply transit through.

Fiji was magnificent, a myriad small islands in an azure sea. On my first night, I stayed on the "mainland" and the next day sailed to tiny Mana, overnighting at a diving backpacker hostel right on the beach, with my own cabin a few metres from the water's edge. Every morning before breakfast I would swim lengths along the beach and coral reefs.

It was a relaxing time, where I managed to do a lot of reading and writing. I was feeling a calling to share my journey and the changes in my being. Just before I had left South Africa, a number of friends had urged me to share my travels in a blog or on Facebook so that they could track where I was and what I was up to.

Under the title "My Journey", I had been regularly updating every two weeks or so since I left, but by now I was writing and journalling quite a bit. First, I wrote it in a book, but my handwriting was so bad that I struggled to read my own scrawl. Then I switched to the Notes app on my iPhone. That proved much easier and I didn't have to worry about all the paper. An added benefit was that I could copy and paste some of that to the My Journey update on Facebook.

All this time I had this strange but deep calling to share more of my personal insights and learnings. I was experiencing so much and thought that if I could plant seeds, these could help others see another perspective. And it seemed to be working. I was surprised by how interested people were and noticed an increasing number of people actually following this crazy journey around the world. Over time, my sharing became increasingly open and personal.

Then, on one of my morning swims on Mana, I had a bizarre experience. I was doing a few lengths up and down the beach, only about 15 metres out because it was high tide, when I felt a hard bump against my side. The first thing that went through my head was "Shark!" I looked around frantically, only to find a dog swimming next to me, barking furiously. I swam out of the way and then spotted two other dogs swimming from the beach towards me. I immediately thought that my swimming must have excited them and that getting out of the water would probably calm them, so I swam around, past them, and got back onto the beach. The thing is, though, they simply followed me and the next moment I was surrounded by three dogs barking and snapping at my legs. When one connected with my knee cap, I realised that they were not just playing. It flashed through my head that I was on an island with limited medical care. The word "rabies" sprang to mind.

I retreated back into the ocean, shouting and kicking, hoping that that would defuse the situation – only to be followed by all of them. That took me completely by surprise. Waist deep in the water, though, I realised that I would have the advantage if I stayed right where I was, my legs protected by water. I had a strong intuition that if I swam further out, they would follow me and, unable to stand and defend myself, I would be even more vulnerable. So up to my waist in the water, I turned around, faced them and proceeded to punch them in the head one by one to keep them at bay. At that point three guys from the village came galloping up with long rubber pipes and started to hit out at them. The result was that two dogs were dead and one fled injured.

I felt really bad that the dogs had been killed. I mean, was that really necessary? But later the chief of the village explained the dogs were feral, living wild in the jungle, and that they had attacked and killed children in the village, and some visitors to the island had been seriously injured. Then, at breakfast later, I was told by the hostel manager that a few weeks earlier the dogs had attacked a couple on the beach and when they fled into the sea, swimming out deep to get away from them, the dogs had followed them all the way. Luckily, there was a boat lying out deep and the couple was pulled aboard to safety. I was dumbstruck. The Voice in my head had been very clear – I was not to swim out because the dogs would follow me.

I had never heard anything quite as bizarre. But then an image from Paulo Coelho's *The Pilgrimage* popped into my head where, on his pilgrimage on the Camino de Santiago, he describes being followed and viciously attacked by a big black dog, which he then has to fight off. Maybe the wild dogs were a sign to trust my intuition.

I left Fiji after a magical two weeks and flew to Australia a week before the training was due to start in Byron Bay. Once again, I had neither booked nor committed to the training – I'd decide once there.

On the way to Byron Bay I received a message from the lead facilitator of the Hawaii TS, asking whether I wanted to share a house in Byron Bay with him and his cousin for the week prior to the training. This was the guy who had started TS, an easy, laid-back kind of guy, and we had become good friends. I felt a strong soul connection with him, so I said yes. So it was that we hung out together and he became Brother Easy. In the week leading up to the training, I attended a few workshops of the sexuality conference taking place at the time, and on other days simply enjoyed spending time on the beautiful beach. A few days before the Level 1 was about to start, I asked Brother Easy for his thoughts on whether I should attend. He wasn't facilitating this specific training, but was promoting it at the conference.

"Feel into it over the next few days," he said, "and then decide."

I was surprised. I thought he'd be determined to sell it to me, to pull out all the stops. That's what my business mind expected. In a way, I suppose I was also testing him to see whether he was going to do a hard sell on me. What he did was pass the power of the decision back to me. And not having any pressure or expectation on me removed all my resistance. I found all of this really amusing. Before, I would "think about something" and now I was "feeling into something". I had become such a hippie!

In the end, I only made the final decision to attend the day before the training was due to start. It was much the same material as in Hawaii because it was also a Level 1, but the facilitators were new and some of the exercises were different.

The experiences that stood out for me were the brother and sister rituals. The whole group, men and women, would perform the brother ritual, a warrior exercise, together and in pairs. Everyone – male and female – would tap into their masculine energies and afterwards you could see the brother in not just the men but also the women. I could walk up to a woman, confident that she was my brother and would have my back. The experience must have been especially profound for the women because, for many of them, there is seldom the opportunity to feel that true warrior brotherhood and how good it feels. What intrigued me most, though, was that after the exercise a number of people, men and women, came over to share how powerfully they felt my masculine warrior energy, the raw African energy coming through in my transmissions. I sometimes forget the energetic power of Africa.

I had a similar experience when, after the sister ritual, I sat with a bunch of girls on the river. I truly felt part of the sisterhood. It was a beautiful way to learn about masculine and feminine energies, irrespective of the gender body you inhabit. One sister exercise that really hit home, in particular, was when we split up into groups of three with at least one woman in each group. The exercise was to tell the other members of your group about your first experience with menstrual blood. I ended up with two women and was astonished by the amount of guilt, shame and fear they had felt.

From them I learnt that many women aren't even aware of menstruation prior to its onset. I could imagine the fear of bleeding unexpectedly, without knowing what was happening to you. Naturally, I shared my own experiences and told them that it had never bothered me making love to a woman when she was menstruating, that I actually enjoyed having a woman's blood all over me. They told me that it was healing for them just to hear that. The lead facilitator explained that in ancient times menstruation was regarded by many as a sacred time and the blood was often placed on an altar; in some cultures the warriors would even drink it before marching into battle. Strangely enough, that made perfect sense to me.

It was through these exercises that I also connected deeply with my Dark Feminine. I encountered Her after one very intense ritual – and she was fucking scary. I had always known that I had a very dark, very powerful Dark Masculine I could call on when needed, a warrior energy that would not have hesitated to kill if need be, and ruthlessly too. Luckily, I had never had to call on it, but I had often tapped into the energy to get me out of situations where I was in physical danger and outnumbered. Simply tapping into it and blasting that energy out in my booming voice, I had often scared off danger without resorting to force.

My Dark Feminine, though, took ruthlessness to a whole new level. She would have chopped a head off without hesitation. I was in awe. I was in love. It was the last ritual before breaking for dinner, so I had a lot of time to assimilate what this meant. On a long lone walk in the forest, I felt this extremely powerful force surfacing within me, one that now appeared so I could see her face. She was dark no doubt, but she was also full of love. A fierce love.

The next day the lead facilitator, a tiny Australian with a strong energy and clearly a lot of wisdom, spoke about her experience with the dark. She revealed that she was brought up strictly Catholic, warned to never explore the dark because if you do you will encounter evil. She explained how pissed off she was when she eventually explored the dark and found power and love there. She said the reason the Church forbids us delving into our own dark is because it knows that that's where the power is. Organised religion wants to keep us from our power, from self-love, so that it can keep us slaves.

I totally related to this, recognising the same kind of manipulation from my schooling years. I also intuitively knew that the one consciousness – God, if you like – is not just in the light, but also in the dark. Then this thought popped into my head: "If you can see God in the dark and what they call 'evil', then you really know God."

Even though the material was much the same as in Hawaii,

I found that I was learning and growing on an entirely different level. I learnt not only to live more from my feminine, but also to grow my masculine. My mature masculine. My healthy masculine. I learnt that the most essential part of the healthy masculine is presence. As simple as that. Pure presence. Not fixing, not solving, just presence.

I wish I knew that 20 years ago. How often did I have women – an ex-wife, a girlfriend – come home and share with me the challenges of their day only for me to respond by "helping" them, to analyse, to fix the problem for them? Little wonder they would get upset and we'd end up fighting. Naturally, my reaction would be: "What the fuck? Now you're fighting with me – I'm just trying to help!" I realised now, of course, that that was not what they needed. They just wanted to be heard. Nothing else. To be present with them, attentive, as strong as a rock in receiving them, listening to them, feeling compassion. Fully present with my gaze, my energy, everything. I now understood how healing that was, to be received like that.

I was now keen to sign up for Level 2. Although I was apprehensive, I was also excited to learn more. This had not been an easy journey, but I felt as though I no longer had any choice in the matter. There was no turning back. I was on it and committed to go where it would take me, no matter what.

When I arrived at the Level 2 initiation high in the Kaimai mountains of New Zealand two weeks later, Brother Easy was already there, even though he wasn't facilitating. He was tall, about an inch more than my six foot, with straight black hair to his waist. Even though he was in his late 50s, he was very good looking, with a youthful look about him and still in incredible shape, lean and fit. He was also very chilled; with his board shorts and sleeveless vests, he looked more like a surfer dude than a spiritual teacher. I think that's what I liked most about him. Brother Easy wasn't trying to impress anyone.

On one of our walks together, he said to me, "I know you have an extensive background and a great record in business and was wondering whether you'd be interested in helping us with the marketing or running of TS. I have a vision of expanding the organisation, taking it to a new level in order to reach more people."

"Aah, brother," I said. "I love what you guys are doing and I'm passionate about your work reaching more people, especially in the mainstream. I have no idea where my life is going, but I'd love to help where I can."

"Well," he said, "feel into it and let's see how it develops."

"Cool, man," I laughed, "I'll feel into it."

"We have a Core Gathering for facilitators and organisers in Greece in September," he continued. "Please come and join us as an 'ally' and then we can explore these ideas further."

I was touched and told him I'd see where I was closer to the time. As usual, he was very chilled. "Sure, man… see how it flows."

The Level 2 initiation was another opportunity to dive deep – and I had to dig very deep.

Although I've had my fair share of challenges in life, – studied for three degrees, some concurrently, had to do 18 months' compulsory military service in apartheid South Africa to defend a system I didn't believe in and been involved in a few tough cut-throat businesses – this was a stretch on another level altogether.

The process involved facing your fears, your dragons, getting to the root causes of your behaviour, seeking your dark side – your shadow – and embracing it. I found it really hard to be so vulnerable; it wasn't part of my make-up, part of my upbringing. Where I came from, you had to be tough, or at least act tough. However when I went there, ventured to the other side, I found such power in vulnerability. I found that beneath my fears and shadows lay the gold. But I had to dig deep to find it.

I enjoyed the pace of learning. Fast. There are so many spiritual routes, but mine wasn't going to be to sit on a mountain top and meditate for 10 years. I found, too, that so many spiritual teachings operate only from the heart upwards. They embrace all the chakras or energy centres from the heart, but ignore or deny anything below the heart: the gut, the sexual centre and the root chakra, situated between your anus and genitals, as though sexuality and spirituality don't mix. I learnt that the root chakra is the energy centre that roots you in this world, grounds you to the earth, and being comfortable and relaxed in that area is vital for success in the physical, material world.

If you don't embrace all energy centres in your body you can never really be fully integrated. Denying your sexuality doesn't mean it goes away, it's just suppressed. This was confirmation for me of the importance of sexuality and the role it can play in raising your consciousness, your creativity and your joy for life.

What was even more fascinating was – as at the Hawaii and Australia training – I stayed celibate for the duration of the week. It seemed that the intention I had set at the start of the Hawaii training was applying to all the other TS trainings too. Here I was at sexuality trainings and not having sex with anyone. And I wasn't forcing it. It wasn't a mind thing – I was just going with the flow.

Unlike the group in Hawaii, the attendants in this group came from many different areas of life and occupations, from sexuality and body workers, to engineers and surgeons – there was even a sheep farmer.

Much like in the previous level, there was also a sacred spot massage for men in Level 2, but I was to learn even more from this one and be challenged right out of my comfort zone again.

The Level 2 sacred spot massage did not require the group to split between men and women. Instead, everyone had to take a look at the two different altars on opposite ends of the room and stand at the one they felt drawn to. In the end, the group had split half-half, but with mixed groups of men and women. I was immediately very nervous, bordering on panic. Having already experienced two sacred spot massages – at the Level 1's in Hawaii and Australia – I was more at ease with the notion, but both had been given by a woman. Not in my worst nightmare did I imagine that Level 2 would not be gender specific. I don't think I would have participated had I known.

Both groups were given trays of nature objects from which to choose and, predictably, we had to walk around in the room to find the partner with the matching object. So, there I was walking with my little leaf in front of my chest when I felt a tap on my shoulder. I turned around and instinct kicked in.

"Oh fuck!" I said out loud.

In front of me, with a similar leaf in hand, was the farmer ... a sheep farmer, at that. I immediately apologised, but I was gutted. I was wondering how I was going to get through this exercise. I had never in my life had a massage from another man, never mind touched a man's genitals or put my finger up his bum or vice versa!

Both receiving and giving were very tense affairs. I don't think I got much further than the inside ring of his anus and neither did he. But, afterwards, I was amazed at how empowered I felt. The experience had seemed almost normal, matter-of-fact and not at all sexual. I wasn't really sure why I felt so empowered, but I suspect it had to do with my conditioning, growing up in a macho environment in South Africa that had entrenched so much fear around men's intimacy and closeness.

I was becoming more aware that, because of conditioning and ruthless competitiveness in life, in business and survival, men had been starved of bonding with other men. I realised that, at a deep level, most men might actually be scared of other men. And I saw how I might have been one of those men. By doing this exercise I had faced that fear and come to some important realisations. This experience forever changed my relationship with men. It allowed me to have much deeper relationships. I still felt no sexual attraction to other men, but now I started to enjoy deeper brotherly heart connections.

On one of the other days, the group shared a shamanic death experience – well, actually four death experiences, because you were given the opportunity to cut someone's head off and they could then later return the favour. Then, with a new partner you would take turns cutting each other's hearts out. Pretty grim business.

I ended up with a tall young guy from Sweden and I had to "go first", performing the beheading. This was a group exercise that included about 40 of us, and the combined energy – the entire ceremonial aspect, in fact – made it extremely powerful. The Swede knelt on the grass in front of me while I stood ready, my large imaginary sword in hand. I waited until he indicated that he was ready to die and when he looked up into my eyes and nodded, I took a full swing with my sword, brought it down on his neck, chopping off his head. He crumpled to the ground, dead. I had no expectation of what would happen or how I would feel, but the moment I sliced his head off I had this clear flash that I had done this in battle many times in what could have been previous lives, or perhaps I was simply tapping into the collective unconscious. I was slightly disturbed by the tingle of pleasure I experienced doing it, erotic pleasure even. Once again, whether this was a deep-seated memory of a previous experience or the collective unconscious, did not matter, but in that moment I experientially grasped that we are all connected, that we are actually all everything, we are both light and dark.

Intellectually, I already knew this, of course, but it's one thing knowing something intellectually, quite another experiencing it first hand. I suddenly remembered Osho saying that "knowledge" is just borrowed, but that "experience" is your own.

After the death exercise, compassion came so much easier to me. I even began to feel for murderers and terrorists. Perhaps their consciousness was not at the level where they were able to act any differently. I knew that, at a different consciousness level or under different circumstances, everyone is capable of doing exactly the same. Although I agreed that they had to face the consequences of their actions, my perspective now came from a different place. I felt immense gratitude that I wasn't one of those killing and having to live with those consequences.

I had experienced that everything out there is also inside you, a part of you.

CHAPTER 14

Africa to Bali – when the going gets tough

I left New Zealand a few days after the initiation and took a long flight back to Cape Town via Sydney and Johannesburg. I intended to spend only a month in South Africa, to spend time with my parents, to see my kids and then resume my journey.

It was really weird being back. In some ways, I felt something of an outsider in Cape Town, a stranger among people I had once connected with but who could not relate to the journey I was on. Old friends in Johannesburg from university days with whom I had kept close contact over the years were a little confused about what I was doing, but were nevertheless supportive. I was surprised by how open they were. These were traditional men who grew up in the rough, tough Old South Africa of the '80s. I imagined they would judge me, tell me that I had gone mad, but they didn't. Instead, they were curious, interested to learn more.

My parents had aged a lot since I'd last seen them. My dad, ill with prostate cancer, was going down fast, but still had his quirky sense of humour. I spent precious time with my mom too, going out for coffee and visiting art galleries, much like we used to do in the old days. She and I had always had a deep soul connection.

After three weeks with my folks and a fortnight reconnecting with my youngest sister in Stellenbosch, I had a magical time with my kids during their April school holidays. We spent time on the South Coast of KwaZulu-Natal, on the beach, swimming, playing golf, cooking together and just hanging, listening to music, reading and talking.

I shared my learnings of the past year with them and we had very open discussions. One day I started a discussion on self-pleasuring or masturbation, explaining how normal it was, a way to honour and love your body. Halfway through the discussion, my daughter interrupted, "No, Daddy, this is too much!" and fled. I suspect, though, that she remained just around the corner, well within earshot, while my son and I continued the discussion. He was surprisingly open and interested to learn more.

Finally, after two months in South Africa, I left for Germany to hang with Brother Easy and Brother Didi, a German friend I had made at the Hawaii TS training earlier in the year. The three of us spent a week together in Cologne, hanging and visiting the sites, before I moved on to Berlin for another week with Brother Easy and a few of his friends. From there I flew on to Bali to meet up with my kids for their July holidays. I was very happy that, after the previous year in South and Central America, when I hadn't seen them for almost a year, I was now seeing them regularly and for long periods.

Instead of checking into some sterile hotel, we backpacked the small island, staying in local homes. I was determined to make sure that the kids became used to my way of travelling, to teach them something about flow and to surrender to the spontaneous. They had had a very protected and structured upbringing at home with my ex-wife and her German husband, where everything was always well organised, controlled and planned. And yet here they were thriving in this new open-to-anything approach, arriving in a strange town with no bookings and absolutely no idea where we were going to sleep that night.

After a week, we jumped on a backpackers' boat with a bunch of other youngsters and their crates of beer and headed off to the Gili Islands between Bali and Lombok, snorkelling every day before finally taking another boat to Lombok. But then my son, riding just ahead of me, crashed his scooter. I almost had a heart attack and was furious with myself for allowing him his own scooter when we rode to fetch supplies in the neighbouring town. He needed 10 stitches in his foot and knees, and I was reminded that there's a fine line between being too protective and allowing kids their space. I was heartbroken when, after three weeks together, of fun and bonding, I saw them off at the airport. Over the years, I had always been sad to say goodbye, but to avoid the emotions that came with waving them off I usually had something to do straight after. This time, however, I went back to the hotel and sat on my own, holding onto the sadness. I didn't block it, or try to escape into another experience; I just sat with it. It was terrible.

The path I had chosen was proving to be a pretty tough road. Often lonely, uncertain and challenging, constantly trying to heal and recondition myself. In a particularly down mood, I even contemplated returning to Cape Town, getting back to my old life. Getting another high-flying job, a mansion on the beach, a new sports car, hanging out with beautiful people, using alcohol and drugs to fuel the fun. That was not the first time I considered turning back and it would not be the last time either.

But I knew that this time there was just no way that I could go back. I realised that that was the catch-22 of waking up. Once you're awake to the fact that you were asleep before and realise that others around you are still asleep, you can't go back to coma land. Because now you are aware, aware that you have been living an illusion. It's much easier to stay asleep when you don't know you are. As they say, ignorance is bliss. But once you have woken, you can only go forward. Alone and not sure what my next move would be, I realised that waking up was both a blessing and a curse.

But, after a day or two, I noticed my feelings start to change. Slowly, the sadness ebbed away, and underneath was a thin line of joy. I even felt grateful for the hole my kids left after they departed – it showed me how much I loved them. I wondered whether this was perhaps the way to deal with all opposing emotions and circumstances in our world.

In Ubud in Bali, I found an amazing bookstore that stocked most of Osho's books, some I had never even heard of. In seventh heaven, I spent most of my days reading and studying him. And the more I studied Osho's teachings, the more layers of conditioning I shed. It finally felt like I was getting to a place where my life could be a blank sheet for me to rewrite it in truth.

CHAPTER 15

Greece – open your heart

After two months in Bali, I knew it was time to move on, but I still had no idea where to go next. Then I received a message from an Austrian girl I'd met at the Hawaii TS training, who mentioned she was going to the summer festival at the OSHO Afroz Meditation Centre on Lesvos island in Greece. She suggested I check it out. The synchronicity of me studying Osho in Bali and then getting this message was the answer I had been looking for.

I was on a plane to Greece a few days later.

The festival was fascinating, filled with workshops, meditations and live music performed by a group of eight international musicians every night. At the end of the festival I decided to stay on at the meditation centre in the hills a few kilometres above the beach town of Skala Eressos. I hired a scooter to get to the beautiful nudist beach on the outskirts of the town and a café called Zorba the Buddha after a phrase coined by Osho that encouraged one to live life with the awareness of a Buddha and the celebration of a Zorba. Half a kilometre out into the sea, in front of the café, was a rock island. I would often swim out to it, all the way around and then back to the beach for a juice or meal at Zorba the Buddha.

At the centre, I put into practice all the Osho meditations I'd learnt at the retreat. The Dynamic Meditation, a truly mind-blowing experience, started at 7 am every morning and I did that for seven days in a row. You had to blindfold yourself before starting. It consisted of five sections and lasted an hour. The first 10 minutes involved rapid breathing through the nose. The second 10 minutes were about throwing everything out that needed to be turfed by going crazy, shouting, dancing, stomping, waving your arms. The third session had me jumping up in the air, hands raised high up above my shoulders, landing hard on the heels of my feet, shouting "Hoo" every time I landed. It was pretty exhausting.

Then at a point the music would suddenly end with a shout of "Stop!". You then remained frozen for the next 15 minutes. And I mean completely frozen – as you were, no matter what. Even if you were standing in a distorted position, or your face pulled weirdly, a drop of sweat running down your nose, a fly sitting on your face or your arms high up in the air. All of this while blindfolded. The only rule was that you do nothing with your mind. Not move a muscle. But if, say, your arm started to fall on itself, you had to allow that and not stop it using your mind. For the final 15 minutes, the music would resume and this was simply for celebration through dance, music and free expression.

I learnt so much doing this meditation. I would, for instance, have a clenched fist when I was meant to be frozen but then, after a few minutes, I would magically feel my fingers open, even though it was my body rather than my mind doing it. I realised then that my body had an intelligence of its own. It beautifully illustrated that we are not just our mind. It was one thing to have "known" this as a concept, but quite different to "experience" it.

My late afternoons were dedicated to doing the Osho Kundalini Meditation, a gentle way to end the day. Then I decided to start practising the Osho No Mind Program, which lasted two hours a day for five days. In the first hour you walked around talking gibberish, expressing or acting out whatever came to mind – but in a language you didn't know. It was pretty crazy watching all these people walking around in circles, jumping against the wall, kicking cushions, rolling on the floor while talking fast and loudly in a nonsense language. The thinking behind this is to rid your mind of clutter.

For the second hour you sat quietly against the wall without moving. Osho designed most of his meditations for the busy Western mind, believing that in Eastern cultures it was easier to sit quietly and meditate.

I made some good friends on the island and slowly started to feel the celibacy thing lifting. In my last few days, I had a tough decision to make. There were two things happening the following week. Firstly, friends from Johannesburg were flying to Ibiza for a week of partying and were egging me on to join. I had always wanted to go and now here I was in Europe only an hour's flight away. I felt a strong pull to go. At the same time, I was invited to attend the TS Core Gathering on the Greek island of Koufonisia, where facilitators and organisers of TS trainings from all over the world were getting together. Again, the pull was strong.

I really had to dig deep to make the right decision because each could potentially move me in two very different directions. It had been a really hard year and a half of learning in which I was constantly pushing my limits and myself out of my comfort zone, so on the one hand I felt like letting my hair down and just having fun. But I also knew that that would entail drinking, sex and drugs and I wasn't sure whether this was the right time to expose myself to that again. It was a close call, but in the end but I listened to a deeper calling and decided to make my way to Koufonisia.

I arrived at the harbour in Koufonisia just as a bunch of the TS guys were disembarking from a catamaran having just completed their Level 3 TS course, shouting my name when they spotted me. It was great to see some of the very good friends I'd made in a relatively short period. I had found that when you share vulnerability, you drop into a very deep level of connection with people. After a week of these intense trainings, you would get to know someone better than after a lifetime of "normal" interaction with so-called friends.

Koufonisia is an enchanting place. During the day, we had the use of a catamaran to sail around in. It was extraordinary, having 30 mostly naked people all over the deck, skinny dipping, swimming to deserted beaches and into mysterious caves. And all without the influence of alcohol or drugs. We didn't even have cold beers or wine on the catamaran. There was no rule against it; it was just that no one brought any on board. It was not needed. The fresh air and the high vibration of all the people were intoxicating enough. In the evenings, over dinner back on the island, one would have a glass of wine or beer maybe, but most of the time not.

There were quite a few women in the group and the celibacy thing was definitely changing. The Voice wasn't gone, but it wasn't that strict anymore. It said: proceed with caution, take it slowly, be thoughtful, be aware, be selective, choose carefully. But at least it was no longer a firm "No".

I felt myself attracted to a number of women, but I noticed a very interesting development. Whereas I would normally have gone for the physical picture of what I thought was attractive, I was now drawn to certain energies. There were a few gorgeous young women in the group and it is to them that I would generally have gravitated, but instead I decided to follow an energy attraction. The result was that I became connected to an Israeli woman in her early 40s. She was older than the women to whom I was usually attracted, looked different to my normal type, but there was a very powerful energy connection between us. We would learn much from each other in time to come. A well-respected spiritual leader and teacher in the areas of conscious and sacred sexuality in Israel, she became Priestess Sharon.

The first night that we made love she lay her hand on my heart and whispered softly to me that my heart was not open and asked that I make sure it was open before penetrating her. I wasn't entirely sure what that meant, but I was really in the mood to make love to her, so I decided to play along and ask my heart to open to her. The amazing thing is that it did. I felt this shifting sensation in my chest cavity and, with that, a receptivity, a feeling of love for her. I could feel it clearly and so could she. That night we made ecstatic love.

Then a profound and life-shifting event changed everything.

Every day, before sailing, we'd get together as a group to discuss different aspects of the organisation – or the "organism", as it was called. One morning we began to discuss money and business. I was confident that I'd be able to add great value to the discussion. These guys were all beautiful spiritual beings but, I thought, not very experienced in business or the material world. But then, as the discussion unfolded, it turned out I had absolutely nothing to add. They were very much on top of it. I resisted the temptation to say something simply for the sake of it, and surrendered to the fact that I had nothing to add.

After, as I made my way down to the harbour to board the catamaran, this weird feeling began to take hold of my entire being. With each step I took, it grew stronger.

I was dying. That's the only way I can describe it. It got so intense that I couldn't even climb into the catamaran, but rested behind a wall trying to recover. I only managed to board when the boat was about to leave. In fact, they had already started moving away when the captain reversed a few metres for me to hop aboard.

As I sat on the back of the catamaran, the sensation intensified. I was terrified. It felt like my body was dying. Eventually, filled with panic, I had to take myself downstairs to lie down in one of the cabins. Priestess Sharon saw what was happening and came to lie beside me, holding me as I shook uncontrollably.

Later I realised that what I had experienced was an ego death. So much of my self-worth had been locked up in my notion of myself as a bright, intellectual guy, a good businessman and sound leader. By not having anything to add to the discussion, but more importantly *surrendering* to that fact, forced me to let go of who I once was. It wasn't a pleasant experience, but I knew immediately that it was profound. I had connected with a deep part of myself, had cracked through layers of ego to catch a glimpse of the soul that was the real me.

I could not help thinking of my dad, the CEO of a big tobacco company until he retired in his mid-50s, and the massive challenges he faced within a few months after he left his position as a Very Important Person to being just ... well, a guy. I wished he had done this type of work before retiring. I felt so much compassion for him.

Until now I had only ever understood ego death intellectually, but I only really got it once I had truly "experienced" it. Little did I know that my world was going to be shaken even further that day.

Later that afternoon as we were navigating a series of small islands, sitting right up front staring straight ahead, I noticed that the captain had begun manoeuvring the catamaran backwards, forwards, left and right – all over the place. I wasn't sure why or exactly what he was doing, but the Voice kept urging me to keep looking straight ahead and to surrender, to surrender to the view that was constantly changing in front of me as the boat zigzagged out of control. The constant weaving motion of the boat meant that I was not able to fix my vision on one thing by looking only straight ahead. So I softened my gaze, which allowed things to float in and out of my vision. It was an exercise in total surrender.

And that is when it happened.

Everything in front of me morphed. The sea, the land and the sky were no longer separate. They all merged together to become liquid. There was no separation. I saw the world ahead of me completely differently, an entirely different reality. I don't know how long the sensation lasted, but when it was over, a silence as wide as the sky descended over me. I felt completely at peace, held and protected. It was magnificent.

CHAPTER 16

The Holy Land – sacred sexuality

After Greece, I travelled with a group of the TS people to Israel. The plan was for me to do another Level 2 TS initiation in Jerusalem.

Priestess Sharon invited me to stay at her place over Yom Kippur, the week before the course began. She lived in a small village just north of Tel Aviv, and behind the trees, a mere 100 metres away from her home, was a massive wall that separated Israel from the Palestine territories. A stark reminder for me of apartheid South Africa in the '80s. It was surreal.

Although I had completed the Level 2 initiation six months earlier in New Zealand, the experience in Israel was completely different, largely, I think, because I had grown in the interim and was open to learning on a much deeper level. The facilitators were lead this time by a tall guy with long grey-white hair from New Zealand who brought a very strong masculine energy to the initiation. Added to the mix was the fact that we were in Israel, which I would soon learn meant that everything was edgier, more challenging, basically more hardcore. What made it even more powerful was that the course was based in the picturesque hills on the outskirts of the ancient city of Jerusalem. Spiritual sexual shamanism in Jerusalem – now that was daring!

On one of the seven days of the initiation, we drove out to the Dead Sea to follow a ritual in an isolated cave. Entry was challenging, to say the least: sliding the first 10 metres or so on our stomachs. I had to dig deep, the claustrophobia almost getting the better of me. I had to stay really low and keep my head down to leopard crawl through, and I was amazed at how some of the bigger participants in the group managed to manoeuvre themselves.

Once through, the cave opened up into a bigger space where we all convened before proceeding deeper. It took a few hours to get to the final destination where the ritual was to take place. At one point a facilitator ahead of me took the wrong turn and a few of us were isolated deep in the throat of the mountain. With no way of knowing where to go, a few "What the fuck am I doing here?" thoughts raced through my mind. Luckily, the tunnel turned and made a full circle back to the main route. I was hugely relieved when we bumped into a group who were initially far behind us, but I seriously started to doubt whether these guys knew what they were doing. I had heard many horror stories of people diving in caves in South Africa never to be seen again.

The walk was endlessly challenging, delving deeper and deeper into a massive mountain of salt that had once, thousands of years ago, been below the surface of the Dead Sea. We had to climb over and under rocks the entire way in; added to the difficult terrain was the pitch darkness. Very few of us had torches or phones to use for light.

But when we arrived at our destination I was awestruck. The cave was much like a big circular room with a high domed ceiling sloping upwards. It was enchantingly beautiful and looked almost man-made. Right at the top, in the middle, a sliver of daylight peaked through a small opening.

We were told to sit quietly until everyone had arrived and, waiting in the dark, panicked thoughts kept flashing through my mind: What do I really know about these people? Will I ever get out of here alive? I had visions of being eaten alive by these crazy strangers.

Finally, after reciting an ancient poem in his deep raspy voice, the lead facilitator explained that the cave ritual was all about facing your demons, your dragons, your shadows, your fears. He reminded us that we were deep in the bowels of Mother Earth, in a cave much like the place where our shadows linger, locked away in our subconscious. He said sternly, "They are not going to come to you – you have to be brave enough to go there. If you don't, they'll stay in the dark but continue to influence your entire life. Only by venturing into the dragon's den and shining a light on it can you get it into your full awareness, thereby healing it. You, nobody else, can do it."

It all sounded very ominous. Then he perked up a little and added, "The good news, though, is that beneath that shadow, under that fear, lies the gold, lies your power."

He then began to explain the importance of the root chakra, not only the source of our power but also the place where fears are trapped. "Oh God, not another sacred spot massage!" my mind raced. And my fears were confirmed when he explained that by accessing that part of the body we can become aware of and unlock deeply held fears. We all laughed nervously when he said, "And the more you relax your arse, the more you'll enjoy life."

Then he hoisted up a big bag of carrots. "We have different sizes here," he said. "Come get one you're comfortable with."

I could not believe what I'd just heard. "We are going to do *what* with the carrots?" I turned to the person next to me.

She stared at me blankly. "I think the invitation is to get a carrot stuck up your arse," she said.

I burst out laughing. There was not much else to do. This had to be one of the most surreal and crazy situations I'd ever found myself in. I decided that if I was going to do this carrot thing, I'd better hurry up and get one I was comfortable with. Thankfully, I found one of the smallest ones, roughly the size of an average finger. I noticed really massive ones, big thick carrots. I shuddered.

Thankfully, this time we were instructed to simply find a partner with whom we wanted to work. I asked a woman I'd had a good

Corporate days – CEO and Founder of the first direct life insurance company in South Africa – 2006

TOP LEFT Start of the journey – Lima, Peru – January 2014

TOP RIGHT Inca ruins high up in the mountains above Pisac, Peru – the Sacred Valley – February 2014

BOTTOM LEFT Coffee on the Plaza of Ollantaytambo, Peru – the Sacred Valley – 13 February 2014

BOTTOM RIGHT Exploring Machu Picchu, Peru – February 2014

Top Medellin, Colombia, where I lived for three months – mid-2014
Bottom Arrival at The Lake – Lago Atitlán, Guatemala – 6 October 2014

Top Road trip in a convertible Mustang from Las Vegas through Death Valley to LA and then up Highway One to San Francisco – November 2014

Bottom Reading *The Seat of the Soul* on the verandah of the wooden house at The Lake – San Marcos village, Guatemala – December 2014

Top Ubud, Bali – June 2015

Bottom Backpacking and exploring in Bali with my kids during their school holidays –
July 2015

TOP Travelling the interior of Bali – August 2015
MIDDLE LEFT Zorba the Buddha café – Lesvos island, Greece – 22 August 2015
MIDDLE RIGHT Inserting my prayer into the Western Wall, Jerusalem – 7 October 2015
BOTTOM Arriving on Koufonisia island, Greece – 13 September 2015

Top left A typical meal for one in Israel – staying over at the Metzoke Dragot hostel high up on a cliff overlooking the Dead Sea – 29 November 2015

Top right Trekking through the Sinai desert and sleeping on the sand in the open air at night – November 2015

Middle Taking a morning bath – camping on the Jordan River in Israel – October 2015

Bottom With my dad on the cliffs of Hermanus, South Africa – 17 December 2015

Top Graduation day – Tribal Tantra Facilitator one-month-long training – Koh Phangan, Thailand – April 2016

Middle left Mcleodganj, India – May 2016

Middle right Regular morning meditations at the Tushita monastery on the top of the hill above Mcleodganj, India – May 2016

Bottom Morning chai teas after meditation at the Tushita monastery, India – May 2016

Top left The Dharamkot waterfalls high above my village – India – 20 May 2016

Top right My moldavite crystal, which I bought at a shop in Bhagsu, India – June 2016

Bottom left Vegetable curry at my favourite spot in Dharamkot, India – 9 May 2016

Bottom right Siddha Kundalini – crystal and sacred geometry energy healing – training and initiation in Bhagsu, India – June 2016

Top left Leaving Sri Lanka for Croatia – 20 July 2016

Top right Living for a month on a large country estate just outside Prague, surrounded by extensive woods – Czech Republic – August 2016

Bottom Prague, Czech Republic – September 2016

Top Sklenářka, Czech Republic – September 2016

Bottom left Standing on top of a rock with my son – three weeks of travelling together as a celebration and initiation into manhood after finishing school – Wadi Rum Desert, Jordan – November 2016

Bottom right Iboga journey – Swiss Alps – December 2016

Top Magical little houses and gardens in Findhorn Park, where I stayed for a week – Scotland – May 2017

Bottom Arrifana, Portugal – 23 July 2017

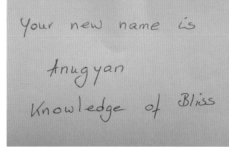

Your new name is

Anugyan

Knowledge of Bliss

Top Cliffs of Moher, Ireland, close to where the two-week TS initiation took place – August 2017

Middle The Crazy Green – West Cork, Ireland – September 2017

Bottom left Being given my new name at the sannyas celebration – Osho Festival in Portugal – 9 July 2017

Bottom right Dancing and flying on Barleycove Beach – West Cork, Ireland – 10 September 2017

Top Cacao dance in the Magic Cave – Ibiza – October 2017

Bottom left I stayed here for a few weeks in a room above a restaurant, writing and swimming 'lengths' in the sea – Cala Boix Beach, Ibiza – October 2017

Bottom right Just picked up my Green Mamba – London – 2 November 2017

Top Back on the farm with *The Heart of the Soul* – Tankwa Karoo, South Africa – February 2018

Middle Travelling the Karoo desert for a few weeks, writing and just being in nature – March 2018

Bottom Lunch with my mom on my birthday – Wilderness, South Africa – 21 May 2018

Journey's end – Cape West Coast, South Africa – 24 September 2018

connection with and we prepared a space for ourselves between the salt rocks. The facilitators advised us to use a condom and coconut oil. Bizarre.

Here I was, deep inside a salt mountain by the Dead Sea, kneeling in front of a woman stretched out naked on her back with a condom-covered carrot in my hand, getting ready to stick it up her arse for her spiritual advancement. Even more bizarre was that, on a deeper level, I saw how it wasn't that crazy at all. I instinctively knew that what these guys were saying was the truth; that, as a society, we have been so conditioned to ignore and neglect parts of our body, how shame, fear and guilt have been used to control us and to disconnect us from our sexuality and our power.

I knew that most of us are terrified to interrogate our deeper selves and will do anything to avoid it. I had done the same for most of my life, distracting myself with alcohol, drugs and unconscious sex just so that I didn't have to delve deeper. The fact that so many of us are afraid to go deep within is a clear indication that that's where the gold is, where the answers lie, where peace may be found. If sticking a carrot up my arse, as ridiculous as it sounded, could help the process, I was happy to at least try it.

I have no idea how long the ritual actually lasted, but I volunteered to massage my partner first. I took my time, sensing that she would be working through deep processes when she was receiving, so by the time I received there was not much time left. I did, however, manage to tap into some pretty deep places and insights but, more importantly, the exercise led me to being more open to practising this ritual with Priestess Sharon and other women in my future.

The session had started mid-afternoon, but by the time we finally got out of the cave, which took us a few more hours, it was after 2 am.

One of the facilitators who really made an impression on me was a rabbi, who after practising Judaism for many years, had become disillusioned and realised that there was much more to life. With a slightly round body, a big beard and long hair on the back of his balding head, he was a fascinating guy. His stories about the holy land in the time of King Saul, a few hundred years before Christ, were spellbinding. He spoke of sexuality temples during that time where priests and priestesses served the people both sexually and spiritually. "On almost every hilltop in Israel," he said, "was a sacred sexual temple."

According to the rabbi, one of the kings who succeeded Saul destroyed all the temples and executed most of the sexual priests and priestesses. Then, later, all traces of sexuality were written out of the Bible. Most other religions also adopted an attitude that was anti-sexuality. Those who ran the show realised that if they were able to cut people off from their sexuality, they could also cut them off from their power, making them much easier to control. I realised then how nothing has changed, that shame around sexuality has become so entrenched that people haven't even realised that they have been disempowered.

At the end of my training in Israel, I made a life-changing decision. In a very powerful ritual, using orgasmic sexual energy, I gave up my sexuality for purely recreational purposes and boldly set an intention to use sex solely for raising my consciousness and helping to raise the consciousness of others. In the language of Tantra, I offered my sexuality to the Goddess, for her to work through me in whatever way she chooses, to empower love in the world and increase awareness and consciousness.

I had had a lot of sex for fun in my day, but I now realised how powerful it could be if used consciously and what a difference this could make in the world. I had managed to harness my power, and with that power came responsibility.

After the week-long initiation, I went off on my own to the hilly village of Ein Kerem on the outskirts of Jerusalem. I stayed in an old convent now being run as a guesthouse and was booked in by a nun, Sister Agatha. The irony that, after the sexual initiation, I had now taken up residence in a convent did not escape me. The contrast was stark and immense. Ein Kerem was teeming with tourists, dashing around with cameras, frantically trying to record everything they saw, looking for divinity outside themselves.

It was during my stay here that I had a strong urge to share my journey with a wider audience, and wrote a piece about my almost two-year celibacy. I made it clear that there had been some lapses in between but the central theme had remained celibacy. I described the confusion I initially felt, but how I'd been guided by my internal voice. I explained how I got to understand that we all have masculine and feminine energies irrespective of our gender, and how it became clear to me to honour my inner feminine first, to get to know her, before looking to the outside feminine. It had been a journey out of the masculine mind into the heart, the gut and the emotions. I wrote that I was finally – slowly and very selectively – starting to interact with the outside feminine from an inner, more integrated place with much greater awareness. I described how sex had changed for me. I no longer needed it – I may want it, of course, but there was no need to look for anything out of myself. It was all inside me. No outside feminine was going to complete me. All the slushy love songs, all the soft-focus Hollywood movies were rubbish. Completeness can only ever be attainable within yourself.

I published my piece on Facebook with some trepidation, and was blown away by how many people commented on my journey update and resonated with it. I realised that, by sharing openly and being vulnerable, one encourages others to open up and discuss ideas and venture into places deep within themselves they may not have been able to go to before.

When I returned to Jerusalem, I visited the Western Wall and, following tradition, wrote my prayer on a sheet of paper and stood for a long time with my head leaning against the wall, meditating on my words before inserting the page in a crack in the wall.

"I ask for the religion of love to spread all over the world and to transcend all religions. I ask for love to shine throughout my being and for me to always be in my full power, authenticity, presence and joy and just *to be*."

I ended up spending three months in Israel, connecting deeply with the Sacred Sexuality community. In that time, I attended a three-day workshop on full-body orgasms, and attended a number of festivals, including the Nataraja Festival in the Negev Desert, workshops and trainings and was often the only non-Hebrew-speaking person there. I was surrounded by extraordinarily supportive individuals who would often sit next to me and translate, looking after me like family.

There was no alcohol at any of these events and the only drug I ever came across was marijuana – the Israelis love their joints. Many regard it as a plant medicine; although it never worked for me in my party days in Cape Town, making me either tired or paranoid, it can be very powerful if respected and used for the right intention. I did try it a few times in Israel, but I preferred to have a completely clear head, with no external influences. I found that, on the few occasions I used it with Priestess Sharon as part of a ceremony with a clear intention, it had an entirely different and positive effect on me and was very helpful in revealing a learning.

When I wasn't attending festivals or workshops, I spent a lot of time with Priestess Sharon, a respected spiritual teacher in Israel with a reputation as a wise woman in the community. She facilitated a number of women's groups and was also a priestess in the Sacred Sexuality community. From her I learnt a huge amount about a woman's relationship – her connectedness – with her yoni. She would often get women in her groups to write letters in the voice of their yonis. What emerged was often life changing, revealing what their conscious minds were not aware of. She also taught me a bag of Hebrew words, which I used to the great amusement of the many Israelis I met along the way. Soon after we met, she gave me an Israeli version of my name: Lenush. When she presented me with a copy of *Vagina* by Naomi Wolf, I did not just read it, I studied it in great detail. It was so accessible, so educational. I remembered Naomi Wolf as a high-profile feminist from years ago – my mother, a feminist in her own right, first introduced me to her. I would later give a copy of *Vagina* to both my daughter and ex-wife as a present on Women's Day in South Africa.

Priestess Sharon and I spent many hours talking about sexuality, sharing ideas and life experiences. I loved her open and direct approach to everything, and learnt a lot about female ejaculation, how to help bring it on and how to give and hold space for a yoni massage. I also experienced first hand with her how a woman can have mouth orgasms as well as a throat ejaculation with a lingam (penis) in her mouth. At one point, in between orgasms running through her body, she took my lingam out of her mouth and said, "Lenush, you know that I am having even more fun doing this than you are."

I was intrigued by the throat ejaculation, and she explained that it came from her thyroid gland. I played with the white sticky fluid between my fingers, astonished how similar it was to semen. She also showed me the spot on the roof of her mouth against which she was rubbing my lingam, which caused her to orgasm. It was such an expanding experience for me.

One day, while licking the line that runs vertically between my two testicles – the same type of tissue that forms the lips of the yoni – she asked me to imagine my etheric yoni. This went on for ages but, after a while, I could clearly sense my yoni, feel the lips and the broader inside of my yoni. It was entirely different to the sensation of male genitals, and lasted for days.

We performed many ceremonies together, making love, a lot of them out in nature, on hilltops, sending healing energy to friends, family and to the troubled world out there. We opened up to each other about our vulnerability and wounds, and I shared with her that I carried a lot of guilt about the number of women from whom I had moved on, but who hadn't moved on from me because they'd kind of got addicted to me. Jade and I, for instance, were still in constant contact. She kept telling me how, because there was still a strong connection between us, she was struggling to make new relationships work. I confessed to Priestess Sharon that even though it was good for my ego, I felt that I might be keeping her back from leading her life. And so Priestess Sharon told me about the Cutting of the Cords ceremony, but warned that I had to be very sure before we performed it because there was no turning back. Once done, it would sever the karmic connection between Jade and me.

We sat across from each other in silence, eyes closed, feeling into our intention. I then announced that I wanted to sever all karmic ties with previous women in my life, but very specifically Jade because I felt that our connection was negatively affecting her. Priestess Sharon and I then started making love with that intention in mind, gradually building the intensity of the lovemaking. At the point of climax, we – with love in our hearts – sent that intention out to cut the cords.

Afterwards, one part of me wondered whether this was all just nonsense, no more than silly child's play, but another part held a deep knowing that what we had just done was profound.

The following morning I woke up to a message from Jade on my phone. It was a long, beautifully written note about how wonderful it had been to know me. She thanked me for our time together, said she would always love and have me in her heart, but that it was time for her to move on. What struck me most were the words, "I hereby release you and myself." Those were not words that Jade would generally use and it was the first time she'd ever mentioned moving on. I was dumbstruck and sat there in silence for a long time. The power and importance of what I was doing and learning was really hitting home. I was beginning to realise how little we knew and how powerful creation is, what powerful beings we are, powerful beyond our wildest dreams.

Soon afterwards, Jade started a new relationship, eventually got engaged and "defriended" me, explaining in a message that, in order to move on with her life and to commit to her partner, she felt she had to. I understood. We have never had contact since. Although there were times that I did miss her deeply, I knew that by releasing her I'd given her a new lease on life.

Priestess Sharon was a mirror to me. I learnt from her the way I made love, with her reflecting it back to me. I realised that my entire life I had been using energetic penetration. I knew that I had been doing something else beyond simple physical penetration, but up until I met Priestess Sharon I didn't know what it was. I thought all men made love that way. During sex I would feel this huge surge of energy and would engulf the woman with it. It just came naturally. I learnt from her that, apart from a physical cock, you also have an energetic cock and that you can penetrate the heart and all the other chakras, the throat, third eye, right through the crown of the head. In other words, you can fuck someone in the heart. She also explained that many women are not able to handle being made love to "energetically" in this way because it often created dependencies. She told me I would have to ask permission before making love this way.

It was as if the lights went on. I immediately knew it to be true. So much of my love life made sense now. All the dependencies I had left in my wake... But how would I have known? It was as though I had held an ancient knowing in my being. And while it was powerful, it was also destructive. I now became conscious – visualising the energy in my energetic cock – while making love to her, fucking her in the heart, looking into her eyes and telling her what I was doing. I could then move the energy up and fuck her in the throat, the third eye, right through the crown of her head, while penetrating her physically at the same time. It was mind-blowing lovemaking. We would reach altered states of consciousness and I would be flying for hours afterwards, intoxicated as though on the most potent drug I had ever experienced.

We spent hours discussing where all of this came from: lineages and previous lives. She was certain that she'd been a sexual priestess in many previous lives, just as many of her friends had clear memories of being burnt at the stake as witches. She believed I had been a sexual priest, explaining how it all seemed to come so naturally to me when clearly I had had no training in this life. The same applied to orgasm without ejaculation – it just happened naturally for me.

One day we tackled the concept of "dark love". She had tears in her eyes when she said, "It's hard to teach men to roar, to get them to connect to their animal bodies. When they do, they are able to ravish a woman. Women want to be ravished. They crave that. Not many men can do that. I often don't approach men I'm interested in because I can see that I won't be met in my power."

She wanted us to do workshops in Israel teaching people "dark love". She felt I embodied the dark masculine and would be able to communicate that to men, to couples. I had always known how to devour a woman, how to ravish her, but now I was doing it with love and with an open heart, which was even more powerful. I was also now secure enough in myself to lie back and surrender, to be ravished by a woman. Priestess Sharon had no problem doing that. She embodied the dark feminine. I think that's why I had been attracted to her in the first place.

We subsequently shared a blissful weekend camping in a tent on the River Jordan just north of the Sea of Galilee. We swam naked in the river, cooked on its banks and made love everywhere in nature. I could imagine that Jesus and Mary Magdalene might have done much the same here 2 000 years ago. We laughed at the thought that we were mimicking them in some way.

One of my most memorable experiences with Priestess Sharon was on another weekend away, in the mountains, where she gave me a long lingam massage that built up and built up until I could not handle it anymore. She assisted by applying pressure with her thumbs to stop me from orgasming. Eventually, I was overcome with an inexplicable fear of meeting my death and I knew I simply had to go through it, to give up control, let go and die. Although I could not – I pulled back at the last moment – I had a very clear knowing that the universe had given me a glimpse of how death was going to be. That you have to meet it and not pull back or lose consciousness because of fear.

Many of the enlightened teachers I'd read say the same thing: that you have to die – give up your identity, fully surrender – before you can really live. I knew I had been given a glimpse of that. I also knew that I needed to practise surrender in order to ready myself for that moment, that day when I would physically die.

I left the Holy Land three months later a changed person. The shift in my consciousness was extreme.

CHAPTER 17

South Africa – foreigner in your own land

I had been on the road, on my soul journey, for almost two years when I decided to return to South Africa for the December/January summer holidays to see my children and parents again at the end of 2015. It was also getting cold in the northern hemisphere, even in Israel.

After spending time with my kids on the Cape south coast, I visited my parents in Hermanus and my sister in Stellenbosch. And then, with trepidation in my heart, I decided to spend some time in my old hood, Cape Town.

But, as I walked the streets, parks and beaches, I felt like a stranger, so out of place. Everything and everyone still looked the same – but I was different. Unlike my old self, I had no desire to go out to restaurants and bars, to socialise, drink alcohol or make small talk. It all felt so boring. I had become used to the deep soul connections I had enjoyed on my travels.

My daughter messaged me one day, asking me how I was doing.

When I told her, she responded with, "Aah, sorry to hear that, Daddy. Think of it as a new start. Look at Cape Town differently, find new friends, create bonds, start anew. Don't be scared. Think of it as just another adventure and you might unlock the part of Cape Town you haven't seen. I'm here for you. Just remember there are a lot of people who love you."

There were tears in my eyes. She was only 16 years old, but already so wise.

Then one day, out of the blue, I received a call from a woman – let's call her Faith – I had known socially before I left Cape Town in January 2014. She told me she'd been following my journey and invited me to meet her for a drink. While we were out, Faith explained that she'd separated from her husband because of his infidelity. She revealed, too, that she'd never had an orgasm while having sex, nor sex that had lasted longer than 10 minutes, because the man would always come first. She had been following my posts on sexuality and asked whether I could help her by making love to her. She hoped it would unlock her, give her the experience and reference points that her body needed. I was completely taken aback – even though Faith was very attractive, I'd never felt any sexual energy with her before. We talked about it a little more while I was feeling into it. For some reason, it did not feel strange to me. I listened for the Voice, but there seemed to be no objection. I felt compassion for her, admired her for her courage. And so I agreed.

So it was that Faith and I went back to my place, undressed and lay down on the bed. I took my time. Kissing her slowly, stroking her chest, moving my hands between her breasts, touching them, but making no contact with her nipples, slowly heating her up. Then I kissed her breasts and when I finally brushed her nipples with my mouth, she moaned, arching her back. When I touched her between her writhing legs, she was soaking wet. As I kissed her stomach, I drew a condom on my very hard erection. I placed myself at her opening, looked deeply into her eyes and very slowly started entering her. Slowly, very slowly … in slow motion. I held her head in my hands to keep her eyes on mine as I entered her inch by inch. Filling her up. The deeper I went the wider her eyes became. She was very wet, and I slipped in easily, slowly. Our pubic bones touched. I slowly pushed further, grinding our bodies together, and her eyes flipped over, her breath gasping. I held it right there, deep inside her, as deep as I could get, holding our bodies tightly together, visualising the energy in my cock, feeling the energy swirling around my cock deep inside her. She felt it too. She started trembling slightly. I held it there for what felt like hours, then slowly withdrew, almost all the way out – only to start the deep entry, slowly back inside her, and then slowly withdrawing and entering again, finding the rhythm, the speed that accommodated both our bodies, not with the mind, but with total surrender to the wisdom of the body. We were dancing the dance of love, in total fluidity, total passion, total surrender. The energy slowly building, rising, increasing, growing, every cell vibrating together towards climax. Her eyes shot wide open as her body quivered uncontrollably, orgasms rippling through her. I felt the contractions in my genitals, the waves pulsing through my body, allowing the orgasm but refusing the ejaculation, more orgasmic energy heaving through me, through my being. Shaking together, slowly subsiding, holding her while still deep inside her, resting, catching our breaths.

We lay like that for a few minutes. Then I lifted my head, looked into her eyes and slowly shifted my hips – I was still hard – so that she gasped and arched her back. I smiled at her, moving my hips even more; she dug her nails into my back, and the rhythm started again, but this time faster and faster... Another rhythm, another dance, another song, all of them perfect in their moment.

We made love for hours that afternoon and she had many orgasms. Later that evening, she stumbled out of the apartment in a daze. I sat at the window, Table Mountain towering high above, my body vibrating, flying high. I could not believe that a woman who was clearly very sexual, could reach her early 40s without ever having expressed that side of herself. It had been so simple.

All her husband had to do was to make love long enough for her to access her orgasmic ability. Ten minutes was not going to do it – a woman's arousal response is usually much slower than that of a man. In my experience, a woman's juiciest orgasms erupt only after an hour or so. That's when they enter an orgasmic state that could last for hours.

Faith and I never met again but she messaged me some time later to say that she and her husband were getting back together again to try to make it work. I thought of my chats with Priestess Sharon and how in Level 2 I'd offered my sexuality up to the Goddess to work through me.

Slowly I began to feel more at home in Cape Town. I started going to events I'd go to overseas but had never while living here. I met like-minded people who, like me, were also on a spiritual path. By February 2016, however, I knew it was time to leave South Africa. This time I decided to head East.

CHAPTER 18

Koh Phangan – Tantra and Zen Beach

I arrived on the tropical island of Koh Phangan in Thailand at the end February 2016, after a deep calling to sign up for a month-long Tribal Tantra facilitator training course. I had become friends with Eugene, who was going to lead the course, the previous year at the TS Level 1 training in Hawaii where he was also a participant. His background was similar to mine, also having been in business before. He had been a mortgage broker but when the markets crashed in 2008 he changed his life completely and started a journey that led him to Tantra.

There was a wealth of alternative things like yo-ga, conscious dancing and meditation to do on the northwestern side of Koh Phangan, where the month-long Tantra training was taking place. As a group of eight men and eight women, we had exclusive use of a beautiful resort right on the beach. And yet, although I enjoyed the training, I was left with a distinct sense that this was all too soft for me – especially after being exposed to four TS trainings and initiations, which were far edgier and more challenging. I did, however, establish a good connection with Eugene and it was inspiring to see how others benefited from the training, to see in action a teacher who was coming from his heart space.

Over the course of the month, though, I died a few ego deaths. I had done a fair bit of that dying – around being a successful businessperson – in Greece the previous year, but as far as money was concerned, I took it to a whole new level in Thailand. I made the shift. I realised how much of my self-worth was tied into me being able to make and have lots of money. I let all of that go. It was a huge shift for me. Huge. This did not mean, though, that I was pushing the option of making lots of money away. On the contrary, I was still very open for money to flow to me in abundance if that was meant to be. I just gave up my attachment to it and the notion that it determined my self-worth. Either way, with or without money, I would be okay. This liberation gave me a sense of freedom I'd never experienced before. I could do anything I wanted to. I was no longer limited to options that generated good money.

Another element that stood out for me in the training was the rebirthing session led by a local island teacher in which we coupled up and spent an hour doing deep, conscious breathing. Being assisted was important because your partner would push you to continue the deep breathing when you were slowing down or drifting off. My partner was a young ex-glamour model from New York who had recently abandoned that world and embarked on her own spiritual journey. She was unbelievably supportive and pushed me hard to continue breathing when I panicked or wanted to stop or slow down when it got too much. I was astonished by how deep the experience of simply breathing was.

Lying in a circle with our heads pointing inwards, after a period of deep breathing, my body began to shake, energy pulsing through it. I felt every cell in my body vibrate and, despite my eyes being closed, became deeply aware of myself within this circle of shared consciousness. It was profound, as though I lost all my labels, my personality and identity.

After the month of training, I decided to stay on on Koh Phangan and found a cheap bungalow right on the beach in a very secluded spot a few kilometres outside the town of Sri Thanu. It was very basic, in essence a hut on stilts on the sand, with just a double mattress on the floor and a small rustic bathroom at the back.

It, however, felt like my palace. I was intrigued by how little I needed and, even though I'd been used to living in luxury in Cape Town, I found I much preferred the basic living I was experiencing now. I could have easily booked into a smart, air-conditioned hotel with sleek white tiles for only a few dollars more, but this felt way more authentic.

I got around on a rental scooter, which I renewed weekly, and spent a lot of time reading. Between books, I attended sunset gatherings at Zen Beach – particularly memorable – and went to ecstatic conscious dancing and five-rhythms dancing, as well as a few more rebirthing breathing sessions, but mostly I hung out and practised to "just be".

I struggled a little in the beginning because all my life I had been conditioned to feel guilty when not doing something, not staying busy and "achieving". But, after a while, everything seemed to slot into place and I began to enjoy taking it easy.

I also went through something of an emotional roller coaster ride. The day after a particularly powerful breathing session, I cracked. I was fragile and emotional. Previously, I would have judged myself, forced myself to snap out of it, but now I was sitting in the discomfort of it. That evening I went to a five-rhythms dance, which allowed me to listen even more deeply to what my body wanted to tell me. I surfed a range of emotions, from deep tenderness to crazy exhilaration. The following morning I woke up in awe of the beauty of the jungle around me, the ocean in front of me, the wail and whistle of the wind through the trees and the love of so many people who deeply touched my heart. I felt so much gratitude for simply being alive.

It was on this island, too, that I saw with absolute clarity that by opening yourself up emotionally, you not only feel happiness and bliss more intensely, but also the ache of tenderness and sadness. I think that's what scares us as humans. That's why we block our emotions. That's why I, as a sensitive teenage boy, blocked all of that shit. It was so much easier not to feel. To get high, to drink, to fuck. Society encouraged me not to feel. That's why so many people take antidepressants: to control, to numb, to avoid the sadness, or the happiness. The kind of fine print that never appears on the labels of bottles of pills.

I realised there was no shortcut. I had to move through my shit, feel the pain of my wounds. But on the other side lay the beauty that came with awareness. I actually felt happy when I was fucking sad! I knew that sounded insane, but it wasn't – it was liberating.

On the sexual front, since the ritual at the TS Level 2 in Israel where I gave up sex for purely recreational purposes, I no longer wanted sex just for the sake of sex. Lying in my bungalow, I decided to jot some of my thoughts on this in my journal and, after thinking long and hard about publishing it, posted it on the My Journey update on Facebook. I wrote about penetration, about the huge responsibility that comes with penetrating a woman. The beauty, the power, the possible destruction and dependency you may leave behind. I shared my experience around energetic penetration and my vulnerability regarding it.

Just before I clicked Post, it occurred to me I may be doing something rash, something I'd regret later. I was worried about the negative consequences it could have on future business or career opportunities. If I ever wanted anyone to give me a few hundred million rand to start businesses in the financial sector again, publishing articles on penetration may not be the wisest move. But my doubt soon evaporated. This was now my truth and I'd live with the consequences. In any event, it was becoming increasingly difficult imagining myself in a traditional business setting again.

The response to my post was inspiring, especially those from women.

I ended up staying on Koh Phangan for another month after the training and then one day I woke up knowing exactly what to do next.

India was calling.

It had started the previous year, but I knew now that the time had come. I'd always wanted to visit the Osho meditation centre in Pune, southeast of Mumbai, in western India. While I was contemplating the possibility, I received a message from Mario, a South African I'd met briefly after one of Dr Bill's morning talks at The Lake. I'd recognised his South African accent while he was chatting to someone on the patio, and we got to talking. We ended up going for lunch in San Marcos, but it was a very brief time together, less than an hour, and I never saw Mario again. So I was surprised to get a message from him. It seemed he had been following my journey and knew I was in Thailand.

Once again, the synchronicity was extraordinary. He was in India. When I told him I was planning to leave for the subcontinent soon, he urged me to join him in the village of Mcleodganj, half an hour outside Dharamshala, in the foothills of the Himalayas.

The call to meditate was strong. Within hours I'd booked my ticket.

CHAPTER 19

India – learning magic

India is big. Very, very, very big. But for the two months I spent there I never moved more than a couple of kilometres, between the villages of Mcleodganj, Dharamkot and Bhagsu. Set in the foothills of the majestic Himalayan mountains, I could walk between them across footpaths, against the backdrop of spectacular scenery. And even though it was summer, you could see the Himalayan snow-capped peaks in the distance.

Mcleodganj is the only village of the three where you can drive cars. A narrow one-way road winds its way up the steep hill, ending at the top on a tiny sloping square with a one-way road parallel to it that sweeps back down the hill to a narrow strip of shops. Taxis, cars, pedestrians and animals compete for right of way along this narrow road, a constant hooting assaulting the senses day and night. Dharamkot and Bhagsu by contrast are serenely quiet because the only way to access them is via mountain footpaths.

I went to India to meditate, but my world was about to expand, to explode into a whole new realm. For a change, I had a soft landing. On most of my travels I'd arrive in a new place not knowing a single person. Meeting up with Mario meant that I was immediately introduced to his circle of friends. For the first week, in Mcleodganj, I stayed in a house called The Freedom Palace, which – despite its name – was far from palatial. But it was also less than 100 metres from the Dalai Lama's residence. Wow. I had always been fascinated by the Dalai Lama and now I was literally within walking distance of his house.

The Dalai Lama is the head monk of Tibetan Buddhism and was traditionally responsible for the governing of Tibet until the Chinese repression in 1959. Along with many other monks who had fled Tibet in 1959, he survived an epic 15-day journey on foot from the capital, Lhasa, over the Himalayan mountains into India, travelling over rough terrain at night to not be detected by Chinese sentries. I love the story of how he slipped out of the palace in Tibet dressed as a soldier. He was given asylum by the Indian government and settled in Mcleodganj with a large number of his followers. He is the 14th Dalai Lama but the first to have travelled to the West, and his charismatic manner has helped to draw much support for Buddhism and the Tibetan cause. In 1989 he received the Nobel Peace Prize for maintaining a policy of non-violence with the Chinese government, the first laureate to be recognised for his concern for global environmental issues.

Mcleodganj itself is both fascinating and over-whelming. Tibetan monks in maroon robes fill the streets, against a soundscape of crazy, consistent hooting. Moving through the village is a fantastical onslaught on the senses: flashes of colours and smells from the shops and stalls on the pavements, vibrant fabrics, sparkling crystals, rich aromas and throngs of people constantly jostling you.

After a week, most of us – me, Mario, his girlfriend and two or three others – moved to the village of Dharamkot in search of peace. You could not really call the accommodation "hotels" or even "hostels" because you rented a room and that was pretty much it. No service whatsoever. If you complained, the owner would simply say, "You don't like here, you move on." My room had a beautiful view over the valley, with my own bathroom, for less than $8 (about R90 then) a night. I quickly learnt that India was a place like no other. She wasn't going to change for you and the only way to deal was to drop all expectations and surrender to her magic.

Every morning before breakfast I would make my way up the hill to join the meditation at Tushita, a tranquil Buddhist centre at the summit, and my walks there were becoming a meditation in their own right. There was a beautiful place, Triund, pretty high up one mountain, just below the snow line, and about a four-hour hike from the village. People would often overnight. By this time, though, I found myself getting more and more introspective, preferring my own company on the hikes. When the group walked up the mountain together, I often waved them ahead, agreeing to meet them up there. I could not for the life of me imagine why anyone would want to hike up in a big group, chatting, when there was this breathtaking scenery and an opportunity to walk in silence and fill up the soul.

It was here in India that I deeply connected with Mother Nature. I could sense her all around me, and I'd be walking along a steep mountain pass and feel as though I were being watched. As if the trees and mountains were watching me. My love affair with rocks deepened. I felt such affinity, such closeness to the rocks on the mountain paths, as if they were talking to me on a deep level. I was experiencing something I had never encountered before, a magical thread linking my inner being to my surroundings. And the longer I stayed with it, the stronger it became.

I also found Mother Earth to be a loving but merciless teacher. I experienced this harsh side of her and was taught tough lessons twice in the foothills of the Himalayas.

I was learning to walk mindfully, to focus my full awareness on the walk and only the walk. To breathe in the mountains, the forests, the streams and waterfalls. To only walk, nothing else. Of course, it was very tempting to stop to take photos because everything around me was achingly beautiful and I longed to capture the moment. But I soon realised that there was a price to pay.

The thing with taking a picture is that it breaks the thread. It's as if you are suddenly yanked from the present moment, distracted from the beauty. I was learning that, like with everything in the "awareness/consciousness space", it's okay if you're not aware but once you *are* and you still ignore it, then there is no mercy.

One day I was walking back from the Dharamkot waterfalls, with a slight drizzle overhead and the grumble of far-away thunder. All of a sudden the magical thread connection happened – and it was otherworldly. Eventually, my mind kicked in and said, "Capture it!" I resisted for a while but I finally gave in and snapped a few photos. Just two steps later, I tripped and fell down hard, slipping a few metres down a slope. I didn't have a scratch on me but I somehow knew that this was a gentle reminder. There was absolutely no reason for me to have slipped – it was a relatively level path and over the last two years of hiking mountains all over the world, I hadn't fallen once.

Then, a few days later, I was walking down the hill to the village below to attend a Kundalini yoga class. It was a clear, fresh morning. In the distance someone was playing a flute and the magical thread connection happened again. After a while, I could not resist stopping to capture this magical time in photographs. *Click.* Boom! The thread connection was gone. And then a second later, *Bam!* I came down hard on the rocky path and slid down a smooth rock step on my back, plummeting to the rock below, my bum and lower back scraping painfully against the exposed stone. It was the hardest I had fallen in a long time. Miraculously, there was no damage, but I had a deep knowing that this was yet another reminder. Except this time it was not that gentle. I knew next time it would be worse.

The message was loud and clear. While there is nothing wrong with taking beautiful photographs, there's a time and a place and sometimes it's more important to stay in the moment and commune with creation fully present and aware.

But it wasn't just nature that was mystical up in the Himalayas. I also kept experiencing mystical, magical encounters with individuals. Once, walking back down the hill from my regular morning meditation at the Tushita monastery, I thought about the one big decision I'd need to make that day: "What shall I have for breakfast and where?"

As I reached the crossroad that leads down to the village, Dharamkot to the left and Mcleodganj to the right, I felt a strong pull right. I suddenly recalled a poster I'd seen of a well-known spiritual teacher who was offering discourses at Hotel Gandhi's Paradise, down the road to the right. There was nothing for it but to follow my instinct.

When I arrived at the hotel, it was deserted because the guru's discourse was only set for the afternoon, so I made my way up to the rooftop for tea. There was only one other person up there so we got to chatting. He turned out to be Shri Prashant, the spiritual teacher I had come to see. It was a magical unfolding on that rooftop, having a one-on-one with the keynote speaker, the snow-capped Himalayas in the distance.

We discussed many issues, but I was keen to check out his view on religion. I was still battling with anger issues when it came to the religious brainwashing of my high-school years. He looked directly at me and said, "Why fight the traditional religions? They have all in essence been defeated and are in decline. Why spend energy on that? Rather spend the energy on the prevailing religion that is taking people away from their truth and freedom, namely the religion of greed and materialism."

His words rang true. Wasn't that the new religion I had so passionately embraced and then walked away from when leaving Cape Town?

Our discussion ended when, after a long period of silence just sitting together, he looked up towards the mountains and sky and, after a few seconds, asked, "You know why this place is so special and powerful? It's not because of the monasteries and the monks and all the yoga places. It's these mountains, that snow over there on those peaks, that eagle circling high up there. If you can, watch that eagle. Really, really, watch that eagle."

In my third week in India I walked from our quiet village of Dharamkot, over the hill, to the madness of Mcleodganj to attend a discourse held by the Dalai Lama. I was really excited to be in the same space as this great spiritual teacher but apprehensive about returning to the craziness of the village. Most of my group of friends hated having to go to Mcleodganj to draw money and shop for necessities not available in our village, and usually returned quite traumatised. On my first visit there I noticed that the same happened to me. How easy it was to lose peace to stress.

But I needed to test myself, to see whether I could hold onto the serenity and peace I had built up in the two weeks of tranquillity I'd spent here since my last visit. Re-encountering the crazy bustle of village life was an extremely rewarding experience. I felt like I was in a movie, observing myself and everything around me. The loud, consistent hooting neither disturbed nor upset me. In fact, it was actually quite entertaining, and I stayed strong in my own inner centre. This was an "A-ha!" moment – it really was about what was happening inside. If one could get to an internal quiet space, then the crazy, noisy outside world cannot disrupt that, whether it's Mcleodganj, Johannesburg or New York.

And you don't need to escape to India to experience this. The real challenge is in staying calm in the middle of the storm, no matter where you are. I was by no means conquering this, but I was becoming more and more aware. I was really starting to enjoy this game of stalking myself.

Sharing space with the Dalai Lama was almost surreal. It really did feel like a dream. At the same time, though, it was so simple, so undramatic. I attended a few discourses held by His Holiness at the Buddhist temple just across the square from his residence. It was fairly easy to get access to them. All we had to do was to register with a copy of our passports for security purposes. Prior to his arrival, there was an electrifying atmosphere of expectation in the air. Maroon-clad monks filled the tight space with throngs of tourists and travellers in between. I went with an Australian friend and we shared a headphone from her little radio, which broadcasted an English translation of his Tibetan discourse as he spoke. We listened to him for a few hours over the next few days.

Because he was reading from the scriptures and then went on to discuss them at length, the discourse was very technical. I wasn't especially interested in the dogma of the faith, so in all honesty I found that a little boring at times. However, sitting there with hundreds of others listening to this remarkable human being was profound. There was something in the air. We all felt it.

On one of the days, when he walked back to his little house, he passed not three metres from where we were standing and smiled at us. It felt like we were zapped. I was surprised at how tiny he was. I am certain that the power of being in his humble presence will remain with me for the rest of my life, the thread of connection much like I felt in the mountains of the Himalayas.

The experience of having shared space with His Holiness would spark an interest in me to research his teachings, and his message to the broader world was beautiful in its simplicity. It encompassed compassion, forgiveness and living from the heart. The Dalai Lama's beliefs are all inclusive, spanning all faiths, embracing non-believers, atheists, all people. In time to come I would return to his teachings and listen to him whenever I felt a contracting in my being or my heart closing. He remains a beautiful reminder for me to live life with an open heart.

Apart from reading, walking and writing, I attended a number of magical workshops in the area. But every now and then I would feel a strong need for intimacy and sex. There were many beautiful women, especially the yogis, but on a deeper level I knew that my time in India was dedicated to learning and sensed that getting romantically involved would hamper the process. The truth was that the Voice would not allow me to go there, and for better or worse I was now past the point where I could just have sex for sex's sake. I really needed to have a deep heart connection before I could penetrate a woman.

I published my thoughts on the My Journey update:

I am starting to get the concept of "non-attachment" now. It's one thing to understand with the mind, another to experience it. And non-attachment is a painful process to go through, to be content without your crutches.

So, what is your main attachment? The one that you spend a lot of time and energy on?

Obtaining?

Maintaining?

Keeping?

Is it a relationship, sex, career, reputation, food, money, alcohol, weed, prescription drugs, legal drugs, illegal drugs, clothes, furniture, toys, yoga, gym, hobbies, sport?

I believe we all have at least one big attachment. I, for sure, have one and that's sex or making love! When our fix is present in our lives, it's easy to be content. But when it isn't, we are miserable. If we are lucky, the universe will take it away from us so that we can learn to live without it, so that we can go deep within ourselves until we are content without it.

And only then will it be given back to us.

In abundance.

But by this stage, our happiness won't be dependent on it. Whether we have it or not, we will be content.

That is bliss.

As inspired as I was to write that post, in truth I was going through deep pain, like withdrawal symptoms. Two months of living in the foothills of the Himalayas without attachment, without making love, without the outer feminine, had been really hard. I was missing the intimacy, the camaraderie, the friendship of a lover.

I often thought, "What the hell was I thinking when I gave up sex for purely recreational purposes and to use it only for raising consciousness?"

My decision was clearly manifesting.

With all these beautiful and willing women around me, I began feeling that the Universe was playing some cruel joke on me. But deep down I knew there was an important lesson in all this abstention.

Eventually I managed to surrender entirely to living with non-attachment. While I was learning about it on a theoretical level in the meditations, readings and teachings in India, at the same time I was getting a practical lesson on a deeper level. And so I got to a point of general happiness without this attachment in my life, something I'd never thought possible. And this gave me a tremendous amount of personal freedom.

Deep down I knew that if I could conquer this then abundance would appear in my future, without me having to chase it. What I didn't realise was how soon it would come after leaving India.

After completing a five-day course on Yoga Nidra – a fascinating practice that helps you connect to your subconscious – I decided it was time for a change in scenery and to move on to Bhagsu. I took my backpack and walked the 500 metres or so further along the hill, down and up the mountain footpaths to get to my new pad, with its spectacular view over the valley and the mountains. It had an entirely different atmosphere to that Dharamkot. Upper Bhagsu was beautifully silent, with steep steps leading up to it from Lower Bhagsu, which was more populated, with shops and restaurants on either side of the road.

I would often go for a chai there. It was a wonderful place to meet other travellers and I made some really good friends and strong connections. It was while I was taking something of a break between workshops that I met three French women – each on different occasions – who all recommended the crystal healing course that was taking place in Bhagsu. They were all so animated and passionate about what they'd learnt. I'd never had any interest in crystals but the more I learnt about them, the more interested I became. So I decided to meet up with the course teacher, Dani, a South African-born Israeli who'd been living in India for 10 years.

We hit it off immediately.

The course, called Siddha Kundalini, was an intensive five days of training and initiation, starting at 9 am and often finishing well after 8 pm. It involved learning about sacred geometry, crystals, the specific Siddha Kundalini meditation and how to channel universal energy to the person you were healing. It turned out to be so much more than just crystal healing; I really got to understand the concept of karma and that time is not a linear process, the way we so often think we're experiencing it in this three-dimensional world. I was so inspired by what I was learning that I made notes:

We are shaping each moment the next moment. Accept karma. Accept everything that comes to you. We are messages of karma. Bow down to karma. Where we are born is no coincidence. It's all pre-planned, a certain place, a specific family, everything, in order for karma to be balanced. Growth is always part of it. Just allow the experience to happen and unfold.

When we are doing healing, we are affecting all of our lives – past, present and future – as well as the lives of ancestors, parents, kids. Sometimes we face issues that are not even ours. We are doing healing then on an even wider scale.

The Siddha Kundalini meditation was itself mind blowing. It involved an hour of alternating between rapid breathing and slow, deep breathing, with eyes closed the entire time. Towards the end of the guided mediation the breathing was so slow that it was difficult to follow. The "in breath" took ages, as did the "out breath". Strange things were happening to the bodies of some of the participants: involuntary twisting, and some were even making strange noises. All of this led to an altered state of consciousness and afterwards I felt as though I was flying high. You had to commit to continuing with the meditation for at least another 21 days once the course had ended, which I did.

As part of the healing sessions, we each built a mandala using a variety of crystals as well as a number of sacred geometry images specifically created for the individual you were healing. The beauty of it was that you did not have to figure out how or where to place the crystals on the mandala; you merely followed your intuition without hesitation. At the start and end of each session, in order to protect the space, you would visualise and place certain sacred geometry images around yourself three times, the person you were healing three times and the whole room three times. The two images we used were the flower of life and the Kryahgenetics Egg. After visualising the flower of life, you would say, "Activate," and after visualising the Kryahgenetics Egg, you'd say, "Turn on." You would then follow certain procedures and start the healing process, channelling the energy to the person's different energy centres. I found the flower of life very effective.

One afternoon I was sitting in a restaurant when I noticed two Indian guys at a table a few metres away. One of them started staring directly at me, and I felt a very strange, uncomfortable energy. To get him to look away, I stared straight back at him but he simply kept at it, staring me down. So I decided to try the sacred geometry. I closed my eyes and imagined the flower of life around me, then softly said, "Activate." Then, when I opened my eyes, the strangest thing happened. As I turned to look at him, he immediately averted his eyes and did not look in my direction again. I noticed, too, that the weird energy had also completely dissipated.

On our next holiday together I would teach my daughter the technique and was delighted when she told me a year later that she often used it to great effect. I often used it at airports when checking in only to be told that I need an outbound ticket for the country to which I was flying. I never bought an outbound ticket because I never knew where or when I was going to be next. Often a return ticket wasn't needed but on the few occasions it was, I would tell them I didn't have one. The matter would then be referred to a supervisor. Whilst standing there I would just quietly, with eyes open, place three flowers of life around me, then around the check-in assistant in front of me, then around the supervisor, even if I couldn't see him or her, as well as around the whole airport. A few seconds later the check-in assistant would inevitably hand me my passport and confirm that I was able to board.

Once the crystal course was over I was exhausted and knew that I was going to have to take a break. But a new workshop soon caught my attention. This one was led by a Frenchman, Demian, who'd been living in India for more than 13 years. After chatting to him, I just knew I had to do his course, a four-day shamanic journey into the heart. Immediately after, I signed up for his next five-day course, which he termed Quantum Field Playfulness. Despite the exhaustion, I could not help myself; I was being driven by a mysterious inner force.

We would often joke that these courses were the Harry Potter School of Magic. Some of the topics included learning to create quantum programmes, time travel, playing with multiple realities, DNA activations, accessing the heart space and quantum healing. We also took a deeper look into quantum physics and scientific research that had not made it into the mainstream media. A whole new world opened up to me.

Then, a few days in, the penny dropped. During one of the exercises experimenting with quantum shifts and quantum leaps, I realised that this was how I had been building and managing businesses. I often knew the answer immediately when it came to deciding what type of business to launch or what brand to go with or what advertising or marketing to use, or even which specific advert would work best. It would often happen that an advertising agency would pitch four different adverts and I'd immediately point to one – I just intuitively knew. Sometimes I did not get that feeling and would send them away to go to work on more executions. We'd publish different telephone numbers on each advert so we knew exactly how successful each one was. The ad I instinctively favoured always did the best.

In the traditional corporate world, people often want to see your market research or the processes of how you came to a conclusion.

I believed, though, that market research could often be more harmful than helpful and that processes are not always important because it's the solution that ultimately matters, not how you got there. Although I was fortunate in that I was almost always surrounded by people who trusted my unorthodox methods and instincts, I knew that in some of the big public-listed businesses the answer was less important than the processes followed. Here, you would not be fired for making the wrong decisions as long as you were able to show that you followed the processes. You were even safer if you contracted some expensive management consultancy to provide the wrong answer. A surprisingly large number of big businesses are run in this way. It's ludicrous really.

It's no secret that most of the game-shifting discoveries in science and tech came about as a result of quantum leaps and intuition, bypassing any procedures or supposed logic. Einstein once famously said, "Logic will get you from A to B. Imagination will take you everywhere." He also said, "There is no logical way to the discovery of these elemental laws. There is only the way of intuition, which is helped by a feeling for the order lying behind the appearance."

On one of the days at Magic School I had a remarkable moment of experiencing myself as so much more than my physical body. We were doing a group exercise in which Demian took us through a guided meditation with closed eyes where we had to imagine activating our 12th chakra, or energy centre, high above our heads, as well our merkaba to the fifth degree. Merkabas are believed to be the same divine light used by ascended masters to connect with and reach those in tune with the higher realms. Your merkaba is in constant communication and connection with all of Source. It is your creative matrix that allows you to combine your soul intention with the spark of god-energy and literally create your reality however you want. I wasn't entirely sure what we were doing but for the first time I clearly felt my "other bodies". Of course, I had been aware of all the different bodies that extend outside our physical ones – the emotional body, erotic body, light body and dark body, for instance – but, as Osho said, knowledge is just one thing and even then it's not your own, it's just borrowed. It's only experience that you can claim as your own and it's only by experiencing something yourself, that you really, *really* get it.

So I now knew *experientially* that my physical body was just a portion of my actual body because, during the exercise, I actually became a 20-metre entity of light and energy and, as I returned to the boundaries of my physical body afterwards, I felt the light and energy getting denser and denser. Once fully back in the physical body and grounding myself with the earth, I placed my hands on my thighs and was astonished by how dense I had become. Now, having felt the high vibration of my extended body, I had a reference point.

There were no drugs involved – legal, illegal, designer, natural, plant – or any external influencer in any other form whatsoever. All that was needed was the innocence and wonder of a five-year-old and the willingness and ability to drop into the heart space, a space that cannot be accessed by the mind.

It was in India that I really learnt about *magic*. I had always felt some apprehension around the notion of magic. Maybe because the Church had conjured up dark images around it in order to scare us so that we would stick to their doctrines or agendas. But now I was opening myself up to that world and was able to *experience* how magical the Universe really is. Here, magic was happening around us all the time and we could create our own.

I couldn't help laughing at my old self. How silly was I to have thought that we were here to make money, to build a reputation, create security, leave a legacy, or whatever other story I'd told myself or that society had sold me.

There was no point in asking: Why are we here? The question itself prevents us from really *being* here, being fully present and aware in every second. Our life's purpose is not to try answer this question, to solve this issue, but rather to experience and live life. To breathe in every second and just be present.

Although I didn't manage to live permanently in the present, when I did, I could feel the expansion of time and see the magic and the wonder of it all. I imagined how life could be if all those present moments were strung together with a magic cord. To live permanently in presence.

Despite all the workshops on yoga forms, meditations, shamanic journeys, energy healing, crystals, dance, chanting and music, there was a very clear absence of anything in the emotional or sexuality space. Even though this was where the most healing was needed, people were generally reluctant to talk about it. I noticed, too, that there was a lot for women exclusively but very little for only men and I could sense a feeling of being left out among many of the guys.

So I decided to facilitate a workshop. I considered doing something in the area of sacred sexuality but quickly dropped that idea because, in many ways, India is such a sexually repressed culture that it just didn't feel right.

In the end, I put together a workshop on emotional expression and release. It was all old school there. No Facebook groups, no Facebook events, social media marketing or anything like that. You simply designed your own flyer, printed it at the local internet shop and walked the mountain footpaths between the restaurants and accommodation houses handing them out. Doing this was both fun and humbling. Previously, when running businesses, I always had a team of operational people and personal assistants to execute these kinds of details. I was the big idea, creative-thinking dude who would delegate operational stuff to others. That same guy was now walking around an Indian village handing out flyers.

No fewer than 16 people pitched up – many more than I expected. Generally, the ratio for workshops is about 70 per cent women and 30 per cent men, so I was surprised that more than half of those attending my workshop were men. There were even a few ex-Israeli army guys who gave it their best, screaming, power stomping and punching and fucking cushions.

By this point I was completely in love with crystals and could not walk past a crystal shop without stopping to take a look and feel. I already had a small bag of them in my backpack, which I got from Dani at the end of the Siddha Kundalini workshop, but felt called to get my hands on a rare crystal called moldavite.

I learnt that moldavite is one of only two crystals on the planet that contains elements from outer space, as it originates from a meteorite that hit the region of Moldavia in the Czech Republic 15 million years ago. The impact caused a gigantic explosion that blasted and sprayed these green-black crystals containing extraterrestrial elements across a vast area. The crystal is believed to accelerate life lessons in a very hard, fast, direct – and not always kind – way. It also allows for a deep connection to the heart. It additionally aids in the expansion of consciousness and the release of that which does not serve one's highest path. Moldavite is a useful stone for star children, those whose origin is not Earth, because it uncovers the reasons why and purposes for which one is here and eases the sense of "homesickness". It's not a power to play with though. Since its vibration is so high, if you're not used to such exposure you can find yourself feeling pretty drained because your vibrational energy quickens to catch up to match it.

Dani showed me a reliable place to buy one, but I had to wait a week for them to get stock. When the stock arrived, there were three. In order to choose the one for me I sat with each of them and closed my eyes, feeling into it. With the first two I could feel the energy but it wasn't that strong. The third, however, was intense and I felt a distinct jolt. I immediately knew that the crystal had chosen me and would be a very powerful ally for me going forward.

The shop artisan encased it in black wiring – rather than drill a hole through it – so I could wear it around my neck. The stone was a beautiful, ominous-looking black, with a rough texture, but when held against the light it had a green translucent quality to it. I wore it for one day but had such an eventful and confusing day that I took it off in order to rest my life journey a little. I was to find out much more about its power in time to come.

Over a vegetable curry one afternoon I thought about how my journey had already affected those in my life, even those thousands of miles away. Two months earlier, while lying in my hut in Thailand, I had sent my ex-wife a YouTube clip of Eckhart Tolle. I was not in the habit of bombarding people with religious or spiritual stuff because I know how annoyed I used to get when I was on the receiving end. I, however, had the urge to send this to her, so I simply followed my intuition. The effect of that single message was astonishing. The clip bowled her over and started her long love affair with Eckhart Tolle. Previously, she had difficulty living in the now, but his words seemed to transform her.

Taking a rest from workshops, I spent more time online to see what was happening in the world and with my friends. I was astonished to see the level of negativity on the planet. It was particularly bad on Facebook and in South Africa where everyone's energy seemed to be spent on attacking the then president, Jacob Zuma. It had become very clear to me that whatever work I was doing in raising my awareness, consciousness and vibration, and any healing or clearing I was doing, I was not only doing it for myself but that every step I took had an influence on those around me to heal, clear and raise theirs. Sometimes I knew that it was not even my own stuff that I was moving but that of someone else or even the collective. It was an automatic energetic process and needed no verbal, written or visual communication. The closer the circle was to me the greater the influence, so the effect was strongest on my children, my ex-wife, my parents, sisters and close friends. Then it extended further into wider circles: Facebook friends, ex-colleagues and acquaintances and, eventually, on the collective consciousness. In return, people in any of these circles raising their consciousness would also affect me. I knew this was true for anyone anywhere. The Ancients and indigenous people across the world all knew the power of collective consciousness. I was truly excited to be living in these times when ancient knowledge was now being released into the wider domain because we were finally ready to receive it. I sensed a quickening of that and knew that we'd have to hold onto our horses because it was going to be a wild, wild ride.

There was no stopping the increase and shift in consciousness taking place all over the planet. It had a multiplying effect. Most people are not aware of this because they are locked into the negative energies that come from, say, watching the news on television. The more you watch, the more you feed that energy and the stronger it becomes in real time out there. The multiplying effect works both ways. Imagine millions of people tuning into the same TV news at the same time. Imagine how powerful that combined negative energy is.

After working in advertising for so many years, I knew that the most expensive TV advertising spots – charged at thousands of dollars or rands per second – are those during and directly after the news. The ARs (audience ratings) are highest at those times, with the greatest number of viewers glued to their screens, hence they can charge the craziest rate. The aim of television stations is to get as many people to watch the news so that they can charge more for the advertising spots. I began to see how they needed to broadcast content as disturbing, negative and violent as possible because they knew – sometimes perhaps sub- or unconsciously – that negativity causes a fear-based chemical reaction in the viewer. The viewer gets addicted to that feeling and comes back the next evening for more.

It was a huge shock to my system to realise that I had unconsciously been part of this system for so long. But it was not all bad. I now realised the power I had in deciding what energies to allow into my life and what energies I wanted to send out and to where.

And so, after three months of the most magical time in my life, it was time for me to leave India. I had arranged to meet my son and daughter in Sri Lanka for a few weeks over the school holidays. Very soon after setting out on my travels back in 2014, I had got into the habit of asking followers on Facebook to guess where I was going next. It was great fun and people following the journey seemed to like it. Little did they know that I often didn't know myself.

CHAPTER 20

Europe – summer of unconditional love

After a fun two weeks of backpacking with my kids in Sri Lanka, I set off for Europe, arriving there in July 2016 and, although exhausted, headed straight to Croatia to catch up with my Peruvian buddy, Amigo Jorge. From there I moved on to Sweden for the Ängsbacka Tantra Festival, then on to Copenhagen where it was impossible to sit still and not explore.

Finally, after a month of travelling Europe, I ended up in the Czech Republic – and even more exhausted. I planned to do a high-level workshop called Wild Love that was to be led by the same teacher who had led the Level 2 initiation in Jerusalem, the main reason I'd come to Europe. As soon as I touched down in the Czech Republic, however, I realised I was way too tired to attend the workshop. I could feel my usual pattern kicking in, one where I'd begin to judge myself for not feeling up to it, the conditioning kicking in saying, "Come on, toughen up. You're just being lazy – get your ass into gear and go do your workshop!"

But I managed to stop myself. I breathed into it, accepted what was happening and made peace with it, even managed to see it in a positive light and to look for the learning hidden in it. And so I decided to drop the guilt, to chill and just be. I was staying on a beautiful country estate an hour outside Prague, hanging with Brother Easy, who'd invited me to stay when he heard I was coming to Prague. It was owned by a friend of his and boasted a lake and forests. I felt blessed to be out here in nature, hanging with my crazy brother and other friends who dropped by as they were travelling through. It felt like I'd landed in five-star heaven. Nothing to do but swim, read, write, cook and braai.

Brother Easy was certainly an interesting guy. I had often been thought of as different, but Brother Easy was on another level. He was his own man and lived on his own terms. He had left school in California when he was just 16, wandered around the desert for a while and then went to live off the land in Hawaii. Later, he moved to New Zealand, started a successful supplements company there, sold it for good money and then, with a portion of the proceeds, started the TS non-profit to spread the teaching across the world. I was very impressed that he hadn't built an earning stream for himself into the model. The only money he earned was the same as any other teacher, the fee for the course he was teaching that week. He had his fair share of shadows and blind spots, just as we all do, but in essence his heart was in the right place; he was passionate and committed to the cause. He did pick up a lot of criticism because he had loads of girlfriends all over the world, but it was all in full authenticity as they all knew about each other. Every three or four days in our time together in the Czech Republic, another girlfriend would arrive to stay a few days, then leave to make space for a new one to come through. Sometimes they would even overlap for a day or so. All of this while there was another girlfriend staying with him the entire period. He had taken the year off as a sabbatical, but the girlfriend thing seemed to be a full-time job. All of this may seem strange, but it all happened so naturally and he handled it well, taking it in his stride. There was a lot of love between everyone. Staying there for almost a month was healing for my soul. It made me feel much more normal.

With both body and soul crying out for a rest, I kept mainly to myself, taking walks on my own in the vast forests and long swims in the pool. I read, wrote and thrived in my own company, although I did socialise a little in the evenings when we all cooked and ate together. I could feel my strength returning. The courses and travelling had been so intense and on such a deep, shamanic level that I realised I had to allow time for all that to settle and for my body to catch up with the dramatic changes that I was going through.

When she thrust her hips hard and fast back into me, I said without even thinking, "I knew there was something about you…"

We were lying in a spoon position but not touching, about a foot apart. We had woken up at the same time and as I opened my eyes I saw the soft skin of her back and placed my hand on her upper arm. The moment I touched her skin her hips shot hard back into mine.

It was as if something clicked into eternity. I had no idea what. But I knew. I wasn't even sure what I knew. It was difficult to put it into words. I had a sense of something magic, something familiar. I recognised something ancient. I recognised myself.

We had met the night before at a full-moon party at the lakeside house. As we all stood around the fire staring up at the moon, taking turns expressing and sharing whatever came up for us personally, it felt more like a ceremony than a party. Later, when I started dancing close behind her, she turned her head around and kissed me full and sweet on the mouth.

We ended up naked in my bed. We didn't have penetrative sex that night, but we did make love. Her name was Anastazie. She was beautiful, but it wasn't her looks that attracted me. It was her energy. So when she pushed herself so aggressively back into me the next morning, it confirmed what I already knew.

We ended up spending a lot of time together, but it was a full three weeks before we had penetrative sex. That was an entirely new experience for me. I'd never been with a woman this long before sex. But when it happened, it felt so right. Waiting allowed us to grow in so many other areas first. Over that time, the energy of anticipation built up to a mind-blowing intensity.

Anastazie turned out to be the mirror I'd never encountered before. We were so similar. She was the female version of me. Everything: sexual drive, mind space, passion. She was me and I was her, a perfect integration of masculine and feminine, which we could switch. Her way of making love was intense, crazy, wild, fast, furious, even violent at times. I could imagine that she must have scared the living daylights out of some men. For me, it was perfect. Here was a woman who could match my intensity, who could fuck me back as hard as I was fucking her. But all with love in the heart. I ravished her and she ravished me back. While we were making love, I would occasionally turn up the intensity and say to her, "I'm going to fuck you dead" – and then really try to do that. She understood and loved it, begging me to go at it even harder.

She would energetically penetrate my etheric yoni with her etheric lingam while sitting on top of me. I would be deep inside her but, as she was moving back and forth, she would be visualising penetrating me energetically at the same time. I had done and received many energetic penetrations in the TS trainings, so I was very comfortable with the scenario. I would be visualising the same and would feel her penetrating me deep inside, deep inside my yoni. I would lie back with arms outstretched, totally surrendering to her. Being properly fucked by her. The combination of physically penetrating her whilst being energetically penetrated by her simultaneously was mind blowing. It was also very healing and allowed for enormous growth for both of us. It allowed her to access her mature masculine, get to embrace it, to grow it and make it stronger. A strong inner masculine meant that her inner feminine felt safe. Similarly, it allowed me to access my mature feminine, embrace and grow it. Having a strong integrated feminine made my masculine even stronger and more mature.

Her wildness echoed mine. I knew I would not be satisfied with a woman who only wanted soft, slow, sensual lovemaking and nothing else. I loved alternating the lovemaking – the full range of expression, from slow and sensual to wild and crazy. Sometimes, in the Tantra circles I moved in, I felt there was an attitude that it was not spiritual to want anything beyond gently moving energy around the body. This was not my truth. It denied the animal part of my being, our beings. We are not just spiritual, we are also very physical. There was nothing more beautiful for me than ravishing a woman with love in my heart and being ravished by her. With Anastazie, I was in heaven. All of a sudden the non-attachment test I had had in India made sense. I had followed the Voice then, and now the universe was giving me abundance. There was never any need to force it or chase it; it just flowed to me naturally.

Anastazie and I would learn a lot together. For the first time in my life I was considering a relationship, albeit one in which I would not require them to be exclusive to me. And vice versa. I discovered that Anastazie was married, with two small kids. She was also seeing someone else, practising Tantra together, moving sexual energy around without penetration. Her truth was that one could love more than one person simultaneously – her heart was big enough for that. She strongly felt that the old paradigm of love or marriage equalling possession was not for her.

And it all resonated with me. All my reading of Osho's teachings, seeing it in practise in the circles in which I was now moving, led me to throw off all the conditioning society and religion had placed on me. I was in the middle of this process when Anastazie and I met, so the timing was perfect.

I was learning about unconditional love because I now had the opportunity to experience how I would feel when she would go back to her partner or someone else after we had spent time together. I found that I could react or feel in two different ways, rather like two parallel highways running together. I could feel jealousy or I could feel the love and freedom that allowed the other person their needs.

I chose the latter. By doing that I shifted something in myself. It was profound. I was amazed that a split-second decision could shift so much and was eternally grateful for the opportunity that our connection gave me to do that. I'd always been in monogamous relationships and although I was never overly jealous, I was nevertheless steeped in a traditional alpha male role with the view that my woman was my woman. The three years on my journey had shifted that but this connection symbolised my greatest shift.

It also made me ask myself whether I had ever really loved anyone unconditionally. The answer was shocking. I realised that, apart from my two children, I hadn't. I realised that I could not say the same about anyone else on this planet, be it previous partners, family or friends. I suspected this to be true for most people. It's easy to love your partner for a long time as long as they love you back. If they don't anymore, then you feel justified to withdraw your love also. But that makes absolutely no sense at all. How can your love be dependent on them loving you? Surely if you really love them unconditionally, then your love will remain, irrespective of whether it's returned?

I was learning a lot about expanding the love in my heart and expanding my capacity to love unconditionally. What added to the learning and exploration was that while on the estate I had also met another woman, Laduška. During the week, I spent time with Anastazie and then some weekends with Laduška, who lived close to the centre of Prague. I also had a deep heart connection with Laduška, but our lovemaking was completely different: mostly slow and sensual but also beautiful. I felt from the moment we met that she was an old friend.

Once again I got a new name to go with a new country. Laduška would call me Lenerdečku, a diminutive of Lenerd. Connecting with both women provided me with another learning in authenticity and open communication because I could tell both women that I was going to the other. I never had to hide anything. What made it more beautiful was that they also sent each other love via me, asking me to pass the love on to the other. It was so normal in many of the circles in which I was moving then, but I was aware that for many it would seem very strange.

This was my first experience of polyamorous relationships where partners have an agreement that they see other people and engage with them at different levels. This was very different to the swinging scene I had come across in South Africa, where it was often purely about sex and not necessarily a heart and love connection. It was also very different to my life in Cape Town, where it was just about sex. Sometimes there'd be no love at all.

Even though Anastazie and her husband explored open relationships, he was never fully committed to it. He knew about our relationship and that we were practising Tantra together, but was not aware of the full extent of our connection. He, she felt, was not ready to handle that. That led me to confront another issue. What I knew for sure was that I didn't want her to leave her partner and that I definitely didn't want to be in the traditional setup of looking after kids. I had a remarkable relationship with my own children and now that they were in their late teens we shared wonderful times together not just as a family but also as friends. Having to take care of young children again was not part of my plan for the future and I knew it would never work.

On one of the last days on the estate we – a group of 18 free, loving spirits – ended up at a concert of Nahko and Medicine for the People in Prague. We were joined by Grace, the English Girl of The Lake, and it was great seeing her and catching up. She had played such an important part in helping put Humpty Dumpty together again when he arrived broken at The Lake. The group took up the whole floor in front of the stage, dancing, kissing and hugging. The free-flowing loving energy was so tangible that even the people behind us couldn't help being moved by it; I could sense how in awe they were, how much they appreciated the love in the air. Laduška and Anastazie were both there and the three of us stood together hugging and kissing – it was a magical night.

Having moved out of the lakeside house, I spent two months in Prague and the surrounding towns, much of it with Anastazie.

It was a hugely transformational and inward-looking time for me, a time for connecting again with my sexual life-force energy after a very long period of off-and-on celibacy, living truly from the heart space without keeping protective walls up. I reached areas of heightened consciousness during and after our lovemaking that I'd never experienced before. I would go for long walks down the river and would be flying high for hours afterwards. I felt almost intoxicated, as if on a strong drug, and yet underlying that high was a sense of peace.

Anastazie was very interested in my crystals and the Siddha Kundalini initiation I had done in India. One afternoon I gave her an energy session and showed her different crystals. She was fascinated by my moldavite necklace and asked whether she could wear it for a few days. Her experience, as it turns out, was much the same as mine. She had a very confusing day and actually lost a few things, including the keys to her house. The next day she was shaken and returned the moldavite necklace to me, suggesting it would be better if she no longer wore it. She had always been a very organised person and had never lost keys or important items before. We both knew that there was a clear message there. That's what moldavite does. It cuts straight through to your truth and brushes away all that is not authentic. I knew that from my time in India. It was clear that her heart was not in the marriage, and so she had lost her house keys.

Even though by now I knew a number of people in Prague, I would often spend weekends there alone. Walking the streets, reading, writing, observing, simply enjoying my own company. It is a fascinating place in which to wander around, to be on your own. There is so much visual stimuli: extraordinary old buildings, the river snaking through the city, narrow cobbled alleyways, castles, cathedrals, cafés, markets, so much. Prague isn't a big city, so you can walk almost anywhere, and if you need to get somewhere fast, then the tram and underground system is easy, quick and cheap.

When I was in Berlin with Brother Easy a year prior, I had met the beautiful Czech Kateřina and had spent time with her again at the TS training in Israel and then again at the estate outside Prague. There was a strong sexual energy between us right at the start; after being introduced by Brother Easy, we were mesmerised and just kept staring at each other. At the time, however, I was right in the middle of my celibacy period so I didn't follow up on it – which was good because by not having sex, we moved the connection to a place of deep friendship and that allowed her to become a true soul sister. She was tall and had once been an international supermodel and there was something in her looks and energy that made me feel like she was my twin. She experienced the same.

So it was then that I was invited by Kateřina to stay at Sklenářka, an otherwise closed community in the woods two hours east of Prague, and I was very honoured to have been granted that privilege. There were around 20 people living there and I was given a cabin furthest away, deep in the woods. My cabin consisted of only one room and was called Wild Boar, with a picture of a boar on the door. Unless there were workshops on the go, I was for the most part on my own because the rest of the families were living either in the big manor house or in cottages close by.

The property was surrounded by woods, and I'd often go for long walks. Occasionally, Anastazie would come visit and on her first stay we spent a beautiful day celebrating life: walking in the woods, hours of lovemaking. I loved most women, but there was nothing for me like the wild, free, dark feminine energy Anastazie possessed. Before she left for Prague, I kissed her black hair framing her beautiful face.

Long after her parting I was still vibrating.

With that energy, I was inspired to write. I had learnt a lot about male sexuality during my long period of celibacy and now, having had a lot of conscious sex with a highly evolved spiritual woman with whom I shared a deep, loving heart connection, my learnings were intense. Soon I posted a piece on what I had discovered to be the man's monthly sexual cycle:

Did you know that men, same as women, also have a

"monthly" sexual cycle?

You only really get to experience and feel it if you are celibate for a period or practising ejaculation choice/control. Depending on the person, from the top of the cycle to the bottom and back to the top again takes about three weeks. It's much more subtle than the women's menstruation cycle, but it's very noticeable once you become aware of it.

So check out your cycle, brother!

What does this mean?

Well, at the top of the cycle you are *"pretty horny, baby"*.

And at the bottom, contrary to popular belief that tends to box all men as constantly wanting and ready for sex, you sometimes can be kinda indifferent to the sacred act.

Over the last 50 years or so, there have been beautiful open debates and discussions about women's sexuality from clits, to G-spots to orgasms, but in stark contrast there's not been much about men's sexuality, as if it's this simple one-dimensional thing, which it clearly isn't. For instance, few men and even fewer women know that male ejaculation and orgasm are two different things and that men can be multi-orgasmic without ejaculating, which means that they don't "crash" and sleep after sex, but want to chat and often cuddle, God forbid! This allows for more intimacy, deeper connection, and they are then also immediately ready for more lovemaking if required, as there is no refractory erection period needed now because they haven't lost all that energy. Between 200 and 300 million sperm, no wonder you want to rather sleep, man!

So why do you want to know where you are in your cycle?

Well, apart from now being aware of why you are sometimes hornier than other times, it can help you decide when to ejaculate, because the fascinating thing is that you lose a lot of energy when ejaculating at the bottom of your cycle, but very little at the top of your cycle, or at least the effect of the energy loss on your body is vastly different at *these different points.*

So, I humbly recommend you make love every day. It's wonderful for creativity. And I recommend retaining your energy so that it can be circulated for more creativity, health and whatever you are focusing on and then consciously gift it to your beloved when you are at the top of your cycle. It's very good and healthy for her body. And, yeah, sometimes you're going to crash over the edge when you don't want to, but that's okay. If you don't crash over the edge every now and then, you wouldn't know where the edge is.

I believe it's critical to communicate, educate and explore much more openly about men's sexuality. It's in a crisis and no one is talking about it. But that's going to change.

Lots of love from the Czech countryside.

I was intrigued by the whole orgasm-without-ejaculation thing. What piqued my interest even further was that I had many women telling me that they had never had a man penetrate them for longer than five or 10 or 15 minutes. None of my friends from the old country, none of the new friends I was making on my journey or the brothers I was connecting with around the world had ever admitted that. The women who confided in me weren't women I was necessarily making love to, just women who were crossing my path or whom I had known before. I think that because of my open articles on the topic, they were comfortable talking to me about it. I had opened a door. In all fairness, I had a few men talk to me about the difference between orgasm and ejaculation and how to split it, but they were not really sharing details of the length of their lovemaking. Traditionally, men didn't really discuss the details with each other.

It became clear to me, however, that there were a lot of sexually unsatisfied, even sexually frustrated, women out there. It also meant that there were a lot of men who had very short, limiting experiences themselves. And it meant, of course, that there was a lot of tension between men and women because of all of this, a lot of it subconscious.

Over the last three years I had been learning about the two ways you can practise orgasm without ejaculation, namely the feminine way and the masculine way. These are just tags and aren't mutually exclusive – you can in fact combine them. One can easily call it A and B, but I have found the masculine/feminine definitions more descriptive.

The feminine is more prominent in Tantra circles and is often referred to as "valley orgasms". You would, while making love, breathe the energy up your spine, away from your genitals and then move it around your body, not allowing yourself to get too close to the peak or crashing over it, but just to stay in that valley. You could then experience full-body orgasms, the orgasmic energy running around in your body for hours without ejaculating.

At first I thought, well, that's news to me ... I had never breathed anything up anywhere, at least not consciously. However, I realised that I must have been doing that to some extent because I definitely had a lot of pleasurable feelings running through my whole body for hours while making love. I was more aware of it now, though, and had been practising it a lot with Priestess Sharon and Anastazie. The first time that I had more insight into it was during a lovemaking session with Priestess Sharon. I was very close to the edge, too close, trying not to go over, when she whispered, "Expand your energy." So I did. I expanded my energy to fill the room, then into the village and then, finally, the whole of Israel. Miraculously, that worked. It pulled me back from the edge and orgasmic energy rippled through my body; I was flying high. I learnt a few precious things in the process too. That expanding my energy pulled the energy away from my genitals, similar to what breathing it up would have done.

Also, doing the Full-Body Orgasm course in Israel helped me bring more of that to the surface, as did the Rebirthing Breathing in Koh Phangan. Especially now with Anastazie, my body would often just start shaking with orgasmic energy while making love.

The masculine way, on the other hand, is the way I'd been doing it all those years prior to my journey. You contract or squeeze your

PC muscle, which runs from your pubic bone to your spine, when you get close to orgasm. Squeezing it – a similar action to holding your pee in – stops the genital contractions, the orgasm and the ejaculation. The more you do it, the easier it gets. My PC muscles got really strong, but then I had a lot of practice... You can then ride that wave, staying close to the edge without crashing over. You need very strong muscles, though, because being so close means that it's really easy to crash over. Then one day I crashed over, had a full-on genital orgasm, but I didn't ejaculate. The first time that happened after hours of lovemaking on the edge, I wasn't trying to do anything. It just happened. I had what felt like this full-on genital contracting orgasm, and yet there was no ejaculation. I did not analyse it much at the time, but I was aware that at the moment of orgasm and just before it I wasn't contracting my PC muscles. I just flowed over the edge with a genital orgasm, but there was no ejaculate. I didn't really understand it and there was no one I could speak to in those years, so I just enjoyed it. This would become natural for me, and happened frequently. It became part of me.

I only *really* got it in Czech when I watched Sasha Cobra's YouTube clip on the topic. She was very clear that for a man to have a genital orgasm without ejaculation he mustn't contract at the moment of orgasm, but rather relax. I immediately realised that that was what I had been doing all along, all those years. Sometimes relaxing into the orgasm. Relaxing my body, going into the orgasm, but with the intention to not ejaculate. The first time was by "accident" – not that anything is ever an accident, of course – but after that my body knew it was possible. I had a reference point: that it was two separate things and I would then just allow myself into the orgasm with the intention to not ejaculate – and often that's exactly what happened.

I never learnt whether there was a physical contraction or whether it was just energetically contracting or whether it just *felt* like a contraction. The fact, however, was that this was completely different to the full-body valley orgasms because it felt like a full-on genital-contracting ejaculation orgasm. Sometimes, I'd even feel something shooting out of my lingam into the body of the woman I was with, but would then realise that it wasn't ejaculation but probably just energy. It felt like ejaculation, almost like a few puffs of air blown in quick succession through a straw. Occasionally, I wouldn't be able to distinguish between the two. It was easy to establish afterwards which it was, of course: one, there would be no fluids and two, I would not lose my erection as one does after ejaculation. What I found strange was that very few men, if any, I came across in Tantra circles were doing it the masculine way. Most were having the valley orgasm, and the "dry genital orgasm" did not seem to feature much as far as I could tell. If it wasn't for Sasha Cobra, it would have been very confusing to me too. I think because she's a young woman and looks even younger she also encountered a lot of scepticism. She clearly is very wise and connected, though.

The second article I wrote and posted over this time was about a man's energetic connection to his genitals and was inspired in part by Sasha Cobra's teachings:

Exercise of the week: Feel your penis.

Can you energetically feel your penis? Can you, without looking at it, without touching it, without contracting any muscles, just quietly sit and, by going inside, feel it? If you can't – and many men, maybe even most men can't – then you are disconnected from your dick. Sounds serious? It is, but the good news is it's easy to get connected again.

I can hear some of you say, "Now he's totally lost all his marbles." But hear me out.

Let's take a few steps back. First try to feel your right foot and then your left hand. Remember, without moving it. Can you perhaps feel a slight tingle in your hand or foot when you think about that part? Now try to feel your penis again. Great if you can feel a tingle or any sensation in your hand. If not, no stress – three years ago I could not feel any part of my body; now, if I think about my big toe, it starts throbbing.

There are many reasons why men become disconnected from their penises in childhood. One reason may be if you're continuously told as a small boy not to play with it; you may then think about it as something wrong and then create a distance between you and it.

It's important for many reasons to be energetically connected to your dick.

One being that it allows energy to easily flow there. Apart from the obviously resultant strong erections, it is very important when making love because it's not the friction-based sex that gives her those mind-blowing internal orgasms, but the amount of energy that is flowing in and around your dick that fills up and interacts with her energy and yoni (vagina/pussy), which builds up more and more and then eventually explodes right throughout her body and even yours.

Energetic connection with your penis also allows you to move out of sex of the mind to a shared harmonious interaction with the woman you are with. Also, your powerhouse is your genitals, your seat of identity as a man, and the moment you connect to that a sense of self-assurance, clarity, courage and discipline become more present in your daily life. I also believe that the way women experience and respond to you as a man is directly related to your relationship – and the strength of your connection – with your genitals.

So whenever you can, try to energetically feel your cock! You can, in the beginning, even put your hand on it when sitting, walking or doing whatever. That will slowly start re-establishing the connection again. And, for God's sake, don't be scared to touch your dick! Don't worry so much about what other people think.

I can see a few people being triggered by this. "Oh, he's

writing about sex again." Yes, you're right. We come from sex – that's how we got here. We are sex. That's our basic energy, our universal life-force energy. But, more than that, you can never have the full spiritual experience if you deny that energy. Or by being neutral to it either. You have to fully embrace it. And the only way to fully embrace it is to be fully aware of your body, your whole body and not exclude any part, to be in your body, feel it, experience it, love it. Eckhart Tolle also says that the body is a point of access to being and that by feeling the inner body you connect to the now and to source.

Lots of love from the Czech countryside.

CHAPTER 21

Prague and the Czech woods

After a few weeks in the woods, two hours east of Prague, I returned to the city. Being back in an urban environment was strange in a way because it brought back all those fears, the uncertainty about what I was going to do with the rest of my life. At times, I could not help thinking that, yes, I have learnt a lot of cool things, but what am I going to do with all of this?

I knew that surrender was the answer and that the "what" and the "how" were not up to me, that the Universe would bring them. It was much easier said than done though. Luckily, I'd already had glimpses of the magic of the Universe, providing what was needed at any given time on my journey. Now I needed to surrender to what was in front of me, to accept that it was perfect just as it was. That I was where I was meant to be. And to have gratitude for that. That the present moment is all I have and to focus not on what is missing but on what is present. That gave me courage.

My instinct was to try to figure it out, to turn it over in my mind, but I needed to avoid all of that, all that overthinking. It was really difficult because all my life I had been so conditioned, so programmed to operate like that, to *think*, not *feel*. And, to be fair, I couldn't complain – I got what I wanted, what I desired. But now I had an opportunity to live my life differently. To open myself up to the mystery, to life. To see what it had in store for me if I surrendered to it.

I had to constantly remind myself, "Be careful what you wish for, be very careful." To remind myself not to set a destination or end goals because chances were that they would come true. Instead, I needed to rather take direction, from moment to moment, because then I would not be defining, creating a specific outcome. I would be opening myself up to an infinite number of options and outcomes that the Universe would continue to provide. That was much more exciting, living fully as opposed to just surviving. It was scary, yes; uncertain, yes; but hell, yeah, it was living fully the gift of life and it was absolutely limitless. So alongside my inherent fear about what the future may hold, I also felt deep gratitude for where this journey had taken me – emotionally, spiritually, physically, all around the world and now to this beautiful city.

On one sunny day in Prague, sitting next to the river, I wrote down my thoughts and published them on the My Journey update on Facebook later that day:

Thank God
For leaving my life in Cape Town
Three years ago
I didn't know what I was doing
Or why
But I knew I had to
Had to
Jump off the cliff
No parachute
No wings
Just threw myself off the cliff
A leap of faith
Falling

Falling
Trusting
I knew I had to build my wings on the way down
And fuck have I been building
Because I didn't want to die
I didn't want to splatter myself on the rocks far below
But I had time
Because this was a fucking high cliff
The highest, scariest one I could find
And I've been building
Growing wings
Slowly at first
I was still plunging head first faster and faster
Then the wings grew stronger
They slowly started to break my fall
Stronger
Bigger
They grew
Until I realised I wasn't falling anymore
I was flying
Well, more like gliding
But now I can feel the power in my wings
I'm slowly starting to flap them
My God, they are powerful!
They are starting to lift me
Am I starting to soar?
I know they are going to get even more powerful
Beyond my wildest dreams
They are lifting me higher
Yes, I am flying
Yes, I am starting to soar.

After Prague, I returned to the woods of Sklenářka, to my cabin Wild Boar, and stayed there for a few more weeks. I never saw myself staying in Czech and Europe that long. It was now already

177

October and getting pretty cold, daily temperatures averaging nine degrees Celsius. I took lightning-fast showers in the outdoor shower outside my cabin in the woods, morning temperatures hovering around four degrees and the water absolutely freezing. I felt awesome afterwards, though, probably because I was just grateful to have survived the icy experience. The muted tones of autumn were appearing fast and the woods were changing daily. One day, on one of my walks, I misjudged the setting of the sun and got completely lost in the dark. Fortunately, I stumbled upon a country road a few hours later and managed to flag down a car. The elderly couple could not speak a word of English, but my pronunciation of Sklenářka was good enough for them to understand, so they gave me a lift back. It was scary being lost in the woods, but it was also a lot of fun too.

On my previous visits to Sklenářka I hadn't done any workshops or training because I'd already done my fair share. On this visit, I did, however, join a men's circle weekend that included a traditional Native American sweat lodge run by an elder from one of the Native North American tribes. I was the only non-Czech-speaking participant but luckily, because of the elder, it was run in English.

It was both humbling and encouraging to see how our world is changing as the mature healthy masculine grows. Here was a group of tough guys not afraid to open their hearts and be vulnerable in their sharing. That open-hearted vulnerability, along with the warrior ability to hold space, was true masculine power. I made deep friends – brothers – that weekend. It never ceased to amaze me how quickly you could drop into a deep connection when you shared vulnerability with another human being. And this is especially true of men between themselves because so little of that happens in the world out there.

At the same time, there was a 10-day women's circle led by Kateřina. I watched from a distance, felt the energy, chatted with some of the women every now and then and was moved by the true sisterhood and the mature healthy feminine I was able to witness.

Our world needed the growth of both these energies.

Before I left the Czech Republic there was one more journey I had to make. A friend had told me about another men's circle taking place in the countryside, one that included a San Pedro plant medicine journey. They say the plant spirits call you when you are ready to journey with them, and I could feel the call from San Pedro. I thought about it for a few more days, to make certain, but knew that I had to go.

The first time I had had a call from a plant spirit was when I did ayahuasca two years earlier in Colombia to purge the parasites from my body, but had ended up on a vivid journey that involved the dangers of cocaine. After that, the ayahuasca plant spirit never called again. Now, two years later, San Pedro was calling me. San Pedro is a columnar cactus native to the Andean Mountains of Peru and Ecuador. Often called The Grandfather, it's been used for thousands of years by the shamans of South and Central America as a spiritual medicine. San Pedro is prepared by slicing and then boiling pieces of the stem for a few hours and the liquid that is left is then ingested orally.

They say that if you decide to do a plant medicine ceremony, the plant spirit has made a deal with your higher self to teach you something. You can either leave that open to be taught what is most relevant to you right now or you can put an intention into the ceremony. I decided to put an intention to connect more deeply with nature and Mother Earth.

When I drank the San Pedro at the start of the ceremony, I found it had a bitter taste, but not nearly as vile as the ayahuasca. I was very happy, too, to learn that this journey did not involve diarrhoea but possibly only vomiting. Not that I was a fan of vomiting either. To my surprise, I was even happier to find that I didn't do much purging and that I had a rather pleasant journey.

At one point, sitting around the fire in the tipi, sharing, drumming and singing with 16 other guys, it hit me what magical adventures and experiences I'd already had on this three-year journey. Here I was, in a group where I was the only non-Czech speaker, participating in a two-day ceremony held in the Czech language, but somehow it didn't matter because so little needed to be translated into English because the universal language of love and brotherhood transcends everything.

A few hours into the ceremony on the first night, a Friday, I left the tipi to go outside to throw up. It was dark out – I had no idea what time it was – but a few candles showed the way from the tipi into the woods where we were asked to do our purging.

After throwing up a few times, I just stood there in the darkness among the trees, feeling so connected with the woods. As I turned to leave, I brushed against one of the low-hanging branches and stretched my hands out to the leaves and was immediately aware of a magical feeling I couldn't explain; I could sense the pulsating life and energy of that tree. The tree wrapped its leaves around my fingers and hands and gently played with them.

I had never in my life felt this before; I was so aware of the aliveness of the tree, similar to the life in a human being. I had this sudden realisation that the life running through the tree was no different to the life running through my body. The intention that I had set prior to the ceremony to connect deeply with nature was manifesting right in front of my eyes. I realised how we as humans, through our arrogance and sense of superiority over other life forms, feel separate to them, superior in our separation. We've been cutting ourselves off from everything, denying ourselves the magic of connectedness with other life forms.

I don't know how long I stood there in communion with the tree, with Mother Nature herself, but it must have been at least an hour or more. I urged myself to never forget this experience, to lock the sensation as a reference point in my body.

During the two-day ceremony, we sat or lay in a circle around the fire inside the tipi. While most of the procedures were in Czech, there was one guy whose English was good so he'd at times lean over to translate critical parts for me. In fact, on the first night there was much sharing in that space, the speaking of intentions, singing and drumming as part of the ceremony. Then, on the second night, the leader holding the space asked whether we wanted to do the same. I responded that I thought it'd be great to do the second night as more of an internal journey. As it turned out, although it was quieter, there was still a lot of sharing and singing. But it didn't bother me because, unable to understand the language, I could really reach inside in my own silence.

The Sunday after the closing circle of the ceremony, we were saying goodbye to each other when the Czech who'd translated for me approached me and said he felt called to share something with me.

"I heard what you said last night about wanting to go into silence in the ceremony and I feel called to tell you about another plant medicine called iboga and this guy called Sean, who's originally from South Africa, who does the journey in a very different way than most, because he does it totally in silence."

I immediately felt something stirring inside me.

He continued, "You also being South African, together with the intention of silence, was just too much a connection to ignore so I had to tell you."

A few days later I received further information from him, did a lot more of my own research on iboga and knew it was something I had to do. It was clearly the next step in my journey.

Leaving the Czech Republic and saying goodbye to Anastazie was hard. We both knew that the relationship would change once I left, in that we would no longer have physical contact, but we also knew that we were deep in each other's hearts and that that love was eternal. We had no idea, however, when or if we would ever see each other again. She dropped me off at the airport and it was very emotional. It was *déjà vu*. I was getting used to women I loved dropping me off at airports, for me to continue my journey without them. It was hard, but I was driven by a force, a voice within me, to keep moving on this journey of learning and awakening.

I was planning to be in South Africa before Christmas to spend time with my daughter for her school holidays, but before that I had two things planned. Firstly, I was going to tour Jordan and Istanbul for three weeks with my son to celebrate him finishing school. He had just turned 19 and the boy had become a beautiful man. Outside and inside. Our trip was not just a father-and-son trip, but friends travelling together. We were seeing it as an initiation for him into manhood. And it would be exactly that.

Secondly, I had committed to being in the Swiss Alps early December for an iboga journey that would turn out to be another life-changing adventure.

CHAPTER 22

Africa in the Alps – the sacred silence

"The deeper I go into my wild heart, the more vivid, striking colours I see all around me, the more beautiful the same music sounds."

I wrote that after a magical, heart-opening and deeply loving experience of making love with Anastazie before I left Czech. I now found myself high up in the Alps in Switzerland feeling the same as I stood in wonder at the enchanting world around me. There were deep green valleys, silver rivers and high snow-capped mountains everywhere. It was overwhelmingly beautiful.

I had come up here to do iboga, to connect with the African root – in the Swiss Alps, of all places. I smiled at the crazy and wild unfolding mystery.

Considering that death would be a central theme, I should have been as nervous as hell for what lay ahead over the next three days, but strangely I was not. I just knew this was the next unfolding of the journey, of the mystery. The calling to be here was strong. And now I was in a small skiing village that was almost deserted because the skiing season hadn't kicked off yet.

I would discover that all the other plant medicine journeys I'd completed up until this point were all just preparation for this. As were most of my other learnings, initiations and readings, especially Osho on the notion of observing yourself from the outside without judgement. All of that had led me to what I would now have to face. Without all that preparation, I think I would've been in deep trouble. Without the learnings on observing yourself without judgement, I would have been fucked.

Iboga is not a journey you want to embark on without being prepared. Very prepared. Neither is it a journey to tackle without feeling a strong calling from the plant spirit. This is not something you do because your buddies are doing it. Because it's hip or cool. It's a tough journey and can be very dangerous.

I did proper research before deciding to do it. The information I got from the Czech guy who recommended the journey included a link to a podcast interview a journalist had had with the iboga facilitator, Sean, and his friend, an English guy. Before I listened, I had read up a lot and spoke to a few people about iboga – or The Wood, as it is often called. What I heard and read made me very nervous. Most people were too afraid to go anywhere near it. Even many of the guys who regularly ventured into the Amazon Jungle to do ayahuasca stayed clear of it. There are stories of people who were pretty messed up after doing it and cases where some were, months later, still struggling to properly come back into their bodies.

However, after listening to the hour-long podcast interview, I knew I had to do it, that the plant spirit had called me. I knew for sure that the plant spirit would not call you if you weren't ready. And I knew I was ready – especially since I still felt the same after listening to Sean talking directly and honestly about how tough the journey was.

I smiled nervously when he said, "With ayahuasca you learn with the mother, you learn the steps, it's a dance, she is like a snake, its flowing. With iboga, he arrives, knocks on the door, you open the door, he steps in and *Bam!* the back door blows off and all the windows blow out. You have signed on the dotted line, there is no escape."

What also appealed to me was Sean's view on the way they do it and why they do it. He said he did not resonate with the fixation on healing. They do it mainly to bring you to a deep silence, to raise your consciousness and awareness. And, contrary to the traditional way of doing it combined with a lot of music and noise, they do it mostly in silence. That really resonated with me.

What I also liked was that they did a Skype or video consultation with you beforehand to assure themselves that you were ready, and prior to starting on the day of the journey they'd chat individually to everyone. This was in stark contrast to some of the ayahuasca journeys I had encountered in South America where they rounded up a few tourists and simply leapt into journeys with them. No questions asked. Often, the participants hadn't even checked whether they were dealing with experienced shamans or con artists.

It is vital to approach plant work with the right energy and with the sacredness it deserves in a ceremonial setting. I had also learnt that it was more important who you do it with than what you actually take. I trusted my intuition that I was going to do it with the right guys.

It was a brutal journey. Brutal.

Firstly, my consultation with Sean an hour prior to the journey was direct, to the point and a little unnerving. At the end of the chat, he looked me straight in the eyes and said, "Up to here you had free will, some control of your life. You were living life, but from here on it will be different – life will be living you."

That made me very nervous, but deep down I knew that that was the reason I'd come in the first place.

Secondly, the journey was extremely rough. I lay on a mattress on my own in the dark with 12 other people in the room, swallowing terrible-tasting ground iboga root every few hours. Now and then I'd throw up in a bowl and didn't sleep for 40 hours, all the time a constant, relentless mind chatter and thoughts coming at me from all directions, at lightning-fast speed, non-stop.

If you are ever in doubt about the insanity of the collective mind and the individual minds of the human species on this planet at this stage of our evolution, do an iboga journey. The only way I could deal with it was to simply observe and acknowledge the thought forms coming at me. You can't judge those thoughts or observations as either good or bad because then you give them energy and durability – and that's what they want; they need the energy you give. You can't repress them, deny them, ignore, reject, judge, hate or love them because all of that gives those manic thoughts the energy to survive and to stay with you. If you just observe them as a matter of fact, they are given no energy and they move on.

The thing is that they continually return and say, "Hey, I'm back because I don't think you looked properly before." They try to get you to interact. And then you just have to do the same again and observe without judgement. But the process repeats itself again and again, returning stronger and stronger: *"Hey! You are not fucking looking! Look here, look at what I'm fucking telling you!"*

Back and forth, back and forth until, eventually, they move on … only for a new thought form to emerge and the whole process starts all over again.

I quickly realised that this is simply an exaggerated illustration of what happens to us on a daily basis, being constantly bombarded with relentless mind chatter. But somehow seeing and experiencing this with such intensity really hit home.

This is just one of the many experiences I worked through on that journey, and it's impossible to put into words what transpired on so many other levels and in other areas. A lot of the work and transformation happens outside the mind space, on a spiritual level, so you can't really describe it or write about it; describing is a function of the mind and the mind tries to box the experience in. The problem, though, is that the experience is much broader than the mind. That's very threatening for the human mind, so it makes up a story of its own. Then, when asked about the experience, it tries to replay that story. And it believes that story and so limits your experience to that story. The experience, however, is much, much wider on so many other levels and dimensions. That's why we were advised not to speak about the experience to anyone else for at least a few months after the journey or maybe even ever.

So the only way to truly understand and experience it is to actually do the journey, but only if you are strongly called to do so. What I can say is that, after all the relentless noise and chatter, I eventually came to a deep sense of silence I had never experienced before, not even in deep meditation. And not just on that journey, but for long after the experience. It really gave me insights and tools on how to deal with the mind chatter we all experience at this stage of our evolution.

To my surprise, I found that many of the thought forms that may have harassed me from time to time were not even my own or those of my ancestors, but just random thoughts drifting through the space that homed in on me because I gave them attention and energy. I realised that none of this was personal. They are just energy forms, much the same as we are, and have their own relation to existence, to God. In fact, I even noticed some of them pissing themselves laughing when they eventually moved on, having messed with me for so long without my realising that I had been keeping them alive by giving them energy.

There are so many stories we tell ourselves about our lives, our past, our experiences, our parents, family, anything actually. A lot of those stories are illusions and don't serve us, but we keep them alive by giving them energy, by retelling them to ourselves and others. Using them as excuses. Becoming aware of that dynamic is really powerful and I realised then how easily we are able to shift things if we need and want to.

There was so much happening in the background on this journey that it was impossible for the mind to grasp it all. For one, I know that right at the end, after not throwing up for a while, that I was throwing up for the last time. Obviously, there was nothing left in my stomach – I hadn't taken any of the root for a while – but I still threw up stuff. In the dark, I couldn't see what it was, but realised that I was getting rid of some deep stuff. I could feel the lightness in my being and my body after that.

With the ceremony having started late Friday afternoon, it was now the early hours of Sunday morning. We still hadn't slept but the effect of The Wood was slowly starting to wear off, which meant that we were getting tired and could feel that sleep was not too far away. I was beyond exhausted.

Sean had warned us that this was a critical part of the journey because what in essence had happened was that we had died and it was now time for rebirth, but to do that and to fully come back into our bodies we had to get up and move.

He said, "You cant go to sleep, otherwise you stay dead. You have to get up and dance yourself into your body again and into rebirth. It'll be difficult, but you have to do it, so I'll be very strict with you to make sure you do. I know of a guy who didn't do it and it took him a good two months to get back into his body." As tired as I was, that got my attention.

Sean started drumming slowly and asked us to get up. I rose and stumbled over to where he had made a small circle of candles in the middle of the room. I could not imagine how I was going to dance. I felt like crawling back to my mattress and sleeping for the next century. I looked around at the others – I was not the only one. Everyone was absolutely finished. I slowly started to move my body, trying to follow the music. It was more of a stumble than a rhythmic dance. We all looked like a bunch of zombies falling around the room. We really looked dead! This carried on for what seemed an eternity. Every now and then someone would go sit against the wall and Sean would walk over, kneel down and urge them to get up again. I never sat down; I was scared that if I did I'd never get up again. So I summoned all my willpower to keep moving, to keep dancing.

I have no idea how long this went on; it could have been an hour, two hours, maybe more. At one point I seriously considered giving up and lying down. I also had no idea what else to expect. Were we just going to dance until we passed out? How do you get back into your body, be reborn? I had no reference point for that.

Eventually, to distract myself, I decided to entertain myself with the candles in the middle of the room. Apart from being dead tired, it was also pretty boring stumbling along for eternity, so I started moving in circles around the candles, changing direction every now and then, waving my arms slowly across the flickering lights.

The next thing I knew I was dancing! My body was moving rhythmically, effortlessly, to the music. I looked down and my feet were stepping lightly all over the place in a funky way. Only thing was, it wasn't me executing those moves. It was magical. I realised that it wasn't me who was dancing to the music, the music was dancing to me. I suddenly remembered Osho talking about not being the dancer, but becoming the dance.

Soon I was swirling all over the place, really enjoying the moment, enjoying the dance. I couldn't believe how that had just happened, without my trying. I looked up and there were a few other dancing figures among the lifeless zombies on the dance floor. And so we continued until everyone was dancing and there were no more zombies. Then Sean stopped the music and said we could lie down. We immediately crashed on our mattresses. I think I was asleep before my head hit the pillow.

Around midday on the Sunday, after a few good hours' sleep and a hearty brunch, we had a closing circle ceremony where Sean strongly advised that for 30 days, in order to deepen the silence experienced, we abstain from tobacco, marijuana, legal drugs such as antidepressants and anxiety pills, illegal drugs, alcohol, caffeine, television, Facebook or anything that could distract us from the discomfort of silence and quietness.

"It's so easy," he said, "to reach for the remote, whatever your remote is, when after a while the silence or quietness becomes uncomfortable. Don't do that – don't escape into another experience. Sit in that uncomfortableness, lean into that, see what happens."

I realised then that, apart from the things he had mentioned, reading and writing were my remotes, so I committed to myself to follow his recommendation. Many of the things Sean had listed were easy for me to abandon; I had never regularly smoked, didn't like marijuana, had never taken or had any interest in legal drugs, had had more than my share of illegal drugs and had lost interest in them, hadn't watched TV for seven years, stopped drinking coffee a while ago. Yes, I enjoyed having a few beers every now and then, but could by now easily go without any alcohol for a few months, and even though I used Facebook to share My Journey updates and learnings, it wouldn't be difficult to avoid that for as long as it was necessary. The challenge for me was not reading, not writing or researching, but I could see the benefit of what he was saying so I committed to putting my books and YouTube viewings aside for a month at least and do only the bare minimum of writing, like WhatsApp messages and emails, when absolutely urgent.

I also instinctively knew that there was no sense in putting a Facebook post out saying I was going to be offline for at least the next 30 days. Just the act of putting that out would have meant I was already online on day one, having broken the whole extension and deepening of the "sacred silence", as Sean called it.

So I stayed offline without any warning and deleted the Facebook app from both my iPhone and iPad, and I did not surface until a month and a half later. After a while, I did receive some worried WhatsApp messages from friends asking whether I was still alive, especially considering that my last update had said something to the effect that I was quite nervous about the following three days seeing that death would play a central role.

CHAPTER 23

The Motherland – can you live it there?

I arrived in the Motherland a few days before Christmas and flew directly to Port Elizabeth to meet my 17-year-old daughter. Our plan was to take a road trip along the scenic Garden Route, down the coast to Cape Town, over the following three weeks.

It would be just the two of us because my son and I had toured Jordan and Istanbul a month prior, in November, to celebrate him finishing his final-year school exams. It was also right in the middle of my 30-day, post-iboga online abstention so there was absolutely no distraction for me and my daughter. We had such a wonderful time, both fully present throughout. Instead of a cold beer or wine, I drank coconut water at our braais, even on New Year's Eve.

In our time alone, my daughter confided in me and discussed issues she had never discussed with anyone before. I did the same. I was very aware and grateful of how my journey was deepening our relationship.

I was also fascinated by how "not reaching for the remote"

– as Sean had put it – but leaning into the "uncomfortableness" of silence deepened that silence, which in turn brought about a deep sense of peace. The longer I sat in the silence, the more beautiful it became. The longer I sat in the uncomfortableness, the more comfortable it became. The more I resisted the temptation to escape from the uncomfortableness of the silence, the easier it became. So I saw the mundane things in daily life as an opportunity to experience and to taste silence.

This time around, my stay in South Africa was so much easier than the previous two visits. I felt comfortable; there was no fear of being pulled back into my old life. There was actually no charge about it in the body either. And I knew from my learnings with Dr Bill that this was the acid test. He had explained it to me very clearly. If there was still a charge in my body regarding anything I was tempted to do or experience, he advised to do it right there and then. And so I took that lesson to heart and rather than *never*, on a few occasions on my travels I did actually take something I'd vowed I'd never do again and found that I was quite indifferent, that I'd kind of lost interest in it. The drug that I mainly came across was marijuana because it was so acceptable in spiritual circles. I also found that with the increasing legalisation of marijuana all over the world, people were smoking it more openly. I would often be with people smoking joints and I'd have no interest in partaking. There was no charge in my body. I simply did not like the fogginess that came with smoking weed, and loved having a clear head. At the same time, though, I didn't have any strong feelings about it, and refused to judge those who did. I never advised anyone not to smoke, although I did start to wonder how regular use could invite a disconnect. I saw how certain acceptability in spiritual circles could be masking the dangers and inducing a numbing effect, an escape of sorts. I could see the potential of consciously using it in a ceremonial setting and I sometimes did, but the everyday habit did not feel that conscious to me.

The same applied to alcohol. Sometimes I wouldn't have a beer for weeks or even months at a time because I liked the clear feeling in my head, but at others I would have one or two and enjoy the slight buzz it gave me. I was a cheap date now. There was no charge in my body either way. I also struggled to drink anything stronger than beer, like strong spirits and even wine. How things had changed for me...

The fact was that my body was so sensitive by now that even a cup of coffee would make me as high as a kite. I had stopped drinking caffeine a year into my journey, but every two months or so I'd have one out of curiosity. I would be flying afterwards, of course, and on the occasions I had two in a row, my reaction would be crazily intense – the same sensation you get when taking too many drugs: hectic, awkward, unpleasant, out of control. I would be bouncing off the walls. And then, after a few hours, there'd be the comedown – and it'd be terrible. For the rest of the day my energy levels would drop right down, along with my mood.

It was very clear to me that, after that initial adrenalin boost, caffeine affects your body's vibrational frequency. I realised that that's why some people have a few cups of coffee a day, in order to keep them on that artificial high, but there would be terrible long-term affects on both the body and the mood. I knew I certainly used to do the same.

The bottom line, I think – mainly because of the iboga journey and the 30-day period of abstaining from the "remote" – was that I became very aware of how anything could take me out of the present moment. It could be the uncomfortableness of silence or some unpleasant emotion. Just one joint, one beer, one coffee or one cigarette could temporarily take you out of that experience. They are stimulants and thus alter something in you, which means you miss out on an experience; you escape. I believe that an unpleasant emotion or experience is vital because it carries with it a message. Escaping it is a missed opportunity to learn more about yourself. I didn't go around lecturing people on what not to have but did become very aware before having a beer or a coffee of why I was doing it. Was I having a beer to escape or was I just sitting in the sun with my son having a good laugh and enjoying the taste of a cold beer? Sometimes, I'd still have a beer or coffee to escape an uncomfortableness or the silence, or something, but the difference now was that I was aware of why I was doing it *prior* to doing it. I had made a conscious choice on the matter.

On the food front, I had become more aware of the effect certain foods had on my body. Even though I liked bacon, I found that after the parasites episode, I could not handle pork in any form whatsoever. I would feel terrible after, with an awful "hangover" for the rest of the day. The parasites were a blessing in disguise on so many fronts. The experience forced me to eat very basic food for a whole year and that cleaned out my system so that I could start from scratch, listening to what my body needed. I experimented with dairy and found that my sinuses were perfect if I stayed away from it but clogged up after taking it. I would also feel lethargic for days. It was an easy decision – I just cut it out completely. I missed normal cheese but found that goats' cheese is a great alternative. I was also eating a lot more vegetables but didn't feel the desire to become a vegetarian. I listened to the wisdom of my body and at that point it was telling me that I needed to eat meat. Also, because I have a very fast metabolism, I need to take in a lot of protein. I knew that vegetables could give me protein, but my body was telling me that meat was necessary too. I ate it with much more awareness, though, and would often thank the animal for sacrificing its life for me prior to my eating and enjoying it. I didn't need to go to a dietician to discover any of this; my body clearly communicated what I needed at any specific time. It was so simple.

The lesson from Dr Bill was such a significant learning that applied to everything, not just alcohol, drugs, caffeine or food. On my previous visits home, I was cautious to avoid headhunters and recruitment consultants contacting me once they knew I was in the country. I was scared of being pulled back into a corporate position with offers of good money and prestige. There was still a charge in my body for that. On this visit there was no charge; I felt indifferent to it and had no problem speaking up when contacted. There was never a rise of interest or desire in the discussions I had.

It felt like a foreign world to me. I could not imagine being in that space again. But because I didn't have a charge for it, I never said I'd *never* return.

It was also great to find that this visit back to South Africa seemed to coincide with my getting back into my flow when it came to interacting sexually again. Even though for at least the last 12 months, it had been flowing relatively well, I sensed that I now needed to reach full balance again. A friend had once said that the longer and further you live your life out of balance, the longer and further it takes to get back into balance. Like a pendulum swinging from the one extreme to the other before settling in balance. I had certainly lived a life out of balance for those four years in Cape Town and it took me roughly four years to get back to full balance.

Because I was radiating integration I found that highly conscious women were being attracted to me without me having to do much. And the wonderful thing was that I didn't have to act sexually on attraction. Often I would not. And even when I did, it often meant moving energy around and playing without penetration. Penetration had become very sacred to me. I only did it if I felt a deep soul calling. I also didn't want to just penetrate; I wanted to bring all of me to it, my body, soul, spirit, everything, to combine the physical penetration with a full-on energetic penetration of not just her body but her heart, soul, spirit, all of her. I would want to crack her open, split her open. To consume all of her and, in turn, allow all of myself to be cracked open and consumed by her. To feel the merging of souls, the merging with existence, the oneness of it all.

The only thing was that I did not come across anyone I felt I could do that safely with. But I was at peace with that. All would happen in due course. How exactly it was going to play out, I did not know, but I knew that the mystery would unfold, that there would be a lot of that in my life. I felt it strongly, a deep inner knowing.

This time round, I spent a lot of my time in South Africa in the mountains and the deserts, writing and reflecting on the journey of the previous few years.

A very good friend, Rix, invited me to write on his farm in the Tankwa Karoo, three hours inland from Cape Town. We had been friends since university days. During the week he lived in Stellenbosch and once a week would go to the farm for a day and night to take supplies through. This time when he returned to Stellenbosch he left me alone on the farm. A couple of farmworkers lived a few hundred metres from the main house, so I was basically on my own. The farm was on a long, straight dirt road, with a mountain range behind the house and, from the front, a view of the stretched-out semi-desert, speckled with hills and another mountain range in the far distance.

I had no idea how long I was going to stay, so I bought food for a few weeks because I had no car and the closest roadside shop, The Padstal, was 40 kilometres away. There was no cell phone coverage, no wifi, just me and a whole lot of rocks. I craved the silence that that brought and was looking forward to quiet time with my beloved rocks and the chance to write.

Most mornings I'd climb the mountain behind the house and perch on a boulder that jutted out on the landscape. The view was magical, mystical and breathtaking: the tiny farmhouse far below, and rocks everywhere – red, white, brown, black. I loved the red ones most. I would sit there for hours. I remembered a book I had read the year before, *Serpent of Light*, by Drunvalo Melchizedek and had watched some of his YouTube clips. What stood out for me was his message that you could only really connect deeply with your higher self once you had, firstly, connected deeply with nature: the planet you were born on and living on, Mother Earth and, secondly, with your ancestors. I immediately knew that to be true and a big part of my journey was exactly that. I had deeply connected with nature and the connection was strong. Good God, now I was talking to rocks... I had also spent time connecting with my ancestors too, especially my parents. On my visits back to South Africa I had spent weeks with them. I knew that I had more connecting to do with them, but I was committed to that.

During the day I would write, read and reflect. In the evenings

I'd have grass-fed Karoo lamb on the fire and write again by candlelight. I stayed out there in the semi-desert for two weeks and only left because I had booked a ticket for a festival that was taking place further north. I organised a small rental car and took the road north into the Cederberg mountains to SpiritFest Africa.

Suddenly I was meeting so many new people, people I'd never come across in all my years in Cape Town. This was because I'd opened myself up to other energies and become much more aware and conscious. There was no doubt that the same shift in consciousness happening all over the world was also happening in Cape Town. It was definitely a different place to the one I'd left three years earlier. But I was, of course, not open to it before.

Getting to know people in the consciousness space meant that I was well informed about all that was taking place. While travelling the desert and mountains, writing in different spaces, I attended a number of festivals and ceremonies in this vast, wild part of the country. It was also a great time to be there because January to April is really the best time weather-wise, with many events taking place in natural settings.

SpiritFest was an interesting four-day event, from Thursday to Monday, with a lot of yoga, meditation, music and dance. I had done so much of that in my three years of travelling, but this was my first event in my own country.

It was also challenging at times. Not being used to so many people around me, the Saturday afternoon I felt overwhelmed, tired and in dire need of my own space, so I took care of myself and went for a long walk along the river and sat on a sandbank for an hour. In the evening, I didn't initially feel like dancing but when I did, I remembered how powerful movement, sound and breath are for the body and soul. Before going to sleep, I stood for a while looking up at the clear, bright stars and magnificent night sky. I consciously decided to open myself and allow the Universe into my being and then expand my whole being out into infinity. At the same time I reminded myself that whatever was happening was just perfect; there was no need to label, to judge; there was nothing "missing". There is never ever anything missing – I sometimes forgot that one. And to surrender. I often forgot that one too. Just surrender to whatever was happening.

Sunday and Monday were magical – and not in the jaded, conventional understanding of the term, but *real* magic, with strange things happening. The dance at midday on Sunday was crazy and wonderful. No alcohol or drugs were allowed at the festival, and yet everyone was on a high. A natural high. People were dancing wildly, the energy tangible and powerful. I was high as a kite, flying. Once again a reminder that I really don't need anything external to be high on life.

It was at the festival that I was invited to join a week-long sweat lodge ceremony in the Langeberg, a few hours away. On my way to the lodge the following week, I was in two minds whether to return to the isolation of the farm or head to the sweat lodge. The farm was roughly on the way to where the ceremony was to take place. At the intersection where I had to decide, I stopped, climbed out of the car and settled under a tree to eat two chicken pies that I had bought on my way. After all the vegetarian food at the festival, I was ready for something unhealthy for a change.

A big part of me wanted to isolate myself on the farm, to be on my own. Another part of me wanted to go to the ceremony, mainly so that I could connect with people in that space and learn more. It was a close call, but in the end I decided to head to the lodge. So there I was in my small rental driving dirt roads, heading over steep mountain passes.

The sweat lodge ceremony, led by a visiting elder from a Native American tribe, was extremely challenging. I had done one before, in the Czech Republic, but this time it was very cramped and claustrophobic. There was one sweat a day, in the late afternoon, and lasted about three hours, over a 10-day period.

At the first one I went to there were 32 of us crammed into a small round structure made of bent reeds with heavy blankets thrown over the roof to keep in all the air. I thought I was going to die. The claustrophobia was overwhelming and I spent much of my time and energy fighting off waves of panic. I crouched in this crammed pit, my knees drawn up against my chest, my head and neck squashed up against the roof, in pitch darkness. The heat from the stones seared my throat and lungs , my breath like steam from a kettle. The guy in front of me constantly complained that my breath was burning his back.

I needed to get out of there – badly – but I knew there was no way to get past or over all these people to reach the flap door, and had to fight the urge to punch and kick my way out. I knew people would be badly hurt if I tried because there were red-hot stones in a hole in the centre of the pit and someone could easily fall in. I tried to ignore the panic in my mind, the thoughts of death, but with no success. It just got worse. I have no idea how I made it to the first break, but when the elder stopped singing and opened the small flap door, a sense of relief washed over me. The limited fresh air that wafted in was heavenly. It was still stifling inside, but at least I could breathe a little easier.

The break didn't last long though – just long enough for the guardian of the fire to haul in another load of red-hot stones and tip them into the pit. When they closed the small flap door again, I wasn't even close to getting my breath back and it wasn't long before the hyperventilation started up again and the waves of panic returned. This time it was even worse and it built up to a point at which I felt myself exploding, leaping up, screaming, kicking and punching, fighting my way to the door. I actually saw it happening in my mind's eye. Then something snapped. I stopped fighting. I surrendered. I surrendered to the fact that I was going to die. I had no choice; I was stuck tight, out of breath, suffocating. With acceptance, a strange kind of calmness washed over me. A reassurance, a certainty that it would be okay if I died. Even though I'd be dead, I'd be okay. My body would be dead, but I wouldn't be. The realisation was clear and, in the midst of the chaos, it brought a calmness to me. It was still fucking hot in there and I was burning my arse off, but I was okay. And, in a way, I did die: another ego death.

For a few days after that, I stayed far from the sweat lodge and just walked the mountains, but I knew I had to go back to face my fears again. I did another sweat a few days later and, again, almost died. It was even more cramped and once again I had to fight the panic attacks, the urge to fight and punch my way out over all the people and the red-hot stones to the small flap door. It was brutal. I went through the whole damn process again, until there was acceptance, surrender and calmness. And, in the process, I managed to learn some things. I learnt that when danger looms near, the mind stops. In that state you are not the ego, the personality, the body, the mind; you are much more, you are eternal. I think that's why people do dangerous things, like climb Everest. They get glimpses of that. Another thing I learnt was that I would probably stay far away from cramped sweat-lodge ceremonies in the future.

In a weird way, there was some similarity in this experience to the moment when my body first experienced orgasm without ejaculation, when I experientially knew that they were two different things because I had *experienced* it, had *felt* it, that it wasn't just a mind thing. It split into two things. Much the same had happened here. I experienced the soul, the personality, as two separate things. I had *felt* it, *experienced* it.

At the end of the sweat lodge week, I arranged to rent a cottage in the mountains and stayed there, isolated and on my own, for a week, mainly writing but also going for long walks. The water I drank, cooked and showered with was from a spring high up in the kloof. There was no cell phone or wifi coverage. There was no electricity, but luckily I had a small solar-powered phone charger, so I wrote on my iPhone with my right thumb only. All my writing over the last few years had been done that way, and I was developing a pain in the joint of my right thumb.

Between being on my own in the vastness of the Karoo, I also spent a lot of time with my parents, three weeks at a time. They lived in the beautiful town of Hermanus, on scenic cliffs overlooking the ocean. The place is one of the best whale-watching spots in the world, mainly due to the vantage points offered by the high cliffs that allow you to look down on the sweeping Walker Bay where the whales gather to birth their young. They take this long journey from the Antarctic waters every year and stay in the bay for the first few months of the calves' lives, roughly from August to November.

My dad was very ill with cancer and Parkinson's disease. My mom had been taking care of him, but because it was getting harder and harder for her, my sisters and I eventually persuaded them to move up the coast to the town of George where one of my sisters lived and there was a frail-care centre.

So on my last visit to them in Hermanus I helped my mom pack up the house and, while we were sorting through her books, I came across one I had read many years ago, *Who Moved My Cheese?* by Dr Spencer Johnson. It was as if the Universe had placed this little book in my hands. I was delighted to find it again. So I opened it and started reading extracts to her because so much of it was relevant to what she was going through. She harboured so much fear around the move, having to leave everything she'd known behind. I felt so much compassion for her because I could only imagine how difficult it had to be for her at the age of 75.

I read out loud to her the part where the mouse, looking for the cheese, peered down the dark passageway and so became aware of his fear. He was scared of what lay ahead and wondered what dangers lurked there, what terrible things could happen to him. He was scared to death. Then he laughed at himself, realising his fears were just making things worse. He then raced down the dark corridor and began to smile. He didn't realise it yet, but he was discovering what nourished his soul. He was letting go and trusting what lay ahead for him, even though he did not know exactly what it was. To his surprise, he started to enjoy himself more and more. He wondered why he was feeling so good, because he still didn't have any cheese and had no idea where he was going, but before long, he knew why he felt good. He had a sudden, clear realisation that when you move beyond your fear you feel free.

As I read, my jaw dropped to the floor. This was relevant, not only to my mother, but to *my* life and to *my* journey. Here I was reading to her in order to help her and *Bam!* it hit me right between the eyes that this was completely pertinent to me and maybe it was me who needed the reassurance.

It had taken me three years to move through that fear. It was only in the last six months or so that I had really begun to enjoy this journey. The three preceding years had been a soul-wrenching slog. Sure, I had travelled to beautiful places all over the world; and, sure, I had fun in between, but it had otherwise been very tough, extremely hard work, with the constant companion of fear by my side.

In my experience, you can't "overcome" fear, you can't "suppress" it; you can only "transcend" it. And you do this by moving through it, acknowledging it, accepting it, living with it, until you have earned your passageway "through" it. And when you transcend it, there is a tremendous sense of freedom, one that grows and permeates everything else in your life.

I still didn't have my "cheese", I had absolutely no idea where I was heading, but what I did know was that I was now enjoying the journey. In fact, that's an understatement – I was ecstatic about the journey; life was magic, pure magic. At the start, I had known nothing but bit by bit the magic, the mystery, had been unfolding. I had experienced things beyond my wildest dreams. I was in awe, everything was changing, reality was shifting and I sensed that this was only the beginning.

I really had no sense of where my life was heading and how my work life was going to look and how I was going to make a living. I still had kids at school and university, so I had financial obligations not just to myself but to them and also possibly my parents. I was also far too young to think about retirement. I was only 49 when I walked away from the old life to embark on my journey.

I felt I was only halfway through my working life. I'd studied full-time for a long time, earning three degrees, and then had to do

18 months' compulsory military training, so I only really started working in my late 20s. And I'd only been working for 20 years or so before I left on my journey around the world. I could see that my remaining working life, bar being hit by a bus, could easily be another 20, 30 or 40 years.

I knew I could go back to financial services, or as I often jokingly said, go back to selling insurance, to make a lot of money again, but that was not calling me at all anymore. I had no fixed view that I would *never* go back, of course, because I had learnt never to say never again, but I definitely did not feel a calling.

I had come to see the insanity of doing something just because there was a lot of money in it. But leaving the safety and security behind often made me feel like that little mouse looking down the dark passageway. I knew that that feeling would come back every now and then, and I'd just have to remind myself to move through that fear. And trust.

I could see how the "regular world" – my parents, my old friends – would not understand how someone at the top of his profession, with many years of "cashing" in ahead of him, could walk away right at his peak. And for no apparent reason. Some people make huge changes when faced by a life-challenging experience, such as the death of a child or a near-death experience. In my case, there had been no external trigger – it had all come from a huge internal shift.

I had left behind everything that I knew, that I had spent my whole life learning about and building up. Of course, I was going to be scared. Terrified, in fact. Like a little mouse peering down a scary, dark passageway. But the mouse had to start moving down that passageway before anything changed. And then it all changed. The forward motion allows magic to start happening. Lights go on. I had got to realise that this whole life thing is not as serious, as personal, as we make it. It's just a game, a dream that we create for our learning, for our expansion, for our enjoyment.

Finally, back from visiting my parents, alone again on the farm in that desolate landscape, I sat at the window looking out over the vastness in front of me, over the sand and rocks of the Tankwa

Karoo. Words flowed easily. Writing about my journey and experiences gave me great pleasure; it lit up my soul. The more I wrote about them and relived them, the more I was able to solidify and integrate all my crazy experiences and learnings. As I wrote, I realised that trust was key to my journey and that it was to play an even bigger part in the future. Trust in existence, trust in myself.

CHAPTER 24

The call back to Europe – dropping in even deeper

Then Europe called me back.

There was more to learn, more to encounter, more to face. I knew that the journey never actually ends, but I sensed it had cycles, journeys within journeys. I knew it was not the end of this cycle, the end of this journey. The Voice said three quarters. That meant another year or so.

But why Europe again?

There were a few obvious reasons. Anastazie was one. I missed her. I missed fucking her. I missed merging my soul with hers. Meditative, deep-soul lovemaking. For hours. Altered states of consciousness, flying high during and for hours and days afterwards. The heightened sense of awareness that that brought. Afterwards, seeing colours so vividly, the definition of everything in such detail, smelling intensely, heightened states of vision, smell, touch, insight, intuition.

I had also been asked by one of the TS lead facilitators to assist at the TS trainings and initiations she was leading in Scotland and Ireland. She asked me to feel into whether I wanted to be involved as a facilitator. I felt honoured. There was a rule in TS that you could not approach them – they had to approach you if they felt you'd be good at it. My mind, my ego, attached to the thought: "Aah, maybe this was some plan for the future." I was aware of this, but I also knew that by putting myself in the situation I'd be able to feel the energy, to sense whether it was for me.

There were other even deeper reasons for the call to Europe. I didn't know what they were, but they were definitely there, hovering in the background. I could feel them strongly, intensely. I had to answer those mysterious calls, just as I had all along. I had learnt not to ignore them. In any event, I could not ignore them. I was in full surrender to life. I had given up control and was listening to the Voice of existence. It was clear and distinguishable now. The more I listened, the clearer it became. The mind would still occasionally butt in and resist, but I learnt the pain in that – I'd feel extreme physical discomfort in my body. A lot of that was lying ahead for me in Europe.

I arrived in Prague at the beginning of May 2017. Anastazie picked me up at the airport, and we fucked like crazy for two weeks. But something had changed. I was losing energy. I was leaking energy. Big time. Before, after spending time together, I would be flying, now I was dead tired. I intuitively knew why. I had come back into a situation where I was required to be unauthentic. Before, it had been different; we had been trying to move it, shift it into authenticity, and she had tried to get her husband to full acceptance of an open relationship. Now we both knew that that wasn't going to happen. He wasn't shifting and it became clear he wouldn't for a long time to come, probably never.

And then something else happened. One day we made love, and when I went down on her, I sensed a slight hesitation in her, an almost indiscernible "uncomfortableness". When my tongue made contact with her yoni, I knew why. I tasted it. I had never tasted another man's semen before, but I knew... The moment it was on my tongue, I knew it was his semen. They had a healthy, active sex life and made love almost every day. She had told me so.

Afterwards, when she left, I took a long walk down the river. Then it came – out of the blue. I did not expect it. I felt connected to her husband. I did not know him, I had never met him, but my heart opened and I felt connected to the man. This was much more than a mind thing; I could feel the sensation in my heart, my chest opening, a feeling of love towards him. Compassion, a closeness, a shared energy. I had his semen, his sperm, in my mouth. Via her pussy. His DNA was in my body, now part of my being. There was a deep connectedness to him. It wasn't repulsive; it was beautiful. I felt love permeating my being. I was aware of the massive shift within me over the last few years. The alpha male of a few years prior would not have been at this place. Not even close.

There was also another dimension: if I was connected to him, I could not hurt him. Now that I was conscious of him, hurting him was more difficult, impossible even. It hit me that this did not come from a place of guilt or shame, but from a place of love. I felt love for someone I had never met or spoken to. Deep down, I knew something had shifted. Shifted deep inside me, shifted in the dynamics of the situation, shifted between all of us. It would take time to manifest, but the shift was there. I knew.

When I left for the TS training in Scotland, Anastazie asked when I'd be back. She knew I had vague plans to be in Europe until the end of the year and there was some expectation that I'd be back in Czech after the Scotland training.

I was honest. "I don't know, my love. Let's see how it flows."

The last day of training in Scotland was 21 May 2017. My birthday. At the end of the closing ceremony, I was called to stand on the mound in the middle of a ceremonial clearing in the woods. The group of 37 international participants and facilitators stood in a circle around the mound. They sang happy birthday in five languages: English, Danish, Hebrew, Ukrainian and the Findhorn version, which was a conscious community just down the road from where the training was taking place. They asked me to sing it to myself in Afrikaans, which I did. So six languages.

It should have been special, but I felt terrible. My body was giving me clear signals. I had for most of the training felt the signals getting stronger and stronger as the week progressed, culminating on the last day at the ceremony. It should have been an ecstatic moment, but it wasn't. The message was clear. This, it said, was not for me. What was difficult was that it made no sense to me. I was passionate about the work and felt strongly that it had to be spread wider. It was also, after all the years of learning the work, a natural, logical progression for me to begin teaching it. So, from a logical point of view, the mind was right. But the Voice disagreed, my heart disagreed, my body disagreed. And it wasn't subtle. I felt dead sick, physically ill. The poisoned sensation in my body was intense and all consuming.

Later, I shared with the lead facilitator that I wasn't sure whether this was for me. I had, however, already committed to assist at another Level 1 and Level 2 initiation in Ireland a few months later, so we decided to use that as an opportunity to feel into it more and make a final decision.

After the training, I decided to stay on in the Findhorn community for a while. I had heard a lot about it and was intrigued. It is situated on the coast of northern Scotland, a conscious community with a rich history that had been birthed in the '60s.

I found myself a room in Findhorn Park, adjacent to the village. It was out of this world, with quaint little houses, beautiful gardens, thick woods, just a short walk over the dunes to the beach and sea. I went for a swim in the Scottish sea on my first day there and was pleasantly surprised. It was cold, but not nearly as freezing as the Atlantic Ocean at Clifton.

It was not an easy integration, though, and I cracked right open. The intention I had set at the start of the week-long training was to always authentically be myself as I found myself in each and every moment; and in the powerful sacred spot ritual, where I was the demo in front of the group towards the end of the week, I set the intention to access my full internal power.

This was all integrating now. It was not pretty. It was a deep journey within, like a sword that cut through all the bullshit, through the stories, through the ego, ruthlessly exposing everything. That was what I had asked for, and I was now dropping into a deep level of self-awareness, facing the full extent of the ego programme that was running. And it was both profound and shocking. It was so easy to confuse what was essence with what was just the operating programme. I realised that almost everything is the programme and it's not real. I was feeling very vulnerable, split open to the world and, worse, open to myself. I was sore from the inside, my insides were on the outside and I felt like crying. But deep down there was a flickering of something else. I wasn't quite sure what, but it was a liberation, a huge sigh, a sense of relief, a realisation that all of it – life, everything – actually doesn't matter, a release of pressure, a sense of a core, deep silence and emptiness, a journey home.

It was while I was going through all of this that I came across a Robert Holden course on the Enneagram and abundance that was taking place that coming weekend in Findhorn. Once again, the synchronicity was mind blowing. The Enneagram is, in essence, about becoming aware and learning about your specific ego programme, the one that's ruling you, and the workshop happened to be at the same time I was at Findhorn, struggling through the same on my own. This type of synchronicity was happening more and more in my life. By now I was almost expecting it around every corner. And so, as exhausted as I was, I enrolled for the three-day workshop. I knew it was no coincidence.

The Enneagram is a set of nine personality types or nine distinct strategies for relating to the self, others and the world. Each has a different pattern of thinking, feeling and acting that arises from a deeper inner motivation or worldview. Determining your personality type helps you see the box from which you experience the world. With this awareness, you can step outside of your limited perspective. Discovering these unconscious patterns can help you connect to your true essence. A quick test can tell which type you are. The nine types are: The Reformer, The Helper, The

Achiever, The Individualist, The Investigator, The Loyalist, The Enthusiast, The Challenger, The Peacemaker.

I did the test the night before and arrived at the Universal Hall in Findhorn Park armed with the result. I immediately liked Robert Holden. He was soft-spoken, humble, witty, clear and direct. He had a very English way of presenting, as opposed to the loud American approach. He was very down to earth and charming in a quiet, shy kind of way. And I immediately fell in love with the topic. It really was an eye-opener and I was excited to learn more.

I very quickly confirmed my finding of the evening before. Yes, as sure as hell, I was number three on the scale of nine: The Achiever. It all rang true, the good, the bad and the ugly.

Threes were described as being self-assured, attractive and charming. Ambitious, competent and energetic, they can also be status-conscious and highly driven for advancement. They are diplomatic and poised, but can also be overly concerned with their image and what others think of them. They typically have problems with workaholism and competitiveness.

I learnt that The Achiever's basic fear is of being worthless; a Three's basic desire is to feel valuable and worthwhile. Their key motivations are that they want to be affirmed, to distinguish themselves from others, to get attention, to be admired and to impress others. They are not known as 'feeling' people; rather, they are people of action and achievement. It is as if they 'put their feelings in a box' so that they can get ahead with what they want to achieve. Threes have come to believe that emotions get in the way of their performance, so they substitute thinking and practical action for feelings.

Good God, all of this was spot on! I liked the good more than the bad and the ugly, but I had to be honest, it was me to a T. I definitely fitted The Achiever label: academic colours at school, three degrees at university, single-figure handicap golfer, youngest director in a large international financial services group at age 33, CEO in my early 40s. And then it hit me ... I was doing it all over again. But this time in the spiritual arena. I was going from workshop to workshop all over the world, reading, studying, increasing my consciousness, my vibration, driving myself to exhaustion. The distance I had covered in growth and in expansion in four short years was astonishing. I was becoming a top achiever in the spiritual space! I took a step back and had to laugh at myself.

The next realisation was not that easy to stomach. I bit my lip and went there, delved into the area of basic fear and basic desire. I stepped inside and faced the dragon. It was painful. Deep down, there in the dark recesses of my being, I found it. A deep fear of being worthless. That was not glamorous at all. I felt shame, shame for being scared of being worthless. I had hidden that very deep, but it was there, part of my make-up. I looked hard and long, hauled it out of the dark recesses and brought it to the light. Somehow in the light it looked less scary, less shameful. It was not hidden anymore; it was now in the open.

And then I remembered what I had learnt on the TS path: that fear and desire are two sides of the same coin. It was often true in the sexuality space too, and it was definitely true here, for me, in this space. My basic desire was to feel valuable and worthwhile and my view of myself was based on a reflection of what others thought of me. That was humbling. I had always thought of myself as a rather cool, laid-back guy who didn't give a shit about what other people thought. I certainly projected that and I was very successful at doing that.

The "put their feelings in a box so that they can achieve" description was eerie and equally spot on. That was exactly what I had done from my teenage years into adulthood.

After recovering from the initial shock of all of this, I started to get excited about the awareness it was giving me. Robert Holden told us there are nine Hero's Journeys in the Enneagram, a different one for each type. Over the three days, we went through each journey for each type. They were very different, but also similar in some ways. The thing was, you could not relate at all to a type that wasn't yours. On the second day, he took us through the Hero's Journey for Type 3, The Achiever. He said we are born a Golden

Buddha, but then we experience a loss of that. In Type 3, the emphasis is on doing. When we feel attended to, we feel seen. But there are times that we don't receive attention, so we learn to stand out, to shine, so that we can feel good again, bask again in the gold light. We are concerned that there is not enough love to go around so, to get attention and love, we carve a position for ourselves. The message is clear: *Be the golden boy*. And so, what do we do? We work out what people value. What's the value that my family likes? What does society value? To feel worthwhile, we absorb all of that. We become the best we can; we compete in every way. We turn ourselves into commercial property to be sold and bought. This is the way we sell out. Our dysfunction is an addiction to work or competition. We work hard on trying to present a shining self to the world. When we lose connection with the gold within, we chase the gold without. Then we hit a place of disillusionment. We may feel fraudulent, terrified that we're about to be found out. In Type 3, we have to look at our relationship with doing. If it can come from the original doer, if we can be an expression of the universal doing, if a Type 3 can feel from the heart, it may seem as though a really bad thing is happening, that the world is crumbling around us, but that can also be a game-changer – it's when you really get into your full power, full potential and full expression. We come to realise that building empires is cool – but what's the real value? Type 3 is a heart type. When we move into our heart, we start touching the gold within. Sometimes we have to just sit there. The attachment is to the doing and the role. The great fear is: if I stop working, will it fall apart? The fear: what is my value? The passion: vainglory. We deceive ourselves that we are separate. The gold is in sitting still. The path of undoing, of allowing these layers to peel off. And that's a scary thing. We are here to shine, but not *our* light, *the* light. We have to find the way, not from a space of shame, but from an authentic soul base. We are trying to get back to the gold, to the authentic self. We are here to be golden, but it has to come from a golden soul rather than the shining ego.

This revelation hit me hard in my core, in my deepest being. I knew it to be true for me. But, more than anything, I felt excitement. I was on the Hero's Journey. A journey into my heart, of shedding layers, so that the bright light of my soul can shine through into the world. That light was starting to shine brighter and brighter. I could feel it.

I laughed when Holden said that a good picture for a Type 3 to remember is a Golden Buddha with the following caption: "Don't just do something, sit there."

After discussing each type, he would give an exercise to do. We all laughed when he said, "The exercise for Type 3 is: we are going to do nothing!"

A classical meditation for Type 3, he said, is to continuously bring your heart into your day and into your work.

I felt great peace when he said, "If we feel unworthy, it's right, the ego will feel unworthy. The ego is not worthy of our true nature. Accept that. Trust me, save yourself a lot of inner work! When that happens, it's a sign to say to your soul: help me remember my true soul's worth, help me remember the richness of my being. We don't have to work on the ego. Accept that!"

Robert Holden's workshop gave me so much insight into myself and what had been happening to me. It also gave me real insight into other people, including family members and friends. I immediately knew the numbers some of those closest to me were, and going through their specific Hero's Journey in detail allowed me to view them with compassion. This knowledge opened my heart wide to them.

CHAPTER 25

London calling

"No, sir, when a man is tired of London, he is tired of life."

I could not have agreed more with Samuel Johnson. London is my favourite city in the whole world. Just walking the streets is an enlightening experience. Invigorating, uplifting, full of zest.

"Sir, if you wish to have a just notion of the magnitude of this city, you must not be satisfied with seeing its great streets and squares, but must survey the innumerable little lanes and courts. It is not in the showy evolutions of buildings, but in the multiplicity of human habitations which are crowded together, that the wonderful immensity of London consists." Johnson again. In detail.

I could walk the city for days, weeks, do nothing but walk, just be. The same way that I could walk in the mountains in an ongoing meditation, so too could I walk in London in an ongoing meditation. London was special. I didn't know why, but it was.

After Scotland, I headed there, went to two book launches, caught up with friends, saw some old business associates, visited my old haunts, met new people, but mostly I just walked the streets.

But after only two weeks, I had to leave. I had made plans to see Anastazie. I took an Uber from a friend's place in West London to a friend in South London. I was going to stay at her place for a night before flying out from Gatwick to Prague the next morning.

At a stop street, I looked out of the car window, and there it was ...
a clear message not to fly to Prague. As we pulled away and made
our way down the road, houses flicking past, I saw the words:
"Don't go to Prague."
"Don't go to Czech."
"Don't go to Anastazie."
"Don't go to Prague."
"Don't go to Czech."
"Don't go to Anastazie."

It was surreal, each house had a line, a message. Now it was
not just rocks, but houses talking to me! I looked ahead, at the
back of the driver's seat. I dropped my chin; I knew in my bones
that I should not fly to Prague, to Anastazie. I felt it in every cell
of my body. I was fucked though. I had promised, after weeks of
delaying, that I'd be there the next morning. I could not drop her
like that.

When I arrived at my friend's place, I got out of the Uber
and reached for my big backpack and small rucksack. My heart
plummeted. My small bag, with my entire life in it, wasn't there.
We searched the whole car, the boot, under the seats, everywhere.
Nothing. I was fucked. Whatever I did not want to lose, could *not*
lose, I had kept in that bag: South African and British passports,
iPad, British driver's licence, medical insurance docs, a few books
and other important items. I could lose my big backpack anytime
– just clothes and toiletries in there – but not my small bag. That
was my lifeline. On a journey, as a traveller, there is one thing you
can never lose. Your passport. I managed to lose two.

Fuck. Fuck. Fuck. A million fucks.

I had kept my rucksack with me at all times. I'd check my big
backpack into the hold when flying, but always kept my small
bag with me. In four years of travelling, I had never lost a thing.
And I had been to some rough places in South America and India.
I eventually worked out what had happened ... I'd basically left
the small bag on the pavement when I climbed into the Uber. I had
put my backpack in the car, but had left the small one. What the

fuck? That was insane. It just did not make any sense. I had got into hundreds of taxis, buses, trains, planes, you name it, in the past four years and not once had I lost anything, never mind left it on the fucking pavement. I was distraught.

Then I was like, "Oh, what the fuck … it is what it is. Accept it."

A weird calm washed over me. My friend and I went out for dinner. I messaged Anastazie and I told her what had happened and that I would not be on the flight to Prague the next morning because I no longer had a passport. She took it well and was, as always, very supportive.

I knew, though, that there had been some divine intervention, that I'd been helped in some way. But "helped" is a double-edged sword, because I'd have a ton of bureaucratic shit to do to get new documents. But, deep down, not boarding that plane was vital for the continuation of my journey. I ended up staying in London for a few more weeks and connected with many new people, accumulating further knowledge and understanding there, and then finally flew to Portugal where some other great learnings were waiting.

Getting my new British passport was easy; I had it in three days. My new South African passport was like having all my teeth pulled out, slowly, one by one. Without anaesthetic. Before I had left home a few months earlier, I had got a brand-new passport and that had been relatively easy. I applied electronically and had it in two weeks. Now, doing the application in London, they insisted it could not be done electronically and would take three to four months.

But there was yet another complication in that the forms I had to fill in were now asking questions about dual citizenship. I completed that correctly. Then they asked for the letter proving that I had requested and received permission from South African Home Affairs to carry dual citizenship prior to applying and receiving British citizenship, when I was living in the UK in the '90s. It was just a technicality back then, but luckily I did request and receive permission. The law had subsequently changed and the penalty, if done incorrectly, was losing South African citizenship. I had followed the rules perfectly, so I could not imagine myself losing citizenship. I informed them that I was travelling and didn't have that letter with me and was sure I didn't have it at home either, but if they just looked on the system, it'd be there. That's when they told me that their system does not go that far back and that they had destroyed all their files predating 1999; essentially, there was no longer a paper trail. I was informed that if I could not find the original letter, I would lose my South African citizenship. I was gobsmacked.

I asked whether I could get an emergency passport so that I could go home and look for it. I also told them that my dad was very sick and that I may have to fly back home at short notice; that I couldn't wait for four months for a passport. But they insisted they needed the letter before they could issue a six-month emergency passport. And so continued the back and forth... I suggested I fly into South Africa on my British passport and then look for the letter there and apply for my new South African passport there. They then informed me that it was a criminal offence to use my British passport to enter South Africa if I was a South African. They would first have to revoke my citizenship and give me permanent residence in its place – and then only could I fly into South Africa on my British passport. I wanted to scream! I wasn't British, I was South African – that's what I identified with. I only applied for the British passport because it made working in the UK, the issue of a visa thing and travelling in Europe so much easier. I knew, too, that once I had given up my South African citizenship and then found the letter later, it would be an administrate nightmare – if not impossible – to try to get back citizenship.

So I took a deep breath. "In other words," I said to the South African embassy official at the counter, "if I want to get back into South Africa, I have to give up South African citizenship."

"Yes." He seemed to get some perverse pleasure from that.

This whole drawn-out process took two weeks; I was back and forth to the embassy, waiting in queues for hours. I was feeling very despondent, and wondered what the lesson in all of this could be. Then my youngest sister, with whom I had stored a few of my personal things, actually found the letter in some obscure place and sent it to me. My baby sister – what a special woman. They accepted it. And so I submitted the full application, hoping that nothing would happen to my dad in the four months that it would take to get the new passport. I decided that if something were to happen, fuck that, I'd just fly to South Africa on my British passport, crime or not.

Finally, with the passport nightmare sorted, I had a new journey ahead of me. Portugal. I boarded a plane a few days later.

CHAPTER 26

Portugal to Prague
to Ireland

"Your new name is Anugyan," she said. "It means Knowledge of
Bliss."

As she said it I felt an explosion in my chest. My heart expanded
and my eyes filled with tears. I could not have – would not have –
chosen it myself, but it was meant to be.

I was sitting in the middle of the room, looking deep into the
wise, ancient eyes of a grey-haired woman sitting in front of me,
foreheads touching. Behind her a band of musicians played. On
cushions in a tight circle around me were six others and, in a
bigger, wider circle beyond, were more than 200 people standing,
clapping and dancing to the music. Everyone was dressed in white
and, with the energy rising, so too did the tempo of the music.
Suddenly I was on my feet, dancing to the now crazy music,
swirling around, looking into the eyes of those around the dancing
circle, feeling the intense interplay of my energy with the energy of
everyone around me. It was bliss. It was intense. I was feeding off
their energy. They were feeding off mine. We were all being lifted
higher and higher and higher. The music swirled faster and, with

it, my legs kicked faster and faster, my arms flying, until I suddenly stopped dead still, lifted my head to the sky, grabbed my balls with my right hand and put my left hand on my heart. The onlookers went crazy, shouting, clapping, dancing even wilder.

I was taking the vow of sannyas, part of the celebration ceremony at the Osho Festival in Portugal. Sannyasa is often described as asceticism, marked by renunciation of material things and a state of detachment from material life, with the purpose of a peaceful, love-inspired, simple spiritual life. I had never been one for dogma and still wasn't, but I could strongly relate to the disinterest in the material life. I had lost interest in what was happening in the world out there, where it did not have a direct impact on me. I wasn't watching or reading news at all. It bored me to tears. I was more interested in peace within, loving and being loved, the simple things in life, the spiritual.

I liked how Osho defined sannyas as, more than anything else, courage, because it is a declaration of individuality, a declaration of freedom, a declaration that you will no longer be part of the mob madness, mob psychology. I could write an entire book on what sannyas means, but in essence for me, in simple terms, it is a commitment to live *your* truth whatever that may mean, irrespective of society, conditioning, religion, security or anything else for that matter. It is a commitment to the journey within.

There were five of us taking the vow. Even though I had lived for two months in 2015 at the OSHO Afroz Meditation Centre on Lesvos in Greece and had read most of what Osho had ever said or written, I had never taken the formal step of joining a sannyas celebration. On Lesvos I had privately committed to sannyas, but now I was celebrating it formally, witnessed by so many of this "living from the heart" tribe. To be given a sannyas name is very special. I loved the sound of mine: Knowledge of Bliss. Loved the power locked into it, the powerful pronunciation of *a-NU-ghi-yan*.

After the Osho Festival, I made my way down to the southwest coast of Portugal where I came across a surfing village by the name of Arrifana. I immediately fell in love with the place. The coastline there has very high cliffs that drop straight down into the Atlantic. The village was right at the top of the cliffs, with access to a long narrow beach far below. It was wild, it was beautiful, it spoke to my soul. There, I wrote and wrote and wrote. By now I had realised that I was writing a book. A book about my journey around the world, about the shift that had started in Cape Town, a book about my life. In the beginning it had just been writing with no specific goal; I don't really know why, but I felt a calling, felt inspired to publish and post articles, journey updates, called to plant seeds where I could. Doing that gave me such pleasure, a deep satisfaction. It lit up my soul. I could not help comparing that to how I felt at the training in Scotland where, when I was considering doing facilitation, I felt actual pain. Now my body was at peace with what I was doing. My spirit was full of light. I was light. I was aligned.

I would wake up around 7 am each morning, write until noon, then go down for a swim in the Atlantic, lie on the beach, swim a few more lengths in the refreshingly cold ocean, go back, write, cook, write until early evening, take a sunset walk on the cliffs, have some fresh seafood in a village restaurant and then go back home and write until after midnight. My days consisted of writing, swimming and eating, but mainly writing.

It was a blissful existence. A very productive time. It was also a time for deep introspection into Anastazie and me. I knew that we would have to change the relationship. We could not continue as we were. I also knew that it would be up to me. We had always said that we would be open and honest and immediately tell each other if we wanted to end it or change it. I knew, however, that it wasn't going to come from her. But now, unlike in London, I did not have the same apprehension. I thought Anastazie would be cool. She was different. I wanted us to discuss it in person, though, not via a video call or texting. She had been asking when I was coming to Prague, so after three weeks in Paradise, I caught a plane.

Prague was deep in my heart by now. Seeing the city, crossing the bridge over the Vltava River and feeling the history in the majestic old buildings filled my heart with joy one moment and made me nostalgic the next. Sad in a happy kind of way.

Seeing Anastazie had much the same effect on me. She looked as good as ever. Fresh, vibrant, strong, passionate, sexy. Her smooth, soft skin was tanned. It was summer in Czech.

God, I loved making love to that woman. She was so confident, so secure in herself. Sometimes a little arrogant, yes, talking over me in her excitement, and I let it go most of the time. Other times I'd be strict with her, telling her calmly but firmly to let me finish, refusing to allow her to interrupt me. She would be quiet, pout her lips and tilt her head like a naughty child who'd been told off and then listen petulantly until I had finished. Like all strong women I'd known, she enjoyed being put in her place now and then. How I loved strong women. Our lovemaking was as intense as always. Time would just disappear into nothingness. Hours of meditative lovemaking that would take me into nothingness, into the void, tasting existence, feeling God. When we stopped to catch our breath, I'd just lie there on my back, my eyes closed, no words, wide awake, super aware, touching divinity.

Lovemaking had become about getting to know God. Touching creation. I savoured this time with Anastazie because I knew I'd come to Prague to let her go. I only had three weeks in Czech because I had to be in Ireland for the TS training at the end of August. Halfway through my time there, I told her. She took it well. I think she knew. We decided that we would make the most of our time together until my departure. We agreed, too, that after my departure we would shift the relationship to a purely platonic friendship. We were brave about it, but we felt the pain deeply. After the talk, we lay in each other's arms for long afterwards.

From Prague, I headed to Sklenářka for a week. It was great to see Kateřina, and all the others in the community. It was home for me. I stayed in Wild Boar again, my little cabin in the woods. Anastazie came to visit me, we made love there, made love in the woods, walked the woods, swam naked in the lake and savoured our time together.

When I left the country, flying out of Prague, I took Anastazie with me, deep in my heart. She stayed in Czech, I went to Ireland, but she was in my heart forever. I did not know whether I would ever see her again, but I was at peace. I knew that it was the right thing. For me. For her. For the journey.

I'd never really experienced the colour green until I went to Ireland. It's crazy – a Crazy Green! Never in my life had I seen a green like that. It was all over, everywhere, overwhelming. Walking in nature was a continuous fascination for me. The colour had an intense quality to it. It was living, breathing. It was alive!

The initiations took place at a consciousness venue close to the Cliffs of Moher on the west coast of Ireland. As always, the TS training was a deep dive. This time I had more energy than I had had in Scotland. After leaving Anastazie and Czech, I felt a huge surge in energy. It was almost as if a blocked energy had been released, barriers lifted. It was still a tough time, though. Two back-to-back trainings meant that we were in the process for 14 days straight, from 7 am to 10 pm every day for a fortnight. You shared accommodation between five others, so you never had time for yourself. That really pushed my buttons. Assisting meant you had even less time for yourself because you were responsible for a pod of six people.

Referring to these events as "trainings" does not really do them justice. Neither can you call them "workshops"; "initiations" perhaps comes the closest. They were deep immersions into ancient teachings, rituals and ceremonies, a dive into the core of one's being, a deep journey with the soul. We were being initiated into a different way of being, a different way of living, a different way of being with the self. One could not be the same afterwards. There was no going back.

I enjoyed delivering some of the work and rituals to the group, but had the same feeling I had had in Scotland that this was not where I should be putting my energies right now. After the two weeks, I met with the lead facilitator and she felt the same, suggesting I first offer some of my own work and then, at a later stage, consider facilitating with them again. I was relieved – and she probably picked that up too. I was relieved for two reasons. Firstly, doing my own thing sounded right to me. TS was growing fast, getting bigger and bigger really quickly, and with that came more structure, more rules. Being on a solo journey and after many years in big organisations, I felt a strong aversion to getting involved in a group thing. So "doing my own thing" sounded like heaven on earth for me. I loved everyone in the group but preferred hanging with them as friends rather than colleagues. Secondly, it took a lot of pressure off me. I could now feel into what it was that I wanted, what my soul wanted. It was very clear. Writing about the journey was what I wanted to do. The message was clear. The Voice told me to write a book.

It turned out that there was another reason I had to be in Ireland. It had to do with Gary Zukav, my guide from The Lake. It was his book, *The Seat of the Soul*, that had taken me over the threshold into a new world. Now it would be another of his books that would guide me into another inner journey and into more ego deaths a few months later.

During the lunch break one afternoon I was sitting in the lounge area when a book on the coffee table caught my eye. I picked it up. It was *The Heart of the Soul* by Gary Zukav. I immediately felt a strange sensation running through my body, a strong message that I had to read this book. Turiya, the organiser of the two-week initiation, was next to me on the couch, so I told her the story of coming across his previous book in San Francisco. I started reading but only had time for a few pages before we had to be back in the Temple space for the next session.

Then I forgot about the book until a few days later when Turiya came over to where I was sitting outside over the lunch break with the book in her hand. "I spoke to the owners," she said, "and they said you're welcome to take the book, if you can maybe just leave another book in its place."

I was taken aback. I hadn't asked for it and didn't expect it. Once again, there was a strange synchronicity that she had taken it upon herself to arrange that. I gave her a big hug. I put the book with the others in my rucksack and promptly forgot about it for the next few months.

After the initiations, I decided to stay on in Ireland and see a little of the country. The Crazy Green was still calling me. Turiya invited me to stay on a vacant farm she was looking after, close to where she was living in West Cork, to do some of my writing there.

So it was that I rented a car and followed the coast south.

The road trip was spectacular. On the west coast of Ireland, as on most parts of the Irish coastline, there are many peninsulas that stick out like the fingers from an outstretched hand. You could follow a finger out on a road closely hugging the coast and then return on the other side of the finger to almost the same spot you started. That journey could take three hours or a few days, depending on how fast you want to do it.

I took my time. I did the Ring of Kerry – one of these fingers – over a week. At the tip of this specific finger, the furthest point into the Atlantic, is an island by the name of Valentia, where I stayed for a few days. I was whisked back in time. Thousands of years. The place felt ancient. My soul felt ancient walking around the little village where I stayed, climbing the mountain, peering down the steep cliffs at the wild Atlantic crashing down far below.

After another week of following the coastline south, I arrived in West Cork and decided to take Turiya up on her offer to stay on the farm. It was so much more than I expected. I was given a big loft room with huge windows with views that went on forever. The house was a little elevated on the side of a ridge and stretching out in front of me was that Crazy Green, flowing into the ocean. In the distance, over the blue waters of the Atlantic, you could see the landmass of another finger sticking out. Looking out over these ancient lands I was transported back in time. The Atlantic was invigorating and wild. I had always found it the wildest, most intense, most energetic, most engaging and most stirring of the oceans. Since childhood, I'd been fascinated by its wild mood. Encountering it now in another hemisphere and witnessing it crashing into the side of an island was mystical.

Apart from a few sheep, I was alone on the farm. A few metres from the house a stream cascaded down the hill, making small waterfalls on its way. I went to the farm to write, but I didn't do much of that, simply because I just could not stay indoors. The Crazy Green kept calling me, rain or shine. I had to see it close up, touch it, smell it, hear the wind whistle through the grass, the leaves, the trees. I would walk for hours in the rain, the wind, the chill, among the green grass, along silver streams, down to the blue Atlantic crashing along the rocky shores.

I went into another deep inner journey. It was impossible not to. There was nowhere to hide, nothing to do but face the demons inside, the mind clutter. I leaned into it, stayed with it. As the weeks went by, it got harder; I leaned into it more and then I realised that I was not just doing it for myself, I was doing it for many. I was playing my role of moving the collective. At some spirit level this is what I must have agreed to. I could feel it. It wasn't just my stuff. It was a lot of stuff for many others that I was helping to move.

The farm was nestled in the triangle of the villages of Durrus, Schull and Ballydehob and on a finger of its own. Following the finger a further 40 kilometres out to its tip sticking out into the wild Atlantic, I found large deserted beaches and steep cliffs dropping down into the ocean. Turiya and I walked in the rain and in the shallows of Barleycove Beach, a vast stretch of pure white sand split by a silver river rushing into the sea at high tide, flanked by those Crazy Green hills. We got wet, very wet. I didn't want to leave. The visual contrast of the pure white, that Crazy Green, the wild blue, together with the rain and the whistles of the wind and the smell of the salty Atlantic, had me floating and swirling like an angel in the sky. How different this was to my walk all those years ago on Clifton beach. That crushing walk. It felt like a lifetime. It was just four years. Four long, long years.

Turiya took me to the Durrus Saturday market where I met the Medicine Lady. When we were introduced and our eyes engaged, locked, an ancient flash exploded out from her eyes. I saw deep into her soul and she into mine. We exchanged numbers and, two days later, she visited. We made love energetically, only half naked, still in our jeans. When she left, she said, "I want to gift you something."

We had been talking about magic mushrooms that grow wild in the hills after the rains in Ireland, and I'd told her I'd never experienced a mushroom ceremony, but that it was calling me.

"I don't usually do this," she said, "but come to my farm tomorrow."

The next day, drinking tea at the table in her kitchen, she asked, "Do you want the heroic dose or a normal, more gentle dose?"

I laughed. "What's the heroic dose?"

"Five grams. It's very intense. Depends what you want to do, what you want to learn."

"I've had an intense last four years," I said. "I'll do the easy journey."

Then she asked whether I knew how to safeguard the space, how to energetically claim the space and protect myself. I told her about my learnings in India, about holding space and energetically claiming and protecting it, inviting and allowing only spirits, entities and guides I wanted. After all my intense training, I felt very confident about that. She explained how to brew the mushrooms as a tea and to pray and meditate while doing so and to set my intentions as part of the preparation process.

As she got up to fetch the mushrooms, I told her, "You know what … I'll do the heroic journey, if that's okay."

She smiled gently at me. "Sure, that's perfect – you'll be okay."

The following afternoon I started preparing for my journey, all on my own. It would be only me, no one else. No shaman to hold space. I was to hold space for myself and undergo the journey alone. I felt comfortable, confident and at peace. I energetically claimed the space of my room, the house and the whole farm. I set the intention to connect deeply with Mother Earth and specifically with the land of Ireland and the spirits of the land. I meditated on that and prayed that into the tea as I was brewing it.

I let the brew cool and then drank two thirds of it consciously, very aware of the spirit of the mushroom plant that was to be my guide. It was 5 pm and the sun shone above. I went outside and stood next to the old stone house overlooking the Crazy Green towards the Atlantic. I closed my eyes – and that's when they came. Playful, colourful spirits danced around me, touching my face curiously, engaging with me. I just stood and smiled, eyes shut, revelling in the moment.

I took a walk in the Crazy Green of the farm, touching trees, their branches, their leaves, feeling the energy in it all. I was so aware of the intensity and beauty of life around me. I stood next to a tree, communing with it for what seemed like ages, then I suddenly became aware of the grass beneath my feet. I immediately shifted to another spot. The blades of grass where my feet had been were flattened under my weight. I bent down anxiously to see whether they were okay, whether they'd survived. They were flat and wet, but still alive. A sense of relief rushing over me. I had not killed the grass. I felt such reverence for life. For all of life. For a single blade of grass. Every single blade of grass was an extension of me, part of me, part of God. I made sure I didn't stand in one spot for too long, so as not to kill or suffocate the grass. That would have broken my heart.

I watched the sun set over the Atlantic, and even when it started to rain I lingered in the Crazy Green. I could not leave. It was getting dark, the rain stayed, I walked further, explored the undergrowth on my knees and hands, sat next to a little waterfall.

My journey home back to the farmhouse was a long one. I was continuously called by trees or plants or flowers to commune with them, touch them, smell them in the silent moonlight and rain. I would try to move on, only to be called by another. How could I refuse? The call was strong, as though my heart was being pulled out of my chest towards the invitation. The hundred metres or so back to the house took me a few hours.

Back home, I was drenched to the bone, my walking boots filled with water. It was 10 pm, and I'd been in the Crazy Green for five hours. I stripped, pulled on dry clothes, lit the fire and drank the rest of my tea, sitting at the fireplace, meditating.

It was a profound and deep connecting with the land of Ireland. It would forever linger in my psyche, in my being.

When I left for another island two days later, I almost did not board the plane. I stood at the door, the pull of the land pleading with me to stay. I had to force myself to step aboard.

CHAPTER 27

On to Ibiza and London

My next stop was yet another island, this one 1 500 kilometres to the south of Ireland, in the warm waters of the Mediterranean. Ibiza. I was there to attend a birthday party, but by the time I touched down I was already missing Ireland. I think, after four years on the road, my body now wanted to stay in one place and not move around much. I landed on Saturday afternoon and that evening I was at the party. It was held at my friend's holiday house – all glitz, glamour, money. I was dressed for the occasion; I still had those types of clothes in my backpack: good shoes, clean jeans and a fancy, long-sleeved, collared white shirt. It was October and evening temperatures were starting to get slightly chilly. I looked as if I fitted in, but I didn't – not anymore. I was bored stiff.

This was your typical northern European rich hangout at an equally typical Ibiza party. Beautiful people, in-shape gym bodies, expensive designer clothes, taking selfie upon selfie, chugging down cocktails, taking drugs, a mosaic of chatter, of superficial conversations. It reminded me so much of Cape Town's high-society parties that it felt as though I was back home. So depressing. The only way I was going to handle this, I thought to myself, was to seek out drugs, but I had absolutely no desire to. I sat next to the pool, thinking about the Crazy Green and wondering why the hell I had left.

Although my first week in Ibiza was extremely hard, I decided to stay because I still hadn't been informed by the South African embassy that my passport was ready for collection. It had been almost three months since applying. The plan was to fly to London whenever the passport was ready and then, from there, back to South Africa before year-end.

I felt the island itself intensely. I was now so connected to Mother Earth and to nature that I felt all energy, and this was a kick-ass island. The energy was intense. No wonder people would gravitate there to party and get fucked out of their heads. I was aware, though, that it had a mystical, mysterious, very deep spiritual side to it too. Interesting how those energies often go together. What had happened to me in Ireland was happening here too. I was connecting with the land and, at the same time, deep within myself. It was really hard; the energy was so different to that of Ireland. Entirely different, but just as tough and beautiful in its own way.

The Ibiza party scene was wrapping up, with a lot of end-of-season parties. I did not go to any of them; instead, after a week, I went up to the mountains in the north and made my way along the coast. I had heard that there were a lot of consciousness events happening there. It was while I was looking for a place to stay that I got completely lost driving the narrow winding roads in my rental car and eventually stumbled on Cala Boix in the northeast corner of the island: an unspoilt, long narrow beach locked in by high cliffs that reminded me a lot of Arrifana in Portugal. The rough open seas meant that you could hear the thunder of the waves crashing down below. There were only two restaurants on top of the cliff, no shops or other buildings. One of the restaurants had a few rooms above it, so I rented one and started settling into Ibiza life. I was mainly writing and would, again, venture out once a day to swim lengths up and down the long beach. It was great getting some exercise again. Turns out that October is a great month to be in Ibiza. Quiet and still warm.

One day I took a break from the writing and ventured over to the western side of the island to a Cacao Conscious Dance in the Magic Cave. You had to descend a flight of really steep steps to reach the cave, which was just above sea level. We danced for hours, high on chocolate, watching through the opening of the cave as the sun set over the rocky islands in the distance. I could not help thinking how different my visit to Ibiza would have been if I had come five years earlier. Instead of suffering a terrible hangover after the dance, I was now flying with the high vibration. I could feel the energy buzzing through my body. There was no come-down, just an appreciation for life and the natural beauty of this magical, mystical island.

Coincidentally, the Ibiza Tantra Festival was taking place at the end of October, and just a few kilometres up the road from me on the north coast. Quite a few of my friends were either attending or teaching there – including my German friend, Brother Didi – so I popped over to attend some of the events, workshops and dances.

Finally, after a month on the island, I had to leave. I didn't really want to, but it was getting colder and I had to get back to London to find out what had happened to my passport application. I still hadn't received an email but was hoping that the passport would be ready by now.

After two months of communing with nature, being back in a city was strange. I stayed in Bloomsbury, just off the West End, close to where I had lived in the '90s when working there. On my second day, I walked down to the South African Embassy at South Africa House in Trafalgar Square. My Green Mamba was ready!

I was now able to get back into South Africa again, but first I wanted to attend the Hay House Writer's Workshop in Bristol that coming weekend. I'm glad I went. As a published Hay House author, Robert Holden was presenting, and he remembered me from the Enneagram workshop in Findhorn in Scotland. During one of the breaks, he said, "Don't try to write a best-selling book

... don't even try to write a good book – just write an authentic book."

I immediately felt the truth in that.

I wanted to stay longer in London, but I had pledged to Brother Easy and the TS guys that I'd produce and organise a Level 1 in South Africa mid-December. The last one in South Africa had been six years previously. I felt the work was desperately needed back there and so agreed to make it happen. I had, in the background, been doing a lot of the work and marketing the course while travelling and initially wanted to be back in South Africa a month or two prior to it kicking off. However, with the passport delay and flying time, the start of the Level 1 was now just three weeks away. So I booked a flight back to the Motherland.

CHAPTER 28

The journey home

I'm on a plane, about to crash into a mountain.

We are flying dangerously low in a valley, the pilot desperately trying to lift the plane to steer it over the mountains. I can see the mountain approaching fast. I must keep my eyes open, not lose consciousness so I can meet death consciously.

A thought flashes through my mind: "Am I dreaming?"

A rational answer: "No, you are not. Remember waking up and going to the loo and getting water from the air hostess earlier?"

Another thought: "And, in any case, you can't take a chance – if this is real death, don't waste the chance of dying consciously."

"It's not a dream! Look at the mountain with open eyes, stay conscious, die with your eyes open, memory intact!"

Mountain rapidly getting closer, heart beating faster... Yes, there is some fear but I'm not terrified. Not really. More a fear of the unknown. More a sense of uncertainty, trepidation, but also anticipation, excitement.

Hitting the mountain, eyes still wide open, no pain, no explosion, just a floating sensation, voices in the background.

"Surely I can't be in a hospital. When you crash into a mountain there is usually not much of your body left!"

With a sensation of relief and achievement, I realise I've succeeded in staying conscious while dying.

"Am I dead?"

Still floating, the scene of the mountain and surroundings still in view.

Suddenly the sensation of waking up, opening my eyes, lying stretched out on the three empty seats of the Egyptian Airlines Boeing on a flight to Cape Town.

Back in South Africa, I knew that I had to make immediate and urgent work of the Level 1 TS training. I only had 12 attendees confirmed, so I threw all my energy into it. I conducted a number of talks, met and had telephone conversations with people who were interested. I enjoyed standing up in front of people, sharing my learnings, and was amazed by how much I could shift in three short weeks. By the time the training had kicked off, we had a group of 31 and it was a massive success.

Even though this was the eighth TS training I'd done, I still learnt a lot. I had decided not to assist but simply to enjoy it as a participant. It was also the first of all the trainings where I had penetrative sex with anyone. Towards the end of the training, I was approached by a beautiful young woman, Isla, one of the international participants, asking whether I wanted to spend time alone together one evening. It felt right, and I agreed. We had a beautiful time together and ended up making love. It flowed naturally, an honest and open heart connection. It felt as if I had come full circle, connecting sexually again, no celibacy, but now from a fully integrated place.

After the training, a group of about 10 of us went to chill in a big house close to a wild beach on the Atlantic coast. The group included Brother Easy, Brother Didi, three co-facilitators and a few of the participants. The three facilitators were women because I wanted a strong female energy in the training – important not only for the training but also to specifically attract women. With its history of abuse by the immature masculine, there was such a huge collective wounding around the feminine in South Africa, and my gut told me that women would be put off by a strong masculine energy in the facilitating group for a sexuality workshop. I was right. Two thirds of the participants were women.

When the group finally dispersed, I went to visit my parents in George on the Cape south coast. My dad had been taken into the frail-care unit just across the road from the house they were living in at the retirement village.

I was shocked when I saw him. He could no longer walk and his speech had slowed quite dramatically. At the end of my previous visit to South Africa, nine months earlier, he had already started to get weaker. He fell a few times on that visit, but was still as tough as nails. He would fall on a pot plant and smash it to pieces but, apart from a few bruises, would be okay. I'd pick him up and carry him to the room – not an easy task because he was a big guy, shorter than me but stocky and very well built. At 76 he still had big biceps. After one of those falls, I sat in silence in the lounge with my mom, and then it happened. I broke down. It was a shocking experience for me, as a son, to have to pick up and carry my own dad around; he'd always been this strong, tough guy. My heart broke for him. What made it worse was that he had had no opportunity to prepare for it. No ego deaths prior. He went from a hundred to zero very fast, no warning. The crying was a release. I felt better afterwards. But it was also the start of the grieving process of saying goodbye.

I was glad that I had decided to get my kids out to George to spend time with me there earlier in the year, so they could also see my parents, especially as I wasn't sure how much longer we would still have with my dad. He still had his great sense of humour and joked around with the kids in his usual way. They always loved it when he did. I stayed in the house with my mom for a month. We would visit him daily and I'd make sure that I took her for drives down the coast, just to get her out of the house. It was really tough on her. She had no life; everything revolved around visits to my dad. I had always enjoyed a very deep soul connection with my mom and I think having me there helped her with what she was going through. She was understandably very depressed but was very interested in the learnings of my journey and asked a lot of questions. Between our long conversations I gave her heaps to read. I tried hard not to go into fixing mode, but just to be there for her and to give her love.

It was also good spending time with my middle sister. I was so grateful to her, for her compassion, for her being there for my parents. I knew it must have been hard on her and her family. She had pressure on two fronts, as a daughter and also as a doctor, because they relied heavily on her for medical advice.

From George, I went back to my magical place in the Tankwa Karoo. This time I followed Rix to his farm in my own rental car because I wanted to be more mobile. When we arrived on the Thursday afternoon, we had our usual Karoo lamb braai with a few cold beers and, as was his style, he asked a million and one questions about the last year of my journey. Rix was a very inquisitive kind of guy. He did not understand most of what the hell I was doing, but he had great admiration for it and was very curious. It was great seeing him again. There is something about knowing someone for 35 years. He, as usual, left the next morning to return to Stellenbosch and I was once again alone on the farm. The plan was that he would only return in two weeks.

My idea was to use the time to finish writing my book. But Gary Zukav had other ideas. When I took my iPad from my rucksack, out fell *The Heart of the Soul*. By now I had an iPad with a little attachable keyboard I'd bought in Covent Garden in London. Using my right thumb to write a book on my iPhone had become impossible, the pain unbearable.

Writing put aside, I opened *The Heart of the Soul* and started reading. And so I embarked on a two-week inner journey. Another one! My God, how many would I have to do? It seemed that once the layers started peeling away, they just kept doing so.

The book is about creating authentic power through emotional awareness. Zukav says that everyone in the Earth school takes the same course, authentic power, but the classes differ from student to student. As you become aware of your emotions, you also become aware of your curriculum in the Earth school. In other words, the emotions in your emotional landscape are your particular course of study.

It starts with being aware of how energy leaves the body from the seven chakras or energy centres – the crown, third eye, throat, chest, stomach, sexual and root – and whether you release it with fear and doubt or love and trust.

It's simple actually. I could clearly feel the difference. The love and trust release is a pleasant sensation in that part of the body. The fear and doubt release is unpleasant and uncomfortable, painful even. I could feel how the unpleasant one was poisoning that part of the body, the organs, bones, arteries and muscles in that vicinity. No sickness or disease just arrives on its own.

I was very aware that I had a choice. To operate from fear and doubt or from love and trust. I had to stalk myself in order to be clear about every decision I made. Was it based on fear and doubt or love and trust?

I was having challenging times out there in the semi-desert. I was reminded by Gary Zukav that below emotions such as anger, sadness, jealousy, frustration, greed, vengefulness and depression lies pain. Below pain lies the fear. You can only access the fear by moving through the pain, by feeling the pain. The pain is excruciating, but you have to go through that in order to get to the fear. You have to get to the fear in order to bring it to the surface, be aware of it, to know it, understand it and thereby heal it.

All of this was terribly hard. But it turned out that that's what I'd come to do here in the Karoo. I thought I was here to enjoy the view, do some pleasant writing, but the Tankwa had other ideas. It got so painful at times that I wanted to jump in my little Corsa rental and hit the dirt road out of there. But I didn't. I stayed. I had come too far. I was working my way through to the fear.

I smiled when I read how courageous it was to choose not to act on an angry impulse but rather to feel the pain that lies beneath it, that that requires more courage than risking your life driving race cars or jumping out of aeroplanes. Zukav writes that most of us do all the things we think of as brave in order to avoid facing the pain we feel. I wholeheartedly agreed. I would, a hundred times over, rather have raced cars or jumped out of a plane than do what I was doing.

In the background a Leonard Cohen song played on my portable speaker, edging me on, telling me how there's a crack in everything and that's how the light gets in.

The stalking I was doing here in the Karoo, the succulent Tankwa, turned into ruthless hunting. Far down into the deep dark. Through the pain into the fear. I conjured up some scary shit. Roots and all. Into the light. Into the harsh bright sunlight of the 40-degree-plus heat.

Zukav was a great guide to do that with. He discussed in depth the different ways we avoid the experience of our emotions. I studied them all in detail with him, all 13: anger, workaholism, pass-through effect, perfectionism, pleasing, vacating, boredom, idol worship, impenetrable optimism, entitlement, alcohol and drugs, eating and sex.

The one that hit me hard in the solar plexus was "pleasing". Surely, no, not me! Not a confident guy like me! But I suppose that's why they call it a shadow. You don't see the motherfucker. It *was* me, though. Spot on. I brought the motherfucker from the dark and into the light. I studied it, scrutinised it and, with that, it began to shrivel in the light.

The Zukav wisdom explained that both anger and the need to please cover extreme pain. The anger, he said, is rebellion against circumstances, the pursuit of external power, which is the ability to manipulate and control. His view was that the purpose of anger is to alter the behaviour of others and to make the one who rages feel better. Interestingly, the need to please is the other side of the same coin because it's an attempt to change others in order to make the one who pleases feel better.

That was a heavy shadow! Pleasing was so effective in avoiding my own emotions because it narrowed my focus on the emotions other people were experiencing, rather than my own, constantly trying to fathom how others felt so that I'd know how to be with them. If someone is unhappy, the pleaser tries to determine how to make that person happy so that he himself will feel safer. It's a technique that isolates you from your own fear of losing love, of your own unworthiness and the terror that comes with that. It's also a way to run from your own greatness and fullness.

This shadow was not news to me – I had come across it in the work I had done in Ireland the year before, but the isolation of the desert definitely got me to drop even deeper into it in order to bring more of it into the light. I realised that this pleasing meant that I was not only being inauthentic with myself but also with others, because it is really just a method of manipulation. It was hard to face, but I looked the monster straight in the eye.

Another way to avoid emotions is idol worship, and I related to that. The idol you worship is an image inside yourself, of what you think you are, what you think you should be. It could be an ideal father, ideal mother, ideal teacher, ideal business person. The idol is the role the worshipper thinks he must play. Fulfilling that role gives him satisfaction and self-worth. The function of idol worship is to avoid living life directly and fully. The idol worshipper does not have the courage to open himself to love, so he mistakes admiration for love. This motherfucker was the one I had done the most work on over the five-year journey. I identified completely with the good businessperson, The Achiever. The CEO title, running a business, making money, being admired for all of that, was important to me. However, on my journey I had died so many ego deaths and had brought so much of this into the light that it had lost its power. By dropping that, I had reached a new depth and richness within me. That depth wasn't in a role. It was in me.

The next motherfucker was a surprise. Entitlement. The perception that you are fundamentally superior. Zukav explains that it is the belief that you have a right to what you desire, regardless of what others desire, that you are not subject to rules that limit others. You see yourself above others, their activities unworthy of you and even boring.

It's a harsh description but pretty spot on about how I had felt and even sometimes still feel. It had softened over the years of my journey, but it was exactly how I had felt before embarking on that journey. Good God, that was honest!

As I learnt more, I had to laugh at the irony of this one. Beneath entitlement is a different reality. A person who feels entitled is not aware of it and cannot become aware of it while he sees himself as entitled. No wonder I did not know!

But it got even better.

Entitlement is a mask someone wears so that others will not know him. It keeps him from knowing himself too. He is unaware that he is wearing a mask or what the mask hides. The mask conceals his fears from himself. The mask is a way of avoiding a deep dynamic: the experience of unworthiness. The fear is of ridicule and rejection. His entitlement is a defence, but he does not know he is being defensive. Rather than experience these fears, he feels entitled.

Entitlement is denial. It is not realising something important about yourself. If you deny yourself a fear, you cannot free yourself from it until you experience it. I laughed when I read that entitlement is an illusion in which disagreement is of no importance because no value is attached to the importance of others; it is a self-imposed sentence of solitary confinement to a cell in which you suffer alone because no one else has the right to enter. I did not laugh, though, when I read that your fear is that they see you as you see them – unworthy.

The beauty of bringing this shadow to the light was that it all but dissolved when the light hit it. I sat with it for days, there in the solitude of the Tankwa Karoo, and worked through the pain and into the fear. Because it was intrinsically a denial, the moment I became aware of it there was denial no longer. It was an "A-ha!" moment for me and it immediately started to lose its power.

I also had another deep realisation of the powerful role this had played in my life. Because I had often felt superior, I would feel guilty about it and, to make others feel better, would sometimes dim my light when with "lessor mortals". That, in turn, would mean that in those situations I would not be in my full power and potential. Once again I had to laugh out loud. That was so fucked up! The Universe has a good sense of humour. Realising now that I was not at all superior meant that all that nonsense dropped away.

The last of the motherfuckers – alcohol and drugs, and sex – were my favourites from my crazy Cape Town days. No surprise that they are signs that you are fleeing painful emotions. I had certainly used them to distract myself from pain and to drown out the Voice in those years prior to starting my journey.

Zukav is very clear on alcohol and drugs, not just in addiction but even mild or occasional use: they are used to mask discomfort too difficult to confront. He says that substances are an apparent remedy for stress, social unease, feelings of inadequacy and fears of being judged, rejected or humiliated. In other words, an effective way of avoiding your emotions.

I recognised this as the one with which most of Western civilisation struggles. It is so acceptable to have one or two drinks in social situations or before stepping onto the dance floor or when you get home after work in order to relax.

Zukav's view on using sex to avoid emotions is that every powerful jolt of excitement you show a person with whom you do not wish to deepen your emotional connection, or whose history and aspirations do not interest you, or about whom you do not care deeply, is an addictive sexual attraction – and that, in essence, is flight from the experience of painful emotions. He suggests that even marital partners, when they engage one another in addictive sexual interactions, are fleeing the experience of painful emotions.

His view is that this type of sexual attraction is a defence against being powerless. It is a manifestation of the terror of feeling unloved and unlovable, the fear of being discovered, at your core, to be inadequate and ugly, the fear of being rejected and alone. It is a flag that signals a craving for meaning, purpose and value.

I realised that was probably why my soul had led me to that period of celibacy early in my journey. It had given me the opportunity to connect deeply with my feelings, without distractions, allowed me to face many of my fears and heal them, to integrate my masculine and feminine energies within me first and to deeply drop into authenticity. When I started engaging sexually again, I came from an entirely different place. I could not imagine myself now engaging with a woman sexually without also wanting to deepen my emotional connection with her.

At this point in my life I was not engaging much sexually, and very seldom with penetration. For me, in many ways, the circle of potential women had shrunk dramatically. I could not be with someone who wasn't aware and conscious – to some extent, at least. I was no longer looking for anything outside of myself, for someone to complete me; I was complete as I was. Interacting with a woman still looking for someone to complete her would have just been too much. I was aware that that would limit my options because many of us – men and women – are still looking for The One, the one who will complete us.

In other ways, however, the circle of women had widened for me because attraction had become less about the visual and more about energy. Whereas before my type was often the most beautiful girl with the best body, that had now become far less important. I would feel the energy of the person and go with that. Age wasn't important either; she could be 24 or 44 or 64, whatever. Interestingly, there are many young women in the conscious circles in South Africa – as it is internationally – who are acutely aware and connected. Clearly, the younger generations are born with a heightened state of consciousness already in place. I was attracted to them and connected easily with them. There are also many older women in those circles who are fast awakening. And I was attracted to them too, and connected with them. I still had a very high sex drive – that had not changed – but I was now combining that with deep soul connections.

It took me, on my own, more than two weeks to work through

the process outlined in Gary Zukav's *The Heart of the Soul*. It was a gruelling time. No doubt there was still some more where that came from, but that was okay too. Ruthless Shadow Hunting is a lifelong occupation.

I felt gratitude for those "negative" painful emotions, those whispers from the soul, that begged:

"Experience me."

"Observe me."

"I have a message for you."

By now, I knew that if I were aware of everything I was feeling all the time, I'd be in continual communication with my soul. The scariest thing for me still was, "You don't know what you don't know", so I tried to listen as best I could.

Gary Zukav was also very clear on the fact that many people would not be able to feel even the physical pain in their bodies and in their different energy centres because they had become so used to the pain. That did not mean that the pain did not exist, but rather that they had to continuously *try* to feel the pain of certain emotions until they could start feeling it again. I could relate to that because my emotional body had also been frozen once. Now it was different. I could feel clearly, in different parts of my body, the sensations that accompanied certain emotions. When I had judgemental thoughts or spoke judgemental words, for example, I'd feel the terrible energy leak from my stomach area. I was grateful for that awareness.

By the end of the book, the message is very clear: looking inward rather than outward, finding the source of pain and changing it into a source of gratitude, is the pursuit of authentic power. And authentic power, says Zukav, is the alignment of the personality with the soul.

That reminded me of my time in the wooden house at the edge of The Lake, four years earlier, when I first read and studied Zukav's *The Seat of the Soul*. In a way, I had come full circle. I realised again that this journey of life is not a linear one, but more of a spiral. We reach the same place but are now more expanded, with the ability to drop in even deeper. We are the same, yet entirely different.

I sat back, breathed in the searing Karoo air. I stayed another week on the farm, then set out northwest to the Great Karoo, a further expanse of wide-open spaces and towering mountains, wandering the terrain for another fortnight.

I left the Karoo via the Tradouw Pass and surfaced on the other side of the mountains at SpiritFest Africa, just outside Swellendam. I had quite a beard by then because I hadn't shaved the entire time I had secluded myself in the Karoo. Not sure why, but it felt right. I had never not shaved for that long. I looked like a wild man. I *was* a wild man. Straight out of the desert. I also had long hair. I hadn't had a haircut for three and a half years, since Medellin in Colombia, when I had tried to no avail to look Colombian. I had no grey in my hair at all, but my beard was almost completely grey.

SpiritFest was fun but also frustrating. Lots of yoga, meditation and dancing, but also so much blocked sexual energy. I encountered almost no intimacy there. It was almost as if yoga sometimes made it worse. As if the body thing, the material thing, kicks in, boosting the ego, blocking vulnerability and intimacy. I sensed a longing for intimacy from most, a longing to be caring, sensitive and loving towards each other. I sensed, too, a fear of doing that, rather blocking it to be safe. Each a little island on its own. Unusually, the handful of men there seemed much more connected to their feelings and more open to intimacy, but not finding much of it here. All this blocked sexual energy broke my heart. I felt intensely all the pain it was causing.

From SpiritFest, I returned to Cape Town and spent a week in Sea Point. Next thing, I found myself travelling into the heart of the country, the conservative farmlands, to give a weekend sexuality workshop. While I'd been on the farm in the Tankwa Karoo, a cousin had messaged to ask whether I could conduct a sexuality workshop for her and her husband and another couple who farmed in the area. I felt into it for a few days and decided to go. I wasn't getting paid for it and there were flights and other travelling costs, but it felt right. I was answering a call. I knew I had to do it.

It was a deep, courageous dive for all. On the Sunday we covered areas we only get to on day five at the TS trainings. I shared my learnings and experiences around sex and magic, explaining how sexual energy can be used for manifestation. We also did it practically, with everyone setting an intention and then sharing what they would like to manifest. I was so at ease facilitating that workshop, and by the time I left I was inspired to explore and experiment more with Awaken your Sexuality workshops for couples. With couples, I knew one could go deep so much faster.

I was also feeling a calling to share and integrate my gifts when it came to manifestation with the same theme of awakening sexuality. Combining orgasmic life-force energy with conscious manifestation was not just incredibly powerful but also fun. There was a deep resonance with my soul there, so I decided to follow that.

As I left my cousin's house that Monday morning, heading for Joburg in my rental car, I played a clip of a Neale Donald Walsch webinar for which I'd registered. The first thing Walsch, the author of *Conversations With God*, spoke about was "do unto others as you would have them do unto you". He explained, very entertainingly, that we have completely misunderstood the Master who lived two thousand years ago, who said the same thing. The lesson has since been simplified to mean "treat others as you would like them to treat you" but, says Walsch, we have missed the point. The Master gave us the key to the Universe. What it really means is that whatever we want, we must give to others first. He used an example: If you want confidence, then go out every day and find three people you can help by boosting their confidence. By doing that, the energy flows through you to the person you are giving it to – it has to flow through *you* to get to them. The more you give, the more it flows and the greater and more powerful the energy flow becomes. Then, one day, you realise that you have grown in confidence. This works for everything.

I was astonished. For me, it was a clear message. The synchronicity... After making my way halfway across the country at my own cost, I was now leaving a place where I had given to others simply because they asked and it had felt right. Confirmation that I was on the right track, that I would continue helping people when they asked and not worry about revenue streams; just give of myself and it would flow where it flows.

It was great to be in eGoli, the City of Gold, again. I had always loved the energy of Johannesburg. Now I knew why. It was sacred land. Especially the Cradle of Humankind, west of Johannesburg, towards Magaliesberg, where the oldest human remains were unearthed. I grew up close to this area but had never been aware of its power. But now that I'd opened myself up to the energetic world, I could feel it clearly. It was really strong. On my last few visits to South Africa and Johannesburg, I'd flown into the much smaller Lanseria airport, close to the Cradle area. I would stay in a country lodge a few kilometres away where many of my friends would visit me rather than meet in the city.

So much more in my life made sense now. When I lived and worked in Cape Town, I would make sure that I went up to Johannesburg at least once a month to go and "get energy there". I would return to Cape Town refreshed and energised. No one in Cape Town knew what I was talking about. I did not either, but I knew it worked. Now I knew why. After a week, I moved into a cottage on Philip's property in Linden, west of Joburg. It was good to see my varsity buddy again. He has a wonderful sense of humour and infectious laugh, and it was fun catching up on our time in Vegas together.

In Joburg, people were working hard, consuming themselves to death. Walking into a shopping centre was surreal. All the glitzy shops, the meaningless stuff people buy. For what? Paid for with money for which they had to work long hours, the time remaining spent on rushed eating and restless sleep.

I could clearly imagine another way: a non-slave reality would be to work three hours or so a day; make love for an hour or two a day; go for walks in nature; really connect with other people, beings and animals heart to heart; soul to soul mindfully savour one's food, consciously consume only what one really needs and end a day in restful sleep. The crazy thing was that we all have choice; we could actually do that, we could denounce all the conditioning. We could collectively do that. We have free will, despite all the manipulation. We have free will.

Staying at Philip's cottage, I came across a video clip of Michael Neill on the inside-out approach to guiding and coaching. Despite my cynicism when it came to coaches, – I always held the view that "those that can, do, and those that can't, teach" – it caught my interest to such an extent that I signed up to his free webinar. I was fascinated. He was using business language, but in essence it was very much in line with most of the shamanic learnings I had done all over the world. He spoke about the innate intelligence of the mind and how our thoughts and beliefs create our reality. That the world was not coming at us from the outside in, but that we are constantly creating our world and reality from the inside out. He said that when he connects to the innate intelligence within himself, while at the same time connecting heart to heart and soul to soul with another individual, that also takes the other person to the innate intelligence within himself. I ended up doing one of Neill's online courses about this type of coaching. I loved the simplicity of it; it was very much in line with my learnings. I could not see myself using a series of clever techniques and dogma – I have a strong aversion to that – and wasn't even sure I would want to do any formal guiding or coaching, but the Voice said to explore it, so I did.

Interestingly, curious about what I'd been up to, many of my old Joburg friends and business colleagues were contacting me to get together. I soon realised that it was more than to just a catch-up. Many were going through a shift similar to what I had experienced five years earlier. There was a lot of confusion within them and many wanted advice or simply someone to speak to.

Having these conversations made me think a lot about where I was. I was not at all interested in helping companies or businesspeople make more money. I was, however, starting to feel that by directly raising the consciousness and vibration of top business executives and shareholders, one could rapidly increase the collective consciousness of the planet because, let's face it, these guys really control everything.

I'm talking about a love consciousness. Love, empathy, compassion, heart. I was very clear that there was no right or wrong. The consciousness of fear, judgment, mind control was also an expression of consciousness. I was not judging it. But I had free choice. We all have. And I was choosing love consciousness. I chose to live in a world where I operated from the heart. I knew in my bones that that was where we all were heading, to ascend into the dimension – or density, whatever you want to call it – of love consciousness.

The funny thing is that if you come from the heart space, people feel it, consumers feel it; you build trust. People know you really care and they want to do business with you, so in essence you will be making more money. But it's not about the money, – that's entirely secondary – and you get to utilise that extra money in alignment with your love consciousness. Now all the marketers (and I was one too) will say that's nothing new, that you have to build a brand on trust, for instance. The thing is, though, that most only get it from the head space; they only do stuff to gain trust from customers, to build a brand, to make more money. This may come across as a simple matter of semantics, that the difference is subtle, almost insignificant. It's not. It's massive. It's everything. Intention is everything. If you operate from the heart space, if you really care, energetically it's an entirely different world. Eventually, everything that is not love consciousness will fall away, burn and fade; it will never be able to survive the high vibration. That means current business and shareholder structures and existing ways of doing business, too. I, though, was not worried or interested in how that was going to look … I was more interested in the first step, in supporting the global wake-up call, in helping and serving to raise the consciousness and vibration on this planet, and have fun doing that.

I was inspired to put a website together and spoke to Brother Lee, a specialist in the internet space. The website told the story of my journey around the world and explained my potential offerings to the world that I was feeling into, namely, sexuality workshops, guiding and coaching, speaking and inspiring and writing a book about my journey. I had no plan or strategy; the Voice simply told me to put it out there whilst I was finishing my book.

In the name of the Father

In the middle of May 2018, my dad's health took a serious dip. I immediately flew down to George. He was very weak. The prostrate cancer had spread all the way up his vertebrae and the Parkinson's was now very advanced. He still liked to spend time outside, though, so we would load him into the wheelchair and I'd push him to a little lake on the estate, sometimes running with him in the wheelchair. He would chuckle and enjoy that.

After my first week home, his condition seemed to improve a little. Although he was still weak, he had kept his quirky sense of humour and thought my big grey beard was hilarious. It had been three months since my time in the Karoo, and I still hadn't shaved. He also found my long hair really strange – he'd never had long hair in his life. One morning, as I appeared next to his bed, he looked up at me, squinting his eyes and then very slowly and deliberately said, "Jesus Christ."

We – my mom and I – burst out laughing. I did look a bit like JC with my long hair and thick beard. I asked him whether he thought Jesus was coming to get him. He chuckled, his body shaking with laughter.

I thought about death a lot when I was in George. This was not something new, of course; I'd spent much of my time on my journey delving into mortality, reading and meditating about living life and dying consciously, but now it was much closer to home. I came across some channelled reading material on ascension. As I read, I had a clear download that brought such clarity to me. It was as if the last piece of the puzzle had fallen into place.

I had a deep knowing that we come to this reality, to this life, to experience separation. The deal is that in order to come here, we have to forget that we are all part of one, so that we are able to experience separation. We have to forget our oneness – that's the pain and suffering of this life. Then, after we have exhausted the experience of separation, we can start the journey back to the one consciousness. Part of that journey back is remembering and awakening to the oneness of it all. That can happen in one lifetime or in many lifetimes. So there is no wrong or right – it's all about our experiences. We can experience whatever we like. We have free choice. We can stay as long as we want on the outward journey of separation, individually and collectively. There is nothing wrong with that. We are all part of Life, of God experiencing God. Experiencing separation is God experiencing Itself as separate. It's an illusion, but it's a brilliantly creative way to know oneself, for God to know God.

I had certainly gone way out there in the experience of separation. It felt like I had lived a million lives in one, just on the outward journey. I had pushed the envelope. Realistically, I should have been dead, but I wasn't … I was alive and kicking. And in the five years since I'd jumped into the journey home, it felt as if I had lived a million lifetimes. I was getting such value from this lifetime, this body, this experience, at this point in space and time. Maybe that's what I signed up for before getting to this place. What I had become super aware of was that there had been an acceleration of consciousness. Everywhere. Rapidly. The world we live in was changing. And I knew it was to accelerate even more. The old structures were still in place, but there was now a lag. There always is. But while the outside looked the same, the internal landscape had already changed for many. And that change was infectious. It was spreading. When enough people had jumped to this new consciousness, the tipping point would be reached and the external landscape would also start to change. I knew that there were big changes ahead in the external world, even in my lifetime.

After three weeks in George, I had to go up to Johannesburg for a weekend writers' course to which I'd committed. When I said goodbye to my dad, I had a strong feeling I may not see him again.

I sat at his bed for a while after he had fallen asleep. It was like a meditation. Eventually I had to get up and head to the airport. I stood at the door for a long time. I knew I was saying goodbye. I did not feel sad. It was time. In this life I had had a beautiful relationship with him. Although I hadn't seen him that much when I was very young because he often worked overseas, he was very present in my teenage years. It was almost as if he had wanted to make up for lost time, and he went out of his way to spend time with me. We played a lot of golf, went on hunting trips together and would often talk late into the night. When I was at university and still living at home, we would regularly enjoy a drink together in the conservatory lounge and bar room he had built with his own hands adjacent to the house, talking about business until late. I learnt so much from him about the people side of business.

As I stood at the door of his room I remembered him saying to me a few days earlier, "I had a good innings, but I want to be bowled out now." I understood and respected that. I gave him one long last look and then turned and walked down the long passage of the frail-care centre, out to my car.

I left George for Johannesburg with a heavy heart, but also with a deep peace, grounded in the connection with my ancestors, those who were alive and those who had passed from this world. I constantly felt them around me. I had a true knowing that a deep connection with my ancestors – and with nature – was an important foundation, even a prerequisite for a deep connection to Higher

Self. It clears the way for open access to the whispers of the soul, conversations with God, the Field of Universal Consciousness, to *all* that *is*.

The main theme of the writers' course in Johannesburg was about dropping deep into your own vulnerability so that you could write from an authentic place. I believed that all my work around the world had already dropped me deep into that, but this course pushed me to a whole new level. It was sweet synchronicity when, on the Sunday, we were given prompts to write about our fathers. I connected my pen to my heart and let it flow.

My father asked me a question that took my breath away and shook me to my core. I was sitting next to his hospital bed, watching him sleep. He would wake up every now and then and turn his head to look at me, struggling to keep his eyes open. The morphine patches on his chest were very strong. They had to be strong enough to dull the pain from the advanced cancer creeping up his vertebrae and the advanced Parkinson's, which made his body twitch every now and then. In one of his lucid moments he turned his head and slowly asked me, "On your travels around the world, have you found out where we go when we leave this earth?"

That was so unlike him; he was never one for discussing emotions or personal things. He was from the Silent Generation. I knew it took a lot for him to ask me. I also knew he was scared. I told him: "There is nothing you have to do before dying. There is no heaven and no hell. That's all the bullshit that we've been told. You are perfect as you are, you are already divine, there is nothing you have to do before dying. Your body dies but your spirit remains forever. My body will also die, but our spirits will always be together, Pappa."

A week later my father died.

I was asleep in the cottage in Johannesburg when the phone rang at 2 am. I knew even before answering. It was my baby sister on the phone. I immediately booked a flight for later in the morning.

My father did not want a traditional funeral. He'd asked that friends and family celebrate his life with a glass of wine. A few days later we arranged a ceremony that I took upon myself to host. It was a beautiful celebration of his life. We cried a lot but we also laughed.

My father's death brought all of us closer.

The day after the ceremony I shaved my beard. It was time. Everyone applauded. They could see my face again. I felt clean and fresh. I had woken up that morning and decided to let it go. In a way, it was closure.

I stayed with my mother for another three weeks. We both knew she would have to come to terms with my dad not being there but that she could only do that on her own. When I finally left for the airport, I caught sight of her frail little body in the rear-view mirror, alone in the road. My heart broke for her. They had been together for 56 years.

CHAPTER 30

Journey's end

I was nearing the end of this journey.

In Cape Town I rented a car, dropped my backpack in the boot, strung my moldavite necklace around my neck and over my heart – the first time since India – and took a slow drive up the West Coast, stopping over in small fishing villages along the way.

The West Coast is an achingly beautiful and barren place. It stretches from Cape Town all the way up to Namibia. The further north you go, the wilder and more beautiful it becomes. Its shores are pounded by the Atlantic Ocean. My beloved Atlantic. She is moody and unpredictable. On any given day she can be four seasons. She stirs and disrupts, tugging emotions from the depths of your being, pulling you to the surface. She magnifies the whispers of your soul. She can be sultry and sexy, but she's always moving, deep blue waters choppy white as she seduces the sand. She forces me to look at all that has been.

It has been said that after death we meet our spirit family, those who died before us and those who are still alive on earth. This is possible because we are meeting in a higher spirit realm. I knew this to be true because as I travelled into the vast unknown, I "remembered" and felt it in my heart.

Since losing my father four weeks earlier, that knowing

had deepened tremendously. I felt union with his spirit, a deep communication. I constantly felt his presence around me, but one that was different since he had passed. As loving as he was before, I now experienced him as a vastly expanded presence, no ego, no earthly limitations, just pure love.

There was no sadness in my heart. Just joy. I did not miss his physical presence because he was still with me. And how could I miss his physical presence when I'd already had a beautiful physical journey with him? Nothing in the same form lasts forever. I understood the benefit and saw the beauty of that.

Change is life. Everything is in constant flux. Rapidly on a subatomic level, sometimes very slowly on a macro level, but everything is in a state of motion. It then follows that everything is alive. There is no real death. Just a change from one form to another. The only death is resisting change. Resistance makes us feel dead while we're still alive. Embracing change and embracing uncertainty is embracing life fully.

As I drove I remembered the story of the Café at the Edge, which someone told me along my travels. It's the tale of a man who heard about a cliff that you could jump off to change your life, based on what your inner truth was telling you. The man travelled far to reach it. When he got there, he stood at the edge, but instead of jumping he decided to sit under a tree and think about it. After a while, someone else arrived at the edge of the cliff with the same intention to jump, but he saw the man under the tree and joined him there. Together, they discussed jumping off the cliff. Over time, more travellers arrived at the edge to jump, but instead of plunging into the unknown, they all joined the group under the tree. Eventually someone said, "Let's start a café here, so we can at least have a cup of tea or coffee while we sit here discussing jumping." They called it the Café at the Edge. It quickly grew in popularity. Great discussions around jumping ensued.

All went well for a while until one day someone arrived at the edge. He did not go into the café, he did not look left or right; instead, he ran up to the edge and without slowing down simply

257

jumped straight over into the unknown. But, rather than crashing to the rocks below, he soared. The crowds in the café were in shock. "What the fuck?" they exclaimed. "That's not allowed. You can't just jump! You have to come and sit here first, have a coffee and talk about it."

I love that story. You can spend all your time talking about jumping or you can jump and fly. I had experienced this so clearly on my journey. I had to make a leap of faith, jump off the cliff to surrender and find my truth.

During my travels I often thought about what Osho had said about "destination" belonging to the ego and "direction" belonging to life and to being, and that to move in the world of direction one needs tremendous trust because one is moving in the realm of insecurity and darkness. He reminded me of how darkness has a thrill to it; without any map, without any guide, you are moving into the unknown and each step is a discovery, of both the internal and external worlds.

With no plans, no goals, no destination, no map, I had set off on my journey. Only a backpack and an open heart.

I was aware that my goal-less approach went against everything in popular belief. So many motivational speakers, coaches, teachers and gurus expound on the virtues of "setting goals" and "believing in yourself", to "go, go, go get what you want". But I was more interested in surrender rather than control. I wanted to fully see what existence had to offer, what else I had committed to do before coming to this life and this place. That required less goal setting and more deep listening. Listening is difficult. It's far easier to set goals and to talk. But once all the fearful internal chatter had died down, I was finally able to listen. I found the place of surrender. And then the magic happened. I began to live in the flow, following the energy, seeing where it led me. I began discovering the world anew, seeing it through unfiltered eyes. With every step I took, I began to discover me. Because every step required a direction. That direction was born out of living the moment and listening carefully. Listening to the Voice, listening to my heart, listening to my soul, listening to existence. The whispers were there. They had always been.

As I stood and looked out over the wild, barren landscape, over the sand dunes and rocks, at the sun setting in the distance over the Atlantic, the following familiar words came back to me: "Up to here you had free will, some control of your life, you were living life, but from here on it will be different, life will be living you."